Criminality and the Common Law Imagination in the
Eighteenth and Nineteenth Centuries

D1427825

edinburghuniversitypress.com/series/ecsllh

Criminality and the Common Law Imagination in the Eighteenth and Nineteenth Centuries

Erin Sheley

EDINBURGH
University Press

For my parents, Janet and Michael Sheley. My mother taught me to love literature even before I could speak or walk. My father taught me to be stubborn and to keep fighting, no matter what. This book would not exist were it not for them.

Edinburgh University Press is one of the leading university presses in the UK. We publish academic books and journals in our selected subject areas across the humanities and social sciences, combining cutting-edge scholarship with high editorial and production values to produce academic works of lasting importance. For more information visit our website: edinburghuniversitypress.com

Edinburgh University Press Ltd
The Tun—Holyrood Road
12 (2f) Jackson's Entry
Edinburgh EH8 8PJ

First published in hardback by Edinburgh University Press 2020

Typeset in 11/13pt Adobe Garamond Pro by
Servis Filmsetting Ltd, Stockport, Cheshire
and printed and bound by CPI Group (UK) Ltd,
Croydon, CR0 4YY

A CIP record for this book is available from the British Library

ISBN 978 1 4744 5010 2 (hardback)
ISBN 978 1 4744 5011 9 (paperback)
ISBN 978 1 4744 5012 6 (webready PDF)
ISBN 978 1 4744 5013 3 (epub)

In Chapter 3, excerpts are taken from Erin Sheley, "The Law of Nature or Nature's God?: Penal Authority in Charles Kingsley's *The Water-Babies*," which first appeared in *Children's Literature Association Quarterly*, Volume 37, Issue 2, Summer 2012. Copyright © 2012 Children's Literature Association.

Contents

Acknowledgments

This book really should not ever have happened. I was told that it was not possible to get a PhD in literature part-time while working full-time in law and then legal academia and that I would be overwhelmed by the attempt. After that seemed to be working out, I was then told, in the midst of a deeply trying, horribly-timed legal academic job market, that it was "confusing" to faculty hiring committees that I had an in-progress PhD in another field and that somehow doing twice as much work, in two fields at once, could be construed against me as a sign of "lack of seriousness." After having finally pulled off both the completed PhD and a tenure-track job in law, I was then told that I certainly should not try to turn it into a book before tenure. Because even if it did not, in fact, reduce my productivity as a legal scholar, it might be perceived as doing so and, again, be counted against me.

Fortunately for this book and anyone interested in reading it, I really, really hate being told what to do.

Fortunately for me, I have been supported throughout the course of an insanity-inducing process by a veritable legion of friends, mentors, helpers, and life-savers. (All of whom are endowed with more patience and kindness than I can personally claim.) To start with the most recent, I am deeply thankful to the University of Oklahoma College of Law. The research support my institution has made available to me to complete this process in the final stretch has, ultimately, made the difference in my actually being able to pull it off. In particular, I cannot give enough thanks to Michael Waters, the editorial advisor to the *Oklahoma Law Review*, for his truly superb skills at citation research, even in a citation style that neither of us previously knew anything about. In my final stretch, I suddenly felt the support of a consummate professional with attention to detail that puts my own to shame. Without these stellar professionals willing to spend the time on this book, I would not have completed it.

A separate category of thanks is due to the University of Calgary Faculty of Law and in particular to Dean Ian Holloway. Ian plucked my job application out of the slush pile not in spite of my side work on law and literature, but because of it. I would not have a career at all were it not for Ian recognizing the value my interdisciplinarity added to a law faculty and supporting it. Two other Calgary colleagues require specific mention here. First, Fenner Stewart, for being interested in hanging out in my office to discuss Foucault, and otherwise creating a scholarly, and personal, community that was very helpful at the time I was creating my book proposal. Second, Ryan Pierson, whose comments on my sample introduction, along with our many productive conversations about literature and theory (and life), were invaluable.

I am also thankful to my series editor William MacNeil, who patiently shepherded this project through the process of submission. It has greatly benefited from both his input and the excellent, detailed comments of the peer reviewers for Edinburgh University Press. Thanks also to all of the editorial staff at Edinburgh for their excellent work.

Some of my most important thanks go to my colleagues in my English graduate program at the George Washington University. This book began as a dissertation in that program; the ideas it developed started as conversations with the talented group of scholars I was lucky enough to get to know, intellectually and personally, during those years. I specifically thank for their comments on this work, and their general camaraderie, M. W. Bychowski, Patrick Henry, Leigha McReynolds, and Shyama Rajendran. Each of them is present in this book in various ways. Thanks also to the members of my dissertation committee, Daniel DeWispelare, Mariah Frawley, Judith Plotz, and Kathryn Temple. It was a lucky stroke of fate that so many of the great experts in the various fields I engaged in this book all happened to be in DC and willing to help me with this project. It was an enormous honor to work with each of them. Thanks also to Marshall Alcorn, who gave me my first introduction to the trauma theory that would become so important to the theoretical contribution of this book.

Next, I owe thanks to the numerous people who supported me personally during the lengthy duration of this book process. First on this list are Paria Kooklan Russo and Scott Shepard. Apart from being two of my dearest, "at-first-sight" friends who have supported me in more ways than I can list, I can specifically credit each of them for decades-long conversations about literature that have impacted everything I have ever written in this field, and specifically this book. Other dear friends have also provided various forms of support during the many years I have been working on this project and are crucial to its existence in a myriad of ways. These include Erin Ashwell, Jessica Begg, Jessica Borelli, Andrew Bradt, Candace Davis, Gregory Dolin, Matthew Hampton, Sarah Joseph, Irina Manta, Anna Muldoon, Christina Mulligan, Christopher Odinet, Lee Otis, William Otis, Mara Rutherford, Thumper Sheley, David Thaw, Kristen van de Biezenbos, and David J.

Williams. The years during which I was writing this book have, frankly, been brutal in many ways. But I do not think it is possible to be more fortunate than I have been in my friendships.

Penultimately, I would like to thank James Engell, my undergraduate thesis advisor. From the first week of my first course with Jim during my freshman year of college I was certain that, no matter what I did in the law one day, I would always want to be a literary scholar as well. Our conversations about Keats and Shelley during the course of my thesis work were the start of my continued passion for literary analysis. His scholarly commitment to interdisciplinary thinking inspired me to think creatively about my own varied interests. And beyond that, he has been the rare undergrad adviser who has remained a lifelong friend and mentor.

Finally, the greatest of thanks are due to Tara Ghoshal Wallace, my dissertation adviser and dear friend. Getting to work with Tara was one of the greatest strokes of luck in my life. At a scholarly level, Tara encouraged me to expand into the eighteenth century, and through her own work in that area opened my mind to the connections I could profitably make between eighteenth and nineteenth-century literature and law. As a scholar I have been inspired by her work and this project would not exist, intellectually, were it not for her input. Beyond that, though, my career and my will to persist in it would likely not exist were it not for Tara personally. She relentlessly believed in me, even when I did not believe in myself, and stepped in at the times when I genuinely did not see the next step, to support me professionally, intellectually, and emotionally. She did so with exactly the sort of tough love I required, in part by modeling the strong, individualistic, increasingly-rare brand of feminism I aspire to. I am so grateful to have had her as a kindred-spirit friend.

This book was both a labor of love for its subject and, biographically, the product of a frequently-tested will to survive. I remain deeply grateful to everyone who stood beside me and helped me to make this a reality.

Introduction: The Tolbooth Door

This ill-omened apparition was of great height, with a scaffold surrounding it, and a double ladder placed against it, for the ascent of the unhappy criminal and executioner. As this apparatus was always arranged before dawn, it seemed as if the gallows had grown out of the earth in the course of one night, like the production of some foul demon; and I well remember the fright with which the schoolboys, when I was one of their number, used to regard these ominous signs of deadly preparation. On the night after the execution the gallows again disappeared, and was conveyed in silence and darkness to the place where it was usually deposited, which was one of the vaults under the Parliament House, or courts of justice.[1]

—Sir Walter Scott, *The Heart of Midlothian*

The narrator in *The Heart of Midlothian* (1818), as in so many of Scott's historical novels, approaches his subject through an immediate sensory perception of the relics left behind by the narrated event. In describing his boyhood memory of the gallows in front of the Tolbooth Prison, the site of the 1736 lynching of Captain Porteous with which the text begins, Scott's narrator underscores the interactions between the criminal law and its representations circulating in the cultural memory, and the potentially discursive relationship between the two across historical time. Scott wrote this description in the early nineteenth century, at precisely the historical moment when Britain's so-called "Bloody Code" was the subject of intense public debate. Across the eighteenth century, Parliament had designated an increasing number of criminal offenses as capital, resulting in a proliferation of hangings for property crimes, particularly in London.[2] While Scotland did not see the same degree of widespread hanging as the capital, the image of the gallows nonetheless captures the trauma of mass-execution that had become an important part of the early nineteenth-century British collective memory, resulting in its abrupt cessation in the face of public opposition in the 1830s.[3]

Scott's literary representation of this phenomenon also came at a time during which the relationship between history and law was already a significant cultural tension. The newly liberalized Enlightenment legal order conflicted with political anxieties over the relatively recent disruption to the royal succession caused by the English Revolution, and with an increasing cultural preoccupation with the archaic and the medieval. As a result, legal discourse in the late eighteenth and nineteenth centuries reveals a particularly fraught relationship with the past. Indeed, Foucault famously characterizes the rise of western liberalism as a sharp break from that past: as a shift from the centralized, state-wielded power to do violence toward the more regulatory-style control over the human subject embodied in such knowledge-producing institutions as the penitentiary, the scientific community, and the asylum.[4] If some version of this change in *episteme* occurred in fact between the time points Foucault suggests (the 1757 execution of attempted regicide Robert-François Damiens and the 1840 opening of the French penal colony at Mettray), then it follows that we might increasingly look to modern, professionalized legal discourse, rather than the might or established character of the sovereign itself, to understand how the modern age produces criminal subjects.[5] Yet in Anglo-American legal culture, the nature of the common law complicates the pure Foucauldian narrative due to its formal power to harness archaic history to produce legal outcomes. In this book I consider how both the criminal common law and its eighteenth- and nineteenth-century cultural representations compressed collective English historical trauma into contemporary legal truth.

I draw on what sociologists call "collective" or "cultural" memory. Twentieth-century French sociologist Maurice Halbwachs first argued that the content of individual memory is dependent upon the social framework within which it is constructed, that an individual memory of subjective experience inevitably becomes subsumed into its group context. Many contemporary theorists go so far as entirely to reject the significance of individual memory as such since it can be expressed only through "the cultural construction of language in socially structured patterns of recall."[6] While it has become uncontroversial to assume the social context in which it is rehearsed has an impact on the content of a memory, this extreme collectivist view has drawn criticism for neglecting the extent to which individual and collective memories may be in tension and the fact that individuals' recollections can challenge official historical accounts designed to attain social unity.[7] A more complete model accounts for the extent to which the memories of individuals, while shaped by collective memory, reciprocally shape it in turn.

The passage from *The Heart of Midlothian* with which I opened illustrates how literary texts may illuminate a cycle between individual and collective memories of law and crime. In attempting to conjure up an episode of past criminality for a nineteenth-century audience satiated with executions, Scott channels it through the individual memory of his narrator, who fashions an image of the Tolbooth Gallows as a dispenser of punishment even as he has been fashioned, in his childhood, by his visceral response to it. (This system implicates Scott himself who, in reality, obtained the door to the Tolbooth Prison after its closure and incorporated it into the façade of his mansion Abbotsford House, thus memorializing the history of punishment as an aspect of personal identity.) This cycle demonstrates a phenomenon first noted by Michael Kenny, who, studying the experiences of Holocaust survivors and Australian Aborigines under colonialism, brought psychological and historical literature together to chart the interaction between personal and collective history "whereby autobiography becomes articulated to influential cultural narratives."[8] Individual memories may shape cultural memory in ways that endure, though their individuality may be threatened by the press of cultural narratives already in place.

It is important to distinguish cultural memory as a repository of shared experience from the concept of official "history" insofar as the former relates to facts as they happened and the latter to a subjective account of the details historians privilege.[9] Theorists have noted the importance of tangible and visual objects such as memorials (such as Scott's Tolbooth door), existing in the present, as a means of accessing the factual past, which produces a problem similar to the signification problems faced by an individual witness testifying to past pain. Because memory extends beyond its present artifacts it is necessarily in flux; when we reproduce it we wind up with only, as Richard Terdiman calls it, "a present past."[10] The content of a memory is never directly accessible and is necessarily shaped by the scene in which an individual memorializes it in the present.

The duality between cultural memory and history creates obvious conflict in legal discourse: upholding the freedoms guaranteed by the rule of law depends upon adherence to a history of "legal truth" that—in order to protect the procedural rights of defendants and for various other reasons —must at times part ways with "factual" truth. Yet the two valences are interdependent in important ways. Personal memories can become part of official "history," and cultural memory can incorporate formal historical narratives, as Marita Sturken has observed in the extent to which World War II movies subsume the stories of individual soldiers into a "general script."[11] Similarly, "official" legal truth can be shaped by cultural memory of real-life events, while simultaneously creating a framework in which individuals form and recall personal memories.

The nature of the Anglo-American common law—with its precedent-based method of reasoning and investment in legitimacy through historical continuity—allows it to function narratively as a bridge between an event and the past. In her study on Victorian-era precedential reasoning in law and literature, Ayelet Ben-Yishai argues that "structurally, precedent works by negotiating a commonality over time" and identifies this logic in both nineteenth-century case reports and Victorian realist fiction.[12] I would add that the *Midlothian* example shows how, at the sensory level, literary portrayals of legal conflict may replicate this common law logic where a present-tense narrative voice contemplates the artifacts of the legal past. Furthermore, because actual legal practice depends upon the reconciliation of an individual case with the weight of history in the present cultural context, these literary representations of criminality which themselves circulate through the culture may logically have a generative effect within the evolution of the law.

Ben-Yishai has also noted the threat to common law reasoning posed by the rise of statutory law in the nineteenth century, and its accompanying implications for English national identity:

> The temporal challenge in applying legal precedent is thus linked to the temporal anxiety of the authority of the common law as the primary source of British law, as well as with the essence ("the very temperament") of Englishness.[13]

I argue that, beyond this particular Victorian epistemological context, the process of common law reasoning tracks broadly with what social psychologists describe as the "prospective" function of collective memory. Scholars of collective memory note that historical discourse is narratively continuous in order to anticipate the future.[14] Others argue that collective memory is characterized by "temporal heteroglossia"—the simultaneous presence of multiple periods of time that collectively form historical representations.[15] Proponents of the "prospective" view suggest that these properties of memory allow the past to function as a resource in the present to determine the future.[16] This sociology supports Ben-Yishai's argument that the Victorians took to precedential reasoning specifically to manage the numerous tumultuous social, legal, political, and theological changes of the nineteenth century while "realizing a continuity with a common past in the form of certainty and the promise of a stable future."[17] These parallels suggest that common law may function as a form of cultural memory.

However, collective memory also contains discontinuity. It may mediate shared negative memories through repression, rather than integration, as when populations collectively repress atrocities committed by their governments.[18] In this book I focus, specifically, on cultural trauma as a particular form of collective memory animating the criminal common law. Like all collective memory, cultural trauma can be understood, as Jeffrey Olick puts it, not only as the aggregate of individual, first-hand experiences but as the damage rendered by a specific traumatic event to shared narratives as they stretch into the future: Vietnam and Auschwitz were traumatic "not just for . . . individuals but for the legitimating narrative . . . that we as individuals produce for us as a collectivity."[19] Yet trauma can also lead to the creation of new group narratives that acknowledge past wrongs while attempting to make sense of them and create a new sense of continuity between the self and others.[20] Some sociologists, however, claim the mere recognition of trauma is, in and of itself, a "socially-mediated attribution."[21] Jeffrey Alexander describes this process as a kind of Foucauldian knowledge production: "Only if the patterned meanings of the collectivity are abruptly dislodged is traumatic status attributed to an event."[22] In Alexander's view, then, cultural trauma is inherently the product of discourse. Regardless of one's views on its relation to facticity, both the productive potential and discursive nature of cultural trauma make it relevant to the common law of crime, which must mediate public and private violence across time.

This book argues that common law jurists and literary authors of both the eighteenth and nineteenth centuries construct criminality through a narrative of historical legitimacy that actively encodes cultural traumas into legal truth. It also explores how literary depictions of what I call "failed history" create space for minority truths even within the hegemonic structure of common law discourse. In some cases, I find that the literary imagination reinforces the static properties of the common law by providing a framework for narrative continuity between historically-specific past and present trauma. However, I also find that many literary texts, by depicting the traumatic failure of history to justify contemporary legal outcomes, create sites of resistance and man-dates for the incremental, Blackstonian evolution also characteristic of the common law. At such moments, the law answers Martha Nussbaum's call for the literary imagination to act "as a public imagination, as imagination that will steer judges in their judging, legislators in their legislating, policy makers in measuring the quality of life of people near and far."[23] I collect, in some cases, evidence of an active causal relationship between cultural and literary narratives and legal development: instances where such narratives drive legal reasoning and others where they assert literal punitive authority in their own right. In other cases, I demonstrate how, at a minimum, the structure of common law thinking as a form of cultural memory organizes the discourse of criminal trauma across both law and literature.

I consider three key components of criminality that were legally in flux during the eighteenth and nineteenth centuries and examine how traumatic historical narratives generated by the common law may have interacted with individual representations in the culture to shape official legal discourse. In Part I, I show how the relationship in the common law imagination between adultery and threatened English sovereignty created a quasi-criminal legal discourse surrounding the private wrong of adultery. In Part II, I examine how the literary "construction" of childhood by nineteenth-century fairy tale writers interacted with the development of the juvenile justice system. Finally, in Part III, I consider common law evidentiary rules governing "proofs" of rape victim character as epistemological components of volatile national identity.

The three topics in this project hardly constitute an exhaustive universe of possible inquiries into eighteenth- and nineteenth-century constructions of criminality. I have selected them in part because the topic of each Part corresponds with one of the three foundational questions a culture must ask in defining the nature of the criminal law. First, what constitutes an *actus reus*—an action that may be morally condemned as a crime as opposed to merely a tort? Second, what "*mens rea*," or state of mind on the part of the accused, is requisite to support a determination of criminality? And third, by what evidentiary standards must we prove these elements as a matter of law? By taking on the subjects of adultery, child criminality, and rape in turn, I hope to consider each of these aspects of criminality in the cultural imagination, as well as a representative swath of cases and manners of crime. Furthermore, in examining a somewhat wider-than-typical range of dates, this book captures the phenomenon of common law evolution in its cultural context without the potential limitations of periodization and complicates the traditional Foucauldian account of the shift from sovereign to discursive authority between the eighteenth and nineteenth centuries. This discussion begins with some preliminary observations on the origins of eighteenth- and nineteenth-century common-law memory in the form of legal materials.

Common Law Documents as Collective Memory

Around the time of upheaval and discontinuity in sovereignty occasioned by the English Revolution, Interregnum, and Restoration, with their accompanying revisions to English law, the great legal commentators of the seventeenth and eighteenth centuries argued explicitly about the importance of temporality and history to the legitimacy of the English common law system. These writers also played a crucial role in constructing a stable version of legal "truth" in their widely-respected treatises. As Peter Brooks has noted, this process is self-consciously narrative: a court must persuade its audience of the inevitability of a given legal outcome flowing from immutable law and precedent.[24] Less appreciated is that the essence of the common law is also extreme fragmentation: in a common law system, judges decide cases one at a time and must look back upon all relevant prior precedent to determine the outcome in a particular case. Despite the aspirational commitment to historical continuity, the decisions of hundreds of jurists presiding over geographically varied tribunals cannot be easily captured by any single judge reviewing a particular case at bar. Thus, the task of treatise writers such as Edward Coke (1552–1634), Matthew Hale (1609–1676), and William Blackstone (1721–1780) is more than simply summary. In attempting to encapsulate the historical trajectories of scattered judicial precedents, even before the widespread acceptance of the doctrine of *stare decisis* in the late eighteenth century,[25] these highly influential writers produced cumulative, yet eventually monolithic, legal truths of their own. Furthermore, editors in subsequent generations amended earlier treatises with new cases and examples, creating a historical pastiche of authority which—like the common law itself—narrates new examples in the context of a long temporal framework.

While some writers, such as Coke, claimed their treatises embodied the static common law as it existed from time immemorial, others were straightforward about the possibility of evolution. Hale, a Royalist jurist whose work became the basis for much Restoration-era legal reform, developed a philosophy of active evolution of the laws, in which the action of historical experience forms a central part. In his essay "Considerations Touching the Amendment or Alteration of Lawes" (1787), Hale claims that "Antient lawes . . . are not the issues of the prudence of this or that council or senate" but rather of "time, which as it discovers day after day new inconveniences, so it doth successively apply new remedies . . . a kind of aggregation of the discoveries results and applications of ages and events."[26] Hale's use of common law "time" indicates how the common law, in general, can be understood as a particular, structured form of collective memory. The tension between textual stability and cultural evolution as sources of legal meaning continues to animate the constitutional debates of the current day and age. Moreover, this particular relationship between law and culture suggests that Foucault's formulation of penal authority as flowing primarily from society, rather than the state, might partially describe aspects of the Anglo-American common law tradition even before the supposed shift in power he designates as unique to modernity. It also indicates that a study of cultural representations of penological change might illuminate this relationship. Nonetheless, the historically-legitimized might of the sovereign necessarily remains legible in legal discourse as such discourse is of and about the formal powers of the state.

Writing a century after Hale and Coke, in his 1769 *Commentaries on the Laws of England*, William Blackstone also describes legal change as a temporally-inflected process in which English cultural essentialism and teleological progress play equally important roles. English criminal law is, he claims, "more rude and imperfect than the civil," though intrinsically superior to that of the other European powers.[27] He stresses the danger posed by the weight of history: where some laws "seem to want revision and amendment" it is due to "too scrupulous an adherence to some rules of the ancient common law, when the reasons have ceased upon which those rules were founded; from not repealing such of the old penal laws as are either obsolete or absurd."[28] For example, he claims that had Parliament referred the law more frequently for revision to "some of the learned judges" then "it is impossible that in the eighteenth century it could ever have been made a capital crime 'as it was for many years' to break down . . . the mound of a fishpond . . . or to cut down a cherry-tree in an orchard."[29] In other words, laws could change but the possibility for absolute correctness remained; so long as the proper authorities were consulted, certain unjust outcomes would be "impossible."[30]

Though the *Commentaries* is ostensibly a treatise on the state of English law as it actually was, Blackstone incorporates the mechanism for change—and, quite frequently, a call for specific changes—into his task of compilation and description. Indeed, the treatise ends with a chapter entitled "The Rise, Progress, and Gradual Improvements, of the Laws of England," which highlights how the articulation of new legal norms can occur at a great historical remove from their realization in fact.[31] For example, he states that it was from the reign of Edward I –"from the exact *observation* of *Magna Charta*, rather than from its *making* or *renewal* [under Edward's grandfather and father] . . . that the liberty of Englishmen began again to rear its head."[32] This interrelated co-existence between archaic practice and evolved norm reveals the potentially schizophrenic cultural effects of common law evolution which will remain important to the rest of my argument.

Specifically, Hale's "new inconveniences" which will purportedly be "discovered" by "time" function like cultural trauma. Whether these inconveniences are individual miscarriages of justice, particularly horrible criminal acts, or simply new shifts in understanding that begin to render particular punishments—like the Bloody Code—socially disturbing, they unsettle the legitimating narrative of the common law in a manner it must shift to accommodate or else risk illegitimacy. Contemporary theorists of cultural trauma have noted that "chronic" crises, such as the Great Depression and the Vietnam War, lack the dramatic beginnings of acute traumas such as the attack on Pearl Harbor.[33] Instead, a chronic crisis grows out of "persisting contradictions within a social system" and the prolonged public response to it becomes part of the trauma itself.[34] In the chapters that follow, I will identify several chronic crises related to crime and punishment and show how they emerge as cultural trauma within the common law.

As Ben-Yishai recounts, the nineteenth century saw a theoretical conflict between the supposed bases for the common law tradition—natural law and custom—and the rise of legal positivism, associated with Jeremy

Bentham, John Austin, and a proliferation of new Parliamentary legislation.[35] She argues that the convention of precedent was adapted to accommodate positivism: where precedent had once been imagined as evidence of custom, "by the nineteenth century, precedential cases were regarded as *rules* made by judges."[36] At around the same time, the business of publishing law reports took off. Private companies hired reporters to attend trials and record the proceedings as a means of informing the legal profession of decisions handed down by the courts.[37] Thus, unlike American judicial opinions, these reports are not direct statements from the courts but the summaries of third parties. While these reports are therefore comprised of piecemeal descriptions of individual trials, they do maintain some structural similarities to the eighteenth and nineteenth-century treatises. As I demonstrate in subsequent chapters, they report on counsel arguing from precedent and conflicts between judges over whether prior cases correctly stated the law. The idea that a case could be wrongly decided implies that the common law system had not transformed into one of pure legal positivism. Many jurists still perceived law as evolving or devolving in ways more or less consistent with a universal right. In documenting the conflicts over the content of such laws, these reports serve as public evidence of the anxieties embedded in the common law.

While most professional Victorian law reports were very sparse when it came to details on the factual history of a particular case—Ben-Yishai describes them as "antinarrative"[38]—their immediate eighteenth and early nineteenth-century forbears were anything but. This book frequently examines early published compendia of trials which—while providing the same legal information as the subsequent Victorian reports—dramatized the proceedings in the courtroom for the presumed entertainment of their consumers. These reports include information about witness demeanor and appearance and sometimes even illustrations intended to highlight dramatic moments in the trial. I will show how such early reporting rendered more explicit the ways in which common law judging processed the cultural trauma of crime and punishment. However functional it eventually became, the tradition of English court reporting had origins in a quasi-literary form. It is not surprising, then, that explicitly literary forms would come to engage discursively with the law.

The Literary Form and the Common Law

A rich body of scholarship has used the Foucauldian lens to reveal how new literary forms, particularly the novel, contributed to the legal and penal discourse of the eighteenth and nineteenth centuries. Several scholars assert that emerging literary structures contributed to a mode of thinking with explicitly disciplinary, real-world consequences. For example, John Bender posits a causal relationship between the rise of the novel form in the eighteenth century and the subsequent reform of physical penitentiaries to focus on the formation and construction of their inmates' characters. For Bender, "Fabrications in narrative of the power of confinement to reshape personality contributed to a process of cultural representation whereby prisons were themselves reconceived and ultimately reinvented."[39] Similarly, D. A. Miller has argued for the "policing function" of the nineteenth-century novel, specifically for the ways in which narrative innovations mimic institutions of social control, such as the police.[40]

A separate debate concerns the evidentiary implications of the novel form. Lisa Rodensky argues that the novel reader's new means of access to the inner lives of characters encouraged re-examination of assumptions about criminal responsibility with an emphasis on individual intent, rather than an evaluation of actions as objectively criminal or not.[41] She suggests that the nineteenth-century novel interacted with and often challenged formal legal discourse by showing the possibility of direct evidence of *mens rea* through attention to individual subjectivity. By contrast, Alexander Welsh claims that the most significant narrative innovation of the novel form in the eighteenth and nineteenth centuries was, in fact, "strong representation"—use of circumstantial evidence to generate the inferences necessary to convince a reader of unseen events.[42] (For example, the rather vapid Tom Jones' literary "acquittal" comes not from his direct testimony in his defense but through the authorial voice, which assembles circumstantial evidence of his basic good character.)[43] While this debate focuses on how the novel facilitates epistemological access to the individual, Sandra MacPherson argues that, in the eighteenth century, the exchange between law and literature had a wholly different effect, attributable in part to the role of chance and accident in driving literary narrative outcomes. MacPherson asserts that the coincidence of novels "that make questions about agency and responsibility central to their formal innovations" and the development of strict liability laws, which impose responsibility for accidental injury without a showing of carelessness or fault, contributed to the objectification, rather than the humanization, of the legal subject.[44] Thus, for all the developments in the history of subjectivity for which the structure of the novel has been credited, MacPherson demonstrates that its themes may, instead, at least in the eighteenth-century, support an action-based objective reality.

Despite the disagreements within this body of scholarship, much of it shares an implicit commitment to what Bender would call "some cycle of generation and regeneration" between law and the literature of its time (discernable, in his case, through the novel's self-conscious preoccupation with some aspect of confinement and the concurrent developments in the realm of penal reform).[45] In particular, the rise of the novel figures heavily as part of a sea change in truth construction, with the range of potential effects on legal problems and institutions just summarized. While all this important work serves as part of my critical starting point, I am less interested in shifts in legal thought discernible in—or even attributable to—literary innovation alone. My focus in this book is, rather, on the effects of the common law's static reliance upon deep history as a form of trauma recalled in the present through law and literature alike.

In Part I, I consider how cultural trauma over the fragility of English kingship contributed to the instability of adultery as a potentially criminal *actus reus*. Adultery was never a crime under English common law, as it has been in many American jurisdictions. Up until the mid-eighteenth century, moral offenders such as adulterers were brought before English ecclesiastical courts, or "bawdy courts," which rarely dispensed corporal punishment, much to the chagrin of Puritan moralists.[46] (In sharp contrast stood early New England law, under which adultery was originally a capital offense). Briefly, during the Interregnum, Cromwell's Adultery Act of 1650 criminalized the offense, but this statute lapsed with the Restoration. By the seventeenth century, however, a cuckolded husband could rely, under common law, on a number of civil causes of action for intentional interference with marital consortium to "punish" his wife's lover; indeed, one of the primary theoretical justifications for such torts was the idea that they served to prevent a cuckold from taking the law into his own hands.[47] Thus, though civil in nature, the legal remedies at common law for adultery originally evolved to serve a quasi-penal purpose.

Indeed despite its non-criminal status, adultery has occupied a uniquely constitutive role in English identity, as far back as the Middle Ages. In the first place, the association of feminine marital fidelity with sovereignty and the threat thereto is central to the English foundational myth. In the *Lancelot-Grail* (13th c), an imposter claims to be Guinevere, saying that she was forced out of Arthur's bed on their wedding night by cohorts of the current Guinevere, and that Arthur's marriage, and his ownership of the Round Table, which was a wedding gift from Guinevere's father Leodegrance, were illegitimate. Arthur believes her to the extent that he arranges a trial by combat between her champion and Lancelot. (Before the development of the common law actions for adultery, indeed, trial by battle had been one of the primary quasi-legal remedies available to a cuckolded husband.) Throughout the ordeal, Arthur repeatedly suggests to Lancelot that—despite being under the enchantment of the new Guinevere, whom he has chosen to believe—he would forget the whole affair if only Lancelot would be reconciled with him. Similarly, in Malory's *Morte d'Arthur* (1485), after the discovery of Guinevere's actual adultery and the bloodshed accompanying her rescue, by Lancelot, from the stake, Arthur says that he would much rather lose his queen than have lost the fellowship of the now-fragmented Round Table. The link between an adulterous queen and the loss of chivalric community and empire is a core feature of the Arthurian saga and remerged in historical reality with the traumas of Henry VIII's reign and the English Reformation. I argue that the relationship between adultery and English kingship in the historical imagination created a quasi-criminal legal discourse surrounding the act of adultery. This discourse reveals the complex rhetorical and political relationship between the ideal of legitimate statehood and that of legitimate marriage. By examining the literary representations alongside the relevant law we can discern the complex social process through which public and private wrongs become distinguished or conflated in the common law.

In Chapter 1, I first trace the cultural history of the tort of criminal conversation through the eighteenth century, illuminating the perceived relationship between adultery and the cultural trauma of violence against kingship revealed in sources as various as political treatises, court documents from Queen Caroline's trial, "murder pamphlets" (accounts written by clergy of notable crimes and their aftermaths), published compendia of criminal conversation and divorce proceedings, and the Henry Fielding play *The Modern Husband* (1732). Despite the formal de-criminalization of adultery, I argue, these texts consolidated disciplinary power in and of themselves, actively participating in the development of the common law on adultery. By collecting and narratizing facts about historical adulteries alongside their modern counterparts, these texts explicitly construct the female adulterer as criminal in her mythic relationship to treason.

In Chapter 2, I consider the relationship between adultery and criminality before and in the wake of the Matrimonial Causes Act of 1857, which made divorce accessible to the middle classes. I show how, because the common law interpreting the Act re-incorporated the older gender inequalities of the adultery cases from Doctors' Commons and Parliament, even the creation of a "modern" divorce system sustained the idea of female adultery as a quasi-crime. Specifically, I argue that the increasing cultural importance of medievalism and chivalric sensibilities throughout the nineteenth century helped re-center the act of adultery in a cultural context as violence against sovereignty and state order, as evident in texts such as Tennyson's *Idylls of the King* (1859–1885). At the same time, however, the literary Gothic genre dramatized failed history as a form of cultural trauma, which put pressure on default adherence to ancient legal norms about women, particularly as reconstituted in modern legislation. Specifically, I demonstrate how Brontë's *Jane Eyre* (1847) may have contributed to the feminist public case for the passage of the Matrimonial Causes Act and how Browning's *The Ring and the Book* (1868) attacked the quasi-criminality of adultery.

In Part II, I examine the relationship between literary child criminality and the evolving concept of *mens rea*. Under sixteenth- and early-seventeenth-century English law, criminal guilt derived almost exclusively from action, as opposed to intentionality, which has today become a critical touchstone for criminal liability. Under the older regime, the fact that a perpetrator's age diminished his capacity to form intent did not matter.[48] Throughout the late seventeenth and eighteenth centuries, penal reformers advocated milder punishments and a greater focus on intentionality, a concern that culminated in the creation of a separate juvenile justice system by the end of the nineteenth century. The notion of children as psychologically "other" than adults frequently recurs in discussions of the cult of childhood associated with the nineteenth century. This fascination dovetailed with the agenda of penal reformation in slightly fraught ways, particularly in the discourse surrounding the Juvenile Offenders Act of 1847. In Chapter 3, I begin by showing how *Yorke's Case* (1748) became a uniquely traumatic image of juvenile crime in the legal imagination due to ten-year-old orphan William York's brutal murder of a five-year-old girl. I argue that the Court's account of York's diabolic temptation generates a cultural preoccupation with the child criminal in a particular grotesque domestic space. This image of the "lost" child tempted by the snake in the garden gives form to many aspects of both the nineteenth-century children's fairy tale and the accompanying, questionable social reforms in juvenile justice. The child protagonists of Victorian fairy-tale writers George MacDonald and Charles Kingsley, as well as the fairy-tale-inflected moments in Charles Dickens's adult novels about children, reflect this cultural anxiety. Their work rationalizes the conflict between the narratively attractive and morally necessary process of thwarting child criminality and the potential moral illegitimacy of earthly penal systems. I show how fairy-tale writers implicitly justified nineteenth-century extra-legal practice by invoking the motif of the royal pardon to resolve what can be understood as a chronic crisis in the collective memory of child discipline.

In Part III, I consider the common law evidentiary proofs of rape and their relationship to chronic trauma surrounding the legal aspects of English national character in the age of revolution. In Chapter 4, I explore the literary and legal discourse around evidence of rape victim character across the eighteenth and early nineteenth centuries. I first survey the centrality of character evidence about the rape victim as proof of rape through the mid-1700s. I show how, given the primacy of "reputation" evidence, cultural texts such as trial compendia actively created legally-cognizable evidence about victim (and perpetrator) character. I then take up the discourse of reputation evidence generated by Samuel Richardson's *Clarissa* (1748) and its critical responses. I argue that this discourse created its own epistemological trauma surrounding collective truth-formation about general character evidence as an element of rape. I conclude with a review of nineteenth-century case law on the relevance and proof of rape victim character to assert that the common law itself came to show signs of repressed epistemological trauma on these questions. These cases leave the legal appropriateness of "general" reputation evidence, as opposed to evidence of specific facts about character, somewhat in flux.

Finally, in Chapter 5, I demonstrate that nineteenth-century literary narratives about evidentiary proofs of rape mediate the particular, the historical, and the national in a rhetorical process similar to the construction of adultery as a quasi-crime. On the one hand, political theorists linked the trauma of the French Revolution to the motif of sexual violence, in a contrast intended to define the superior rationality of English (and, eventually, American) systems of government. Yet nineteenth-century authors used evolving legal ambivalence about the existing common law system of rape adjudication to cast doubt on the truth of this nationalistic dichotomy. For example, at a moment when it was an open question whether the United States would adopt English common law, American gothic writer Charles Brockden Brown linked common law rape adjudication to national identity in his novels *Wieland* (1798) and *Ormond* (1803). On one level, he imports many of the same concerns over victim subjectivity that Richardson uses to complicate common law understandings of character and force. Yet by placing them in a historically specific, Founding-era American context, he also politicizes and problematizes the underlying structure of common law truth construction, suggesting it may have more in common with its French revolutionary equivalent than is comfortable. Rape and revolution collide again decades later in *A Tale of Two Cities* (1859), in which Dickens dramatizes the dual traumas of both *ancien régime* rape and its faulty evidentiary proof in a Revolutionary tribunal as a testament to the superiority of English procedural justice over the French, both before and after the Revolution. However, the text also depicts rape as a product of failed history and national identity, with implicit parallels to the legal and cultural systems of English injustice Dickens extensively chronicles in the rest of his work. I conclude with Thomas Hardy's *Tess of the d'Urbervilles* (1891). I focus on the role of failed history throughout the novel, as an ultimately destructive motivation for events and related to the historical justification of unjust developments in the common law of rape. Throughout the text, Hardy uses relic in precisely the opposite fashion from Walter Scott. While Scott's relics establish history as a source of legitimacy, Hardy's relics reveal that a faulty cultural faith in the importance of historical continuity victimizes Tess. By reading the text alongside Victorian developments in the common law of rape, I show that the unanswerable question of "what happened" to Tess challenges the very modes of legal discourse used to construct her as either a victim or a criminal. And, like Brockden Brown's work, *Tess* demonstrates how the common law imagination—through its imperative toward evolution—facilitates individual, subjective truth by traumatically disrupting the very historical, national truth that sustains it.

These case studies demonstrate the capacity of the common law imagination both to normalize injustice through the reconciliatory mechanism of collective memory and its potential for incorporating minority voices present in chronic cultural trauma. Toward the end of his life, Foucault took a more optimistic view of the potential for individual self-construction to carve out a space for freedom against the regulatory apparatus of truth-formation he had spent most of his career theorizing. He had, he claimed, been overemphasizing discursive power in relation to individual conduct and asserted a new individual ethical imperative to speak truth to power. This book will explore how the common law imagination facilitates both these phenomena, the pessimistic and the optimistic. On the one hand, the structure of common law historical reasoning allows for static mythologies about criminality to shape and resolve contemporary conflicts. On the other, the space for individual trauma narratives created by the focus on specific cases and the incremental incorporation of culture allows for some resistance on the part of non-normative subjects, particularly where cultural and legal discourses collide. By following these threads through two centuries of common law development we can begin to understand the complex relations between the individual, the culture, trauma, memory, and history that produce common law "truth" about crime.

Notes

1. Scott, *The Heart of Midlothian*, pp. 34–5.
2. Linebaugh, *The London Hanged*, p. 54.
3. In V. A. C. Gattrell's history of English execution, *The Hanging Tree* (1994), he asserts that more people were being hanged in early nineteenth-century England than at any time since the early modern era, but that the practice became so unpopular that it was abruptly limited to murderers in the 1830s.
4. Foucault, *History of Sexuality*, p. 144.
5. Differences between English/French experiences?
6. Schudson, "Dynamics of Distortion", pp. 346–7. For example, in an analysis of women's oral narratives about life during World War II Perry Summerfield examines the ways in which the narratives of individual women's experiences relate to public representations about women's lives at the time, fitting them into cultural frameworks such as "heroic" and "stoic" narratives.
7. Green, "Individual Remembering", p. 41.

8. Kenny, "A Place for Memory", p. 437.

9. Nora, "Between Memory and History", p. 15.

10. Terdiman, *Present Past*, p. 3.

11. Sturken, *Tangled Memories*, p. 5.

12. Ben-Yishai, *Common Precedents*, p. 5.

13. Ibid. p. 37.

14. Brescó de Luna, "How the Future Weights on the Past", p. 109.

15. de Saint-Laurent, "Thinking Through Time", p. 59.

16. de Saint-Laurent, "Uses of the Past", p. 9.

17. Ben-Yishai, *Common Precedents*, p. 3.

18. Alexander, "Toward a Theory of Cultural Trauma", p. 26, suggesting the Rape of Nanking as an example of such a collectively repressed atrocity.

19. Olick, "Collective Memory", p. 345.

20. Hirschberger, "Collective Trauma and the Social Construction of Meaning", p. 2.

21. Alexander, "Toward a Theory of Cultural Trauma", p. 10.

22. Ibid.

23. Nussbaum, *Poetic Justice*, p. 3.

24. Brooks, *Law's Stories*, p. 17.

25. Ben-Yishai, *Common Precedents*, p. 32.

26. Hale, "Amendment or Alteration of Lawes", p. 254. According to James Boyd White, Hale thus "conceives of the law not as a series of particular rules or decisions but as a cultural process, with its own modes and standards of transformation". *Acts of Hope*, p. 129. White says that by "time" Hale means "the community and culture over time" and that it is "Hale's word for our collective experience, the test of a rule or practice in many contexts, from many points of view". Ibid. p. 135.

27. Blackstone, *Commentaries*, vol. 4, p. 2.

28. Ibid. p. 3.

29. Ibid. p. 4.

30. It is important to remember that, unlike judges in civil code jurisdictions, common law judges thought of themselves, at least until the twentieth century, as engaged in the process of "finding" the law, rather than creating it.

31. Blackstone, *Commentaries*, vol. 4, p. 263.

32. Ibid. p. 275.

33. Neal, *National Trauma and Collective Memory*, p. 7.

34. Ibid.

35. Ben-Yishai, *Common Precedents*, p. 35.

36. Ibid.

37. Ibid. p. 41.

38. Ibid. p. 49.

39. Bender, *Imagining the Penitentiary*, p. 11.
40. Miller, *The Novel and the Police*, p. 3.
41. Rodensky, *The Crime in Mind*, p. 33.
42. Welsh, *Strong Representations*, pp. 9–10.
43. Ibid. p. 73.
44. MacPherson, *Harm's Way*, p. 4.
45. Bender, *Imagining the Penitentiary*, p. 5.
46. Ramsey, "Sex and Social Order", p. 203.
47. Ibid. p. 219.
48. Brewer, *By Birth or Consent*, p. 182.

Part I

Adultery as *Actus Reus*

1

Adultery, Criminality, and the Myth of English Sovereignty

On June 5, 1820, Lord Liverpool delivered a message to the House of Lords concerning the impending trial of Caroline of Brunswick, wife of the recently ascended King George IV, for divorce on the grounds of adultery. "The King," the Lord Chancellor read aloud, "has felt the most anxious desire to avert the necessity of disclosures and discussions, which must be as painful to his people as they can be to himself," but Caroline's decision to return from self-imposed exile in Italy to claim her place as Queen of England "leaves him no alternative."[1] From both a social and a political standpoint, Caroline's trial was one of the most notorious and divisive episodes in the history of the modern British monarchy; many witnesses testified to her romantic relationship with her Italian steward Bartolomeo Pergami, and a bill of divorce passed the House of Lords.[2] Nonetheless, due to Caroline's immense popularity as a figure of reform and George's reputation as a cruel husband and dissolute monarch, the bill was not submitted to the House of Commons.[3] (George did console himself by having Caroline refused access to his coronation, at bayonet-point.[4]) Beyond its much-discussed political significance, Queen Caroline's trial was also an important moment of cultural ferment surrounding the nature of adultery as a legal wrong.

The King's message for Parliament on that first day of the divorce proceedings, alluding to the harm to "the people" arising from disclosure of Caroline's alleged indiscretions, is clearly a case of political grandstanding. Yet he made the statement in the context of a trial that was, due to the parties involved, at once a private divorce and a proposed public bill. It should therefore also be understood as a particular sort of legal claim, with relevance to the basic classification of a wrong as a tort or a crime. When Blackstone distinguishes between "public" and "private" wrongs at the start of Book Four of his *Commentaries,* he states that English criminal law is known as "the doctrine of the pleas of the crown" because

> the king, in whom centers the majesty of the whole community, is supposed by the law to be the person injured by every infraction of the public

right belonging to that community, and is therefore in all cases the proper prosecutor for every public offence.[5]

In many cases, the public/private wrong model is a useful, if oversimplified, means of distinguishing between a crime and a civil injury such as a tort or a breach of contract, and in democracies it does not depend upon the physical body of a monarch. Individuals may recoup losses for civil injuries, while the government prosecutes a crime to redress the harms it imposes on the polity as a whole. When one commits an intentional assault on another person, for example, he has wronged that person and may owe him compensation under civil law, but he has also done violence to the whole community by violating the collective moral prohibition on assault; he, therefore, may also be prosecuted by the sovereign (styled as either the crown or, in a democracy, the people). Some torts—such as unintentional injuries caused by negligence —may not expose an individual to criminal liability on the theory that they do not rise to the level of moral opprobrium necessary to constitute an injury to the crown or community. [6]

Yet Blackstone's turn of phrase suggests something in the English common law imagination that sees a potentially interdependent relationship between tort and crime, centered on the body of the sovereign. Contemporary torts scholars John Goldberg and Benjamin Zipursky suggest that one way to distinguish between a tort and a crime is the "relational" component of the tort. As they put it, where "a criminal prohibition states 'For all x, x shall not A,' a tort occurs when someone violates the directive 'For all x and for all y, x shall not do A to y'."[7] Blackstone's famous dichotomy is striking in that—counter to this modern understanding—it relies upon the language of relationality to describe criminal liability as well as tort: x shall not do A to the King. In most cases, this legal fiction will not matter much in the common law's disposition of wrongs, either public or private. But King George's invocation of the "people's" wellbeing in his divorce proceeding brings to light a very specific legal wrong that, I argue, has been fluid in nature at common law precisely because of the body of the king: adultery.

In Britain over the course of the eighteenth and nineteenth centuries, the understanding of adultery as a tort is complicated by an accompanying discourse of what I will call "quasi-criminality." On the one hand, the removal of criminal punishment for adultery reduced it, at law, to a manner of commercial wrong. Foucault might call this new, business-like understanding part of a system of "normalization" as opposed to a system of law or personal power: a system with the ability to "qualify, measure, appraise, and hierarchize, rather than display itself in murderous splendor."[8] The law is present but functioning to redistribute wealth among litigants; it is increasingly incorporated, as he said of the modern judicial institution generally, "into a continuum of apparatuses (medical, administrative, and so on) whose functions are for the most part regulatory."[9] Nonetheless—while formally trivialized, or at least privatized—adultery remained discursively linked to a threat to British kingship: the ultimate symbol of personal and legal authority. As a result, the tension between the weight of relevant monarchical history and the absence of criminal enforcement creates a new cultural discourse of adultery which attempts, itself, to serve an explicitly penal function.

In their influential nineteenth-century treatise *English Law Before the Time of Edward I* (1898), Sir Frederick Pollock and Frederic William Maitland open their chapter on the distinction between crime and tort by describing the discursive authority of ancient law as uniquely powerful on this question, noting, "[o]n no other part of our law did the twelfth century stamp a more permanent impress of its heavy hand than on that which was to be the criminal law of after days."[10] They also state the importance to English criminal law of Richard Terdiman's "present past," describing their task of twelfth-century law gathering as "building a bridge" between the "continuous and well-told tale" of the Teutonic law of *wer* and blood-feud that preceded the English, and the more recent English criminal law compiled by treatise writers such as Hale and Fitzjames Stephens.[11] My project in this chapter will be to use this awareness of history to shed light on the dialectical relationship between official and social constructions of adultery, and the specific elements of cultural trauma at work in each. When the law defines a particular sexual wrong as "criminal," it is an instance of what Foucault would call the production of "truth." For Foucault, "truth" is "a system of ordered procedures for the production, regulation, distribution, circulation, and operation of statements," which is "linked in a circular relation with systems of power which produce and sustain it."[12] The cultural texts I consider participate, in a particularly self-conscious way, in just such a circular relationship with the legal systems they seek to define.

This chapter will first provide a brief overview of the legal standing of adultery up until the mid-eighteenth century. It will then trace, alongside new legal developments, the narrative history of adultery through the late eighteenth century. Specifically, it will take up a variety of legal and cultural texts that participate in the discourse around adultery as a quasi-crime and identify the traumatic narratives about threatened sovereignty that motivate it. By examining the development of this discourse alongside the relevant law, we can discern not only an interesting legal narrative in a particular time and place but an instance of the complex social process through which public and private wrongs become distinguished—or conflated.[13] We will also see how the new conception of adultery as a relational wrong (generally between one man and another) contributed to the legal construction of women as contested commercial property.

The History of Adultery

In the medieval period, adultery fell primarily under the penal jurisdiction of the ecclesiastical courts as opposed to the crown. Generally, the church treated both adulterous parties as equally culpable, and typical punishments included the prohibition on future relations, some form of public penance—often beatings or a pilgrimage—or the imposition of a fine.[14] As historian Caroline Dunn notes, however, because adultery frequently implicated concerns about the inheritance of property, a subject for royal jurisdiction, it therefore "transcended the boundary" between the two spheres, as both a "sexual sin" and "secular crime."[15] In 1285 the Second Statute of Westminster provided a civil cause of action for husbands whose wives had committed adultery, by blending the tort into the same chapter intended to establish the tort of wife abduction: a husband could sue for the value of any goods that had been taken away with his wife and, if the wife had "willingly" left to "live with her adulterer," then she was permanently barred from seeking her dower upon her husband's death (unless he had willingly "and without the coercion of the Church" reconciled with her).[16]

Although these claims were tort actions benefitting the husband, the law styled them similarly to criminal prosecutions. In the first place, the blurry line between the crime of abduction and the tort of adultery suggests that in the law's conception these were similar sorts of relational wrongs against the husband which, like the crime of theft (also a relational wrong), the general public might nonetheless have a simultaneous interest in avenging. Furthermore, the statutory language put it that "the king shall have suit" in such cases and, indeed, secular authorities would frequently make arrests that facilitated the husband's practical ability to bring suit.[17] After the Statute of Westminster took effect, the number of suits for adultery rose dramatically, though declined a century later.[18] This decline may have been due in part to the passage, in 1382, of the Statute of Rapes, which created another theory of liability and increased the punishment for wives who "consent" to their "ravishers."[19] Due to the apparent perception that women were increasingly faking their abductions to escape from undesired marriages, the new statute provided that in such cases, both wife and lover forfeited not only the wife's dowry but also her landholdings in jointure.[20] This statute, like its predecessor, blended the provision of civil remedies for the tort of adultery with the description of serious crimes: the felonies of rape and abduction.

The medieval understanding of adultery thus had two legal dichotomies. First, there was the conception of gender-neutral sexual sin in ecclesiastical court as compared to asymmetrical relational tort against a husband in secular court. As Dunn puts it

> [e]ven if adultery and self-divorce were matters for canon law courts, references to both marriage formation and dissolution appear regularly in the common law records. The centrality of property in late medieval society is the key to understanding the overlapping ecclesiastical and secular jurisdictions.[21]

It is clear even at this juncture that the increasing importance of secular courts and their property-based conception of the offence contributed to the discursive process that made women, to use Nancy Hartsock's phrasing, "objectified subjects."[22] Second, even in secular court, there remained a shadow of criminality floating around the definition of the civil wrong, which would come to haunt both the legal and cultural understandings of adultery in the centuries to come.

This relationship would become more complicated due to the increasingly tenuous status of ecclesiastical courts themselves after the political upheavals of the seventeenth century. In the late sixteenth and early seventeenth centuries, the dual sacred and secular regulation of adultery continued, abetted by a variety of communal shaming rituals.[23] During the Interregnum, however, ecclesiastical courts temporarily ceased to operate, and the puritanical Cromwell regime dramatically criminalized adultery in secular courts: the Adultery Act of 1650 imposed the death penalty for adulterers.[24] This draconian punishment proved unworkable, and the statute lapsed; nonetheless, ecclesiastical courts were severely weakened by the English Revolution, and the project of redressing the moral wrong of adultery fell increasingly to secular authorities.[25] As David M. Turner, who has written the most comprehensive history of adultery during this period, puts it:

> The Restoration project of enforcing moral unity and returning to an antediluvian order after the mid-century upheavals was perceived to be under threat from a number of inter-related forces: from the much publicized adulteries of King Charles II and his courtiers, from the open scoffing at religion by "wits" and "atheists," and from the fragmentation of religious allegiances marked by the rise of Protestant dissent and the insidious threat of Roman Catholicism.[26]

In reaction to the perceived sexual excesses of the Restoration Era, the Glorious Revolution brought with it the creation of numerous Societies for the Reformation of Manners, which cropped up across England and sought to utilize the court system to prosecute sundry morality crimes. The Societies attempted to criminally prosecute adulterers in the late 1690s, but by the 1740s such criminal prosecutions were extremely rare.[27]

Nonetheless, the image of adultery occupied a curious position in English political discourse throughout the Revolution and Restoration and the accompanying ideological struggles as to the sources of royal authority. Stuart apologist Sir Robert Filmer famously analogized the relationship between a subject and his sovereign to the subjection of Eve to Adam, and James I—the king who knighted Filmer—declared to Parliament "What God has conjoined let no man separate. I am the husband and the whole island is my lawful wife."[28] The discourses of marital relations and kingship have been intertwined throughout the development of Anglo-American laws related to adultery.[29] In refuting the Filmerian view of absolute monarchy, however, John Locke engaged him at his Edenic point of departure, arguing that the picture of marital sovereignty taken from Genesis was no more literal than the other aspects of Eve's curse articulated there, asking incredulously:

> [W]ill anyone say, that Eve, or any other woman, sinned, if she were brought to bed without those multiplied pains God threatens her here with? or that either of our queens, Mary or Elizabeth, had they married any of their subjects, had been by this text put into a political subjection to him? or that he should thereby have had monarchical rule over her?[30]

The Lockean position—laying the groundwork for a more egalitarian marital union incidental to that of a liberal legal order—points to the fact that one of the notable cultural effects of the Revolution was a move away from a view of the individual household as a microcosm for the state.[31] At this moment, the traditional patriarchal formulation, in which the father occupied the structural role of sovereign, began to be supplanted by ideals of domestic love.[32] Nonetheless, Locke's argument demonstrates the inescapable discursive relationship between marital freedom and kingship.[33] And Foucault saw the outcome of this broader philosophical de-emphasis of sovereignty in favor of domesticity as simply power redistributed and running in reverse. The process of "totalization," he says, is the systemic effort "to introduce this meticulous attention of the father towards his family into the management of the state."[34] Perhaps the family was no longer itself a miniature body politic, but it remained discursively crucial to the newly-decentralized liberal political order. In any case, despite the liberalizing shifts, it remained the case that a woman's murder of her husband constituted petty treason, punishable by burning; thus, adultery-related murders of husbands by wives were inescapably reiterations, in the public sphere, of the husband-as-sovereign legal trope.[35]

Indeed it was precisely this potential relationship between adultery and violence that reinforced the cultural narrative of adultery as a public concern. The seventeenth century saw the increased popularity of "murder pamphlets" —accounts, often written by prison clergy, of notable crimes and their aftermaths, sometimes purporting to contain the final words and confessions of the condemned criminal. These crime biographies, which many scholars have explored as the antecedents to the novel form itself, had both didactic and salacious purposes, which sat in awkward tension.[36] Pamphlet writers would attempt to impose narrative order on the relationship between an underlying adulterous affair and the violence that spun out of it—usually the murder of the innocent spouse by the adulterous one. (Before the Civil War, these pamphlets more frequently featured female murderesses; after the war, the trend moved toward tales of adulterous husbands murdering their wives.)[37] As Turner puts it, "[i]n constructing events to illustrate a cultural and moral commonplace, that one sin led to another, pamphlets articulated a set of 'moral truths' about crime and its consequences recognizable to all."[38] In Turner's view, adultery-related homicide generated such interest because it "fed into wider concerns that, in what was for the majority of people a divorceless society, adulterous lovers might use foul means to break the marriage knot."[39]

Adultery-related homicides, of course, also included cases in which a wronged spouse exacted vengeance by killing his wife's lover; these scenarios raised a more complicated set of moral and legal problems. Before roughly the eighteenth century, prevailing social norms understood such murders to be at least somewhat acceptable actions to restore one's lost honor. In 1617 English courts first recognized honor-related motivation as a formal factor in mitigation of a murderer's culpability.[40] By the eighteenth century, however, courts moved away from the "honor"-based formulation and considered such murders in the more contemporary "heat of passion" framework. In other words, the question shifted from whether a wronged husband was motivated by the fact of his wife's adultery to whether the crime had occurred so immediately upon discovery of the same that he could not be said to be fully in control of his actions.[41] The coincidence of the popular genre of prison house confessional with the changing story deemed legally relevant to a wronged lover's defense of inability to form intent (a concept discussed in greater detail in my treatment of *mens rea* in Chapter 3) is an example of how law and culture worked together toward what Foucault might have identified as the formation of the criminal subject. Certain subjective stories, of sufficiently "normal" reactions, led to exoneration, while others led to the gallows.

In any case, while adultery was for the most part formally beyond the jurisdiction of the criminal law by the eighteenth century, as a cultural phenomenon it had become rhetorically linked with it. Turner argues that

[i]n narratives of petty treason, cuckoldry was portrayed as a portent of the catastrophic events that lay in store for the injured husband . . . In the pamphlet narratives a wife's power to cuckold her husband became synonymous with the power to kill him.

Or, as Laura Gowing puts it, "[m]urder was the culmination of the economic, material, and physical consequences of adultery . . . it was the last danger that adulterous women posed to their husbands."[42] These descriptions drive home a particularly interesting feature of this understanding of adultery: the importance, to its quasi-criminality, of the narrative that gave rise to it. In other words, adultery straddles the theoretical border between crime and tort precisely because of the increasingly powerful understanding of the causal link between adultery and inevitable violence. Adultery is thus most criminal at the moment it generates a particular traumatic narrative trajectory.

In light of this relationship, it is perhaps unsurprising that the famous eighteenth-century cause of action in tort for adultery was known as "criminal conversation." A form of trespass, the cause of action was first recognized in the latter part of the century and exploded in popularity immediately.[43] It is important to understand, too, that due to the complicated pleadings, this tort action was only available to the very wealthy.[44] Regardless, the very name of the action compresses the criminal into the commonplace; "conversation" suggests a congenial social setting. The cause of action recognized both the quasi-criminality and the basic impoliteness of seducing someone's spouse. Indeed, in the courtroom, lawyers for plaintiffs in these cases expended a lot of effort to play up harm to the public morality occasioned by an act of adultery, even though such public concerns are traditionally the territory of the criminal prosecution which, as Blackstone would have it, is concerned with the rights of the king, not the plaintiff.[45] Because none of the primary parties to the suit were allowed to testify in court, counsel for the two sides sought, as Turner puts it, to "reduce the individuals involved into preexisting roles which illustrated universal 'truths'."[46] Simultaneously, however, proof of damages in such cases required the exact opposite argument. It was important not that the adulterers had violated some objective standard of morality, but that their actions had affected the plaintiff husband. To that extent, the greater the degree of affront taken by the husband—whether, for example, he had been friends with the defendant before the adultery took place—the more likely he was to collect.[47] Unlike a crime, then, this aspect of criminal conversation was highly relational. However, as a social matter, a plaintiff walked a "thin line between taking proper action to restore honour, and petty-minded vindictiveness."[48]

Adultery as Narrative

The increasing popularity of the criminal conversation lawsuit resulted in a new form of popular literature in the tradition of the murder pamphlet: the publication of the proceedings of trials for both criminal conversation and divorce. In these cases, observers attended the trials and took shorthand notes on the attorneys' arguments and the testimony of each witness. These were then collected into volumes containing the proceedings of multiple trials, which were often illustrated like novels, with detailed drawings of the various pairs of lovers at their moment of discovery. With such aesthetic packaging and intended so obviously for entertainment, these compendiums belong alongside the murder pamphlets squarely in the genealogy of the novel.[49] Yet these compendiums share two less-discussed features that shed light upon the development of the tort of adultery itself as quasi-criminal. The first is the manner in which they rhetorically locate their subject matter—with varying degrees of explicitness—against a set of background cultural concerns about the instability of British sovereignty. The second is their tendency to assume a formal punitive function themselves, self-consciously.

The seven-volume *Trials for Adultery: or, the History of Divorces* (1799) is a representative example. Even the title strives for a particular sort of legitimacy. While the contents are indeed a series of unrelated trials, the claim to being a comprehensive "history" echoes the vision of the past as continuous and cumulative that motivates common law judging.[50] The frontispiece elaborates, explaining that it is

> A complete History of the Private Life, Intrigues, and Amours of many Characters in the most elevated Sphere: every Scene and Transaction, however ridiculous, whimsical, or extraordinary, being fairly represented, as becomes a faithful Historian, who is fully determined not to sacrifice *Truth* at the Shrine of *Guilt* and *Folly*.[51]

This passage suggests that a theatrical lens—in which events and people are "scenes" and "characters"—is the best means of access to "Truth." It is also the reader's first hint at the intended public function of the work: to bring to light the "private" lives of "elevated" people.[52]

The introduction puts a finer point on the matter, lamenting that "[c]onjugal infidelity is become so general that it is hardly considered as criminal; especially in the fashionable world."[53] It goes on to note that "a Right Reverend Prelate" has tried to introduce a law criminalizing adultery, which passed the House of Lords but not the House of Commons. Adultery, therefore, is not merely a subject for entertainment, nor even for moralizing, but an actual crime that has fallen into a gap of non-enforcement. The author then contemplates the particular penological challenge presented by adultery: that "[i]t is indeed a difficult matter to deter those of an abandoned disposition, from the commission of crimes where the punishment is trivial."[54] Having thus identified a failure of the law, the text states plainly that it might, itself, rectify it: "[t]his publication may effect what the law cannot: the transactions of the adulterer and the adulteress will, by being thus *publickly circulated,* preserve others from the like crimes, from the fear of shame."[55] The author speculates furthermore that the compendium may also "be of service to the practicers in the law, as they may have recourse to these trials for information, which will answer the same purpose in this, as the Law and Equity Reports in other courts."[56]

This language makes a startlingly powerful suggestion about the role of cultural materials in shaping the law. Not only can publication of adultery narratives serve a deterrent function the law cannot, but these texts, it is suggested, may themselves occupy a place in the development of common law precedent. In other words, the narratives of adultery generated in these texts may form a continuous history with the law reports and therefore contribute to the accumulated legal materials upon which judges decide individual cases. Such a process renders startlingly explicit Foucault's claim, in *Discipline and Punish*, that surveillance techniques—here in the form, essentially, of tabloid gossip—supplanted aggressive state power in the regulation of the human body. That said, the formal legal machinery for determining guilt remains central. The compendium seeks to assist in the legal process as much as it may partially replace it.

In any case, having stated this general claim for his work, the author of the introduction then directs us to a particularly important narrative emerging from the compendium: the public effects of an upper-class woman's fall from grace. "[F]rom her situation," he asserts, "it was incumbent on her to have been an example of purity to the rest of the sex: she is indeed become the object of the scorn, pity, and derision of her relations, her former associates, and the public."[57] He thus argues that adultery imposes a public harm, which is often the threshold at which the law recognizes a tort to be a crime as well. If these compendiums do indeed claim a place in the common law itself, their contribution may be the idea that the fall of a noblewoman causes sufficient public harm to justify the criminalization of adultery. While this observation immediately raises a number of class and gender questions, many of them are beyond the scope of this project. What is clear, however, is that the broad focus on upper-class female adultery indicates the particular salience of the highest-profile instances thereof: the adultery of queens such as Caroline.

The first trial included in this history is the famous 1730 suit brought by Lord Abergavenny against Richard Lydell for criminal conversation with

Katherine, Lady Abergavenny, which—in the attorneys' attempts to characterize the wrong that had occurred—provides a clear example of the legal
status of the tort. The pair had been caught in the act by Abergavenny's
servants, after which he expelled the heavily pregnant Katherine from their
home; she subsequently died two weeks after giving birth. The record of the
Lydell trial bears much in common with many of the other transcripts in the
compendium. Most notably, much of the evidence given in these proceedings
is testimony by the servants of the involved parties (who, whether by their
own initiative or at the direction of their employers, were frequently said to
be the first to "discover" the adultery). Abergavenny's servant Osman testifies
that upon discovery of the lovers he had said to Lydell "[f]or you, Sir, to come
so frequently, in such a shew of friendship, and to wrong his Lordship after
such a manner as you have done, is a crime for which you can make him no
satisfaction," a claim with which Lydell himself apparently agreed.[58] Osman's
characterization of adultery as a crime, which somehow transcends vindication, typifies the slippery legal identity ascribed to the act during these tort
proceedings. The Lydell account emphasizes the criminality of adultery by
noting that the defendant had been "carried away to the county gaol" upon
discovery, for Lord Abergavenny's securing civil process.[59]

The closing summations of both parties' counsel further emphasize
the rhetorical confusion surrounding the quasi-criminality of adultery. The
defense counsel opens with the largely monetary considerations frequently
associated with tort compensation, arguing that "damages ought to be pro-
portioned to the circumstances of the person offending" and that in this
case Lydell was only possessed of "a life estate under great incumbrances."[60]
He makes the further dispassionate point that because Lady Abergavenny
did not live very long after her discovery "the injury his Lordship sustained
in his health could not be very great" as he would not have been able to
enjoy her company much longer in any case.[61] Yet he then makes the sort of
intentionality-based arguments more relevant to the sphere of the criminal
law, suggesting that "it seemed as if an agreement was made to lay a snare and
temptation to draw [Lydell] into a criminal action."[62] This argument, which
today we would recognize as the defense of entrapment, essentially suggests
that Lydell should not be liable for actions he was encouraged to commit by
the prosecuting authority. If not originally possessed of the intent, or *mens
rea*, to commit a crime, a person should not be deemed a criminal for being
tricked into it by the government. (The comparison, of course, fails in this
case even on its own terms, as Abergavenny's servants did not trick Lydell into
committing the act, they merely failed to prevent him so as to be able to catch
him red-handed.)

The defense counsel raises yet another point that seems better suited to a criminal sentencing proceeding than a tort action: Lydell is already miserable and has therefore suffered enough. In a purely relational tort framework, the mental state of the defendant should have nothing to do with the amount of damages he owes the plaintiff; the only question should be the plaintiff's losses. In the criminal context, however, the defendant's state of mind has long been cited as relevant (albeit controversially so) to determining the degree of punishment he deserves. Remorseful defendants, the argument goes, are already good examples to society of the ills of crime and are likely therefore to deter others from committing the same.[63] Under a retributive theory of criminal punishment, they also have less moral desert than the unrepentant. Finally, the defense presents witnesses who testify to Lydell's reputation as "a very civil, modest, well-bred gentleman, and could never have thought he would have been guilty of anything of this nature."[64] Lord Abergavenny's counsel, however, responds somewhat curiously to all of these arguments by conflating tort and criminal logic into a general rebuttal. He points out that the criminal law imposing capital punishment for adulterers is still on the books and that therefore, "there is nothing here can make satisfaction, but a pecuniary punishment."[65] This response is inherently illogical: the justification for criminally punishing adultery lies in the public harms it causes, which cannot be rectified through remuneration to one private individual. Yet with respect to Lydell's encumbered estate, he again avoids the purely monetary logic of tort law by making a wholly desert-based argument: "it is but reasonable, if a person destroys the happiness of another, his happiness ought to be disturbed as long as he lives."[66]

Throughout the compendium, the ecclesiastical origins of adultery prosecutions become clear in the various courts' repeated observations that the adulterer was "instigated and seduced by the devil" and "[d]id not have the fear of God before his eyes."[67] In the suit of J. G. Biker against Mr. Morley, his wife's gynecologist (or, as plaintiff's counsel describes him, "male midwife") the compendium editor took great care to transcribe (or possibly embellish) the plaintiff's melodramatic description of the defendant's behavior. According to the transcription, the plaintiff

> thought himself happy in the possession of a wife, young, beautiful, virtuous and affectionate; when all at once this happiness was dashed, by the discovery of a piece of management of the defendant, in seducing her from those paths of virtue, in which she had been brought up from her infancy, and continued to walk, 'till her unfortunate acquaintance with the defendant'[68]

Plaintiff's counsel goes on to note that Mrs. Biker was "surprised into a breach of her duty" but in the end, she "looked back upon her false step with contrition and horror" and "so great was her remorse that she expired in a mad-house."[69] The conflation of legal terms like possession and breach of duty with the dramatic rendition of innocence spoiled and subsequently exterminated manifests the theatrical approach to legal history promised in the introduction. The editor of the compendium further emphasizes the plaintiff's narrative of guilt by wholly omitting the defense case, noting only that defense counsel "made some observations upon the evidence for the plaintiff, and some upon their own; but as they arise for the most part on the plaintiff's evidence we omit taking notice of them."[70] With these editorial choices, the compendium foregrounds the public dangers of fallen women, suggested in the introduction as one of the text's motivating concerns as a contribution to the law reports. Further—by highlighting the dangers to fallen women, such as death and madness—the text assumes the deterrent function associated with the law itself.

An even loftier public purpose appears throughout the two-volume *A New and Complete Collection of the Most Remarkable Trials for Adultery &c* (1780). This collection takes a form closer to that of the novel, noting on its frontispiece that it is "[g]iven in the way of a narrative and not in the tedious forms of depositions."[71] The author thus eliminates the mechanism of eyewitness transcription. Even more notably, this work is not purely a collection of eighteenth-century legal proceedings. Freed from the transcript form utilized by other works of the time, the text's editors more explicitly locate their subject matter as part of a deeper historical project. While including several of the same famous adulteries chronicled in *The History of Divorces,* this "Complete" collection begins with the 1542 trial and execution of Henry VIII's fifth queen, Catherine Howard. While *The History of Divorces* is concerned with presenting the criminal relationship between aristocratic sexual behavior and public morals, this collection takes it a step further. In using an English queen's trial for treason as the starting point for a project on eighteenth-century tort cases, the text's editors reify the relationship between adultery, criminality, and sovereignty.

Consequently, the chapter on Catherine Howard explains:

> This trial is put at the head of this Work, not only on account of its being the earliest in point of time, but on account of the dignity of the party tried. It is a trial of a most curious and interesting nature; the principal facts proved were committed before marriage; the punishment of the Queen's relations, who were no way accessory to her lewd practices, was contrary to every rule of law and justice; and the act of Parliament that passed, in order to oblige any lady the King intended to marry, to reveal any former incontinence she had been guilty of, was considered a most extraordinary effort of tyranny.[72]

From this introduction, it is clear that Catherine's trial is significant in part because she is the archetypical adulteress: as she is the queen and therefore "first" in "dignity," Catherine's adultery has the most important general effects on the kingdom, its legal order, and its security vis-à-vis the rest of the world. The editors of the compendium emphasize this by including a long extract from a letter sent by the king's privy council to William Paget, the English Ambassador in France, which states that the King had desired in the first place to marry Catherine so that "his Majesty might have some more store of fruit and succession, to the comfort of his realm."[73] The inclusion of his fifth queen's adultery trial at the start of this compendium demonstrates how the criminality of adultery had come to function as a form of English legal origins story. In addition, at least in respect of Catherine Howard's affairs before her marriage to the king, the text notes that investigations "shewed that the Queen had thrown aside all sense of modesty, as well as all fear of discovery."[74] As I will discuss, the concept of "discovery" as the touchstone for legal liability remained deeply important to the eighteenth-century discourse on adultery. When closely considered under the logic of those who would criminalize the offense, it is, in fact, the discovery of the private sin that brings it into the public sphere and thereby causes the harms complained of. In this case, Catherine's heedlessness of discovery, perhaps even more so than the original impropriety, becomes the strongest indication of her lawlessness. Finally, the chapter closes noting that Catherine was condemned to die for "[t]he act of defiling her sovereign's bed," a succinct statement of the act of political insubordination presented by an adulterous wife.[75]

Yet the text nonetheless takes a complex view of the relationship between sovereign authority and sexual sin in its treatment of Catherine's trial. In the first place, the author describes Henry as a "jealous and despotic monarch."[76] Thomas Cranmer, the author, notes, "was in extreme danger; for if full evidence was not brought, his ruin was inevitable," a fact which calls into question the procedural fairness of the investigation.[77] Most significantly, the author considers tyrannical Henry's *ex post facto* law forcing a woman and her relatives to disclose her prior sexual history before she marries the king, noting "the excessive severity of parliament to the Queen's relations was greatly censured by the public. It was thought unnatural to punish a father and mother for not discovering their daughter's shame."[78] The new statute was consequently:

> Looked on as a grievous piece of tyranny; since, if a King, especially one of
> so imperious a temper as Henry VIII, should deign such an honor to any
> of his subjects, who had been guilty of miscarriages . . . they were reduced
> to the shocking alternative of making themselves infamous by publishing

so scandalous a secret, or exposing themselves to the danger of being afterwards attainted of treason.[79]

Here, again, the "discovery" of adultery is cast as a quasi-crime in and of itself, comparable enough to treason to render the choice between incurring the guilt of one or the other a "shocking" dilemma.

The Catherine Howard narrative emphasizes both the threat to sovereignty posed by adultery and an eighteenth-century concern over the threat to liberal legal order posed by the extreme criminalization of spousal insubordination. This dichotomy, in a sense, represents both poles of cultural trauma remaining in a post-Restoration constitutional monarchy, where threats both to and from the King can unmake the fabric of society. Yet most of the rest of the compendium focuses almost exclusively on the first set of concerns. Most notably, the author says of the suit for criminal conversation brought by the Irish Viscount Bellfield against his brother Arthur Rochfort that, of all recent cases, "none for the opprobriousness of the act itself or the many horrid circumstances attending it comes anything near."[80] According to most historians, Bellfield's accusations against his wife and brother were specious, and his cruelty to his wife Mary, whose own family had forced her to marry him against her will, was legend.[81] After the supposed affair, he had her locked in a tower for the thirty-one years until his death; she was so mentally and physically debilitated by her imprisonment that she died soon thereafter. (Arthur died in debtor's prison, from which he never escaped, having never been able to pay the judgment in his brother's favor.)

Yet the text presents Bellfield as dramatically wronged and the alleged affair as a uniquely specific failure of Irish identity and sovereignty. The author describes Bellfield as the consummate Irish nobleman: from a "very ancient family," with "considerable possessions in the kingdom of Ireland," and so handsome and talented that he "was looked upon as a match for the first woman in the kingdom."[82] His young wife, too, the daughter of Lord Viscount Molesworth, was notably beautiful "even in that country, remarkable for pretty women."[83] As superlatively Irish as both parties were, Mary's downfall was similarly so: "[t]he pernicious Irish custom of drinking and carousing at each other's houses . . . frequently forced his lordship into company where my lady could not decently go" which "left her alone, at her own disposal."[84]

After Bellfield confronts Mary (who is never actually mentioned by name in the text itself) with purported love letters from Arthur, and she sees the "criminal lines"—which also supposedly (and most likely apocryphally) contained plans to poison Bellfield—she cries out "O my lord, kill me yourself, but do not discover me to my father."[85] The horror of being "discovered" again appears tantamount to—or even worse than—execution among the various outcomes of adultery; in this case, the discovery has national significance as "[t]he affair was now the conversation of the whole kingdom."[86] The narrative then goes on to sugarcoat the remainder of Bellfield's actions, stating that he only sued his brother "to clear himself from unjust imputations" and consented to let the affair stand without demanding monetary judgment. In the text's account, he pursued the judgment eventually only because his brother returned to Ireland against his wishes, while it appears to have been the case historically that Rochfort fled to escape the debt.[87] Further, the text states erroneously that Lady Bellfield "was removed to a country seat of his lordship's"[88] where she remained shut up till about three years after, instead of the thirty-one she endured in reality.[89] Most curious, perhaps, are the last lines of the narrative:

> When Mr. Rochfort in defiance of his brother's lenity having returned to Ireland, his lordship renewed his proceedings ... Mr. Rochfort was confined for the debt, in the King's bench prison of that kingdom. The title of this family is now Earl Belvedere.[90]

The sudden narrative leap from Bellfield's successful suit and his brother's imprisonment to the fact of the former's creation as the first Earl of Belvedere sublimates the entire adultery drama into an entry in the Irish peerage. The law, by providing these points of official significance, works to repress the trauma of Mary's abuse and imprisonment, as well as the legal circumstances that made them possible.

This sampling of accounts of criminal conversation has served three primary purposes. First, it has demonstrated that such texts troubled the de-criminalization of "criminal" conversation, and functioned, themselves, as punitive authorities, actively participating in the development of the common law discourse on adultery. Second, it has proposed that when adultery operates in the English cultural imagination, it necessarily implicates the collective trauma around threatened sovereignty, which contributes to its quasi-criminal status. Third, it has shown how the English, rights-bearing subject itself developed—both legally and culturally—against a conception of dangerous femininity with the potential to disrupt both the property interests of the individual and the physical stability of both the local community and the state itself.

The Sale of Sovereignty and the Literary Criminalization of Adultery

We now turn to the question of how purely literary representations of adultery in the eighteenth century interact with the legal and cultural landscape just discussed. Henry Fielding's *The Modern Husband* (1732) is a useful starting point, both due to its subject and to the fact that Fielding eventually became an important figure in London law and policing[91] after his career as a dramatist was effectively ended by the Theatrical Licensing Act of 1737.[92] After he was forced to return to the practice of law, he eventually availed himself of political connections to become Chief Magistrate of London, from which position he founded London's first formal police force, the Bow Street Runners.[93] Throughout his career as a jurist, he was deeply interested in the reform of prison conditions and the elimination of the spectacle of public hanging.[94] Due to his role as a judge and penal reformer at the very time Foucault argues such reforms gave rise to a new form of bodily control through incarceration and cultural discourse, Fielding's literary take on the question of adultery is of particular interest in any discussion of adultery and the law. Few other authors of the period participated equally in both the legal and literary discourses on the subject.

Fielding's official judicial authority makes it particularly significant that his satirical work transmits an awareness of the policing function of literature itself. For example, in *The History of the Life of Mr. Jonathan Wild the Great* (1743), ostensibly an account of a well-known seventeenth-century highwayman, Fielding sends up Horace Walpole as the parallel to his condemned antihero, noting on the occasion of Wild's execution "whether [Fortune] hath determined you shall be hanged or be a prime minister, it is in either case lost labour to resist." Fielding makes a parallel between Wild's dominion over his crew of bandits and Walpole's leadership of the Whig Party in Parliament, by explicitly comparing the "prig" and the "statesman:"

> [A]s the prig enjoys (and merits too) the greater degree of honour from his gang, so doth he suffer the less disgrace from the world, who think his misdeeds, as they call them, sufficiently at last punished with a halter, which at once puts an end to his pain and infamy; whereas the other is not only hated in power, but detested and contemned at the scaffold; and future ages vent their malice on his fame, while the other sleeps quiet and forgotten.[95]

Fielding implies that both Wild and Walpole deserve capital punishment and the latter greater dishonor. Furthermore, by describing the ongoing public hatred of the failed statesman, Fielding's words themselves participate in the envisioned punishment. This interest in the explicitly penal function of satire—similar to that manifest in the compendia of adultery trials discussed earlier—would also motivate his literary treatment of adultery. Through satire Fielding critiques the use of criminal conversation actions to exploit and pervert the justice system for personal gain, in a manner he considers generally threatening to England itself as an imperial power. As Foucault observed, "the idea of justice in itself" has been "put to work in different types of societies as an instrument of a certain political and economic power or as a weapon against that power."[96] Reading Fielding with that claim in mind, we can see how he uses the quasi-criminality of adultery to critique a set of privatized commercial arrangements in the service of a broader construction of English identity within the newly flourishing mercantile system.

While several of Fielding's later novels, such as *Amelia* (1751) and *Tom Jones* (1749), took up the question of adultery, *The Modern Husband* is the work most entirely devoted to it. The play opened at the Royal Theatre, Drury Lane, on February 14, 1732, the same year as the *Abergavenny* v. *Lyddell* criminal conversation litigation, and it is generally agreed that Fielding shared the public's belief that Abergavenny had intentionally tolerated his late wife's affair in the hopes of making money in court.[97] The play ran for an impressive thirteen nights, after which it was forced to close due to the illness of one of the lead actresses. According to the *Daily Post*, it was performed "with Applause, to very good Audiences," though it was never revived, possibly due to the difficulty of finding other actors willing to tackle the material.[98] The play contains two overlapping legal discourses regulating the practice of adultery: business law and criminal law. Lord Richly, the wealthy nobleman who sits at the top of the economy of wife-selling in the play, summarizes the relationship between crime, adultery, and money succinctly: "Poverty makes as many Cuckolds as it does Thieves."[99] Fielding thereby indicates that adultery is regulated by a separate economic system from thievery, parallel to but apart from criminal law and that it can be commoditized as monetary damages to complaining husbands. Mr. Gaywit summarizes the situation in the economic language of the time:

> I am mistaken if many Husbands in this Town do not live very comfortably by being content with their Infamy, nay, by being Promoters of it. It is a modern Trade, unknown to our Ancestors, a modern Bubble, which seems to be in a rising Condition at present.[100]

Gaywit compares the cause of action for adultery to the South Sea Bubble, which in 1720 led to severe nation-wide economic losses amidst the aggressive fund-raising by promoters of various joint-stock companies looking to do business overseas.

In *Maria* (1797), Mary Wollstonecraft also identifies this sexual economy, making the feminist critique that the relationship between property, power, and sex serves primarily to debase and subjugate the females participating in it. Due to Maria's father's mistress becoming "the vulgar despot of the family" after the mother's death, Maria and her sisters are helpless, a situation which her uncle attempts to alleviate by paying George Venables 5,000 pounds to marry her.[101] Wollstonecraft expresses the fluidity between the commercial and the marital in explaining that Maria's uncle genuinely believed he had made a good match because Venables "had the reputation of being attentive to business" and "habits of order in business would, he conceived, extend to the regulation of affections in domestic life."[102] In reality the relationship between business and "affection" becomes toxic, precisely because it results in the commoditization of women: Venables offers to sell Maria's sexual favors to his friend Mr. S___ for 500 pounds a week, expressing in a letter "that every woman had her price, and, with gross indecency, hint[ing], that he should be glad to have the duty of a husband taken off his hands."[103] Maria protests that the double standard governing sexual policing of the genders turns on the legal status of men as property holders. "Such is the respect paid to the master-key of property" that a man may "rob [his wife] with impunity, even to waste publicly on a courtesan" while a mother "cannot lawfully snatch from the gripe of the gambling spendthrift, or beastly drunkard, unmindful of his offspring, the fortune which falls to her by chance."[104] By contrast, a woman "resigning what is termed her natural protector" is "despised and shunned, for asserting the independence of mind distinctive of a rational being, and spurning at slavery."[105] While Wollstonecraft thereby critiques the propertization of women created by this system of sexual incentives, Fielding critiques the commoditization of masculine honor.

In *The Modern Husband*, Fielding presents the alleged cuckold's abuse of tort law for profit to be, like the economically innovative joint-stock corporations that contributed to the Bubble, a "modern" legal innovation. The rise of the mercantile system marked a change in *episteme*; under the new rules, knowledge of how economic systems interact translates into power, displacing (though not, I will argue presently, to the extent Foucault suggests) the older view of power embodied purely in sovereign territory. Foucault argues that in the new order

> the things which the government is to be concerned about are men, but men in their relations, their links, their imbrication with those other things which are wealth, resources, means of subsistence, the territory with its specific qualities . . . men in their relation to other kinds of things which are customs, habits ways of doing and thinking, etc.[106]

In this view, the legal system transfers power to those who understand how to use it to consolidate capital; an adulterous wrong is a fungible good to the extent that it translates into a monetary judgment.

Here Mr. Bellamant's reply to Gaywit reinforces this relationship to mercantilism:

> [i]t is a Stock-jobbing Age. Eve'ry thing has its Price: Marriage is Traffick throughout; as most of us bargain to be Husbands, so some of us bargain

to be Cuckolds; and he wou'd be as much laught at, who preferr'd his Love to his Interest, at this End of the Town, as he who preferr'd his Honesty to his Interest at the Other.[107]

Indeed, literal money circulates through the economy of the play, facilitating adultery in the same way that it facilitated slavery in the transatlantic trade. Lord Richly reveals that "I have succeeded often by leaving Money in a Lady's Hands: she spends it, is unable to pay, and then I, by Virtue of my Mortgage, immediately enter upon the Premises."[108] In this case, he does indeed leave Mrs. Bellamant with money, which she lends to her husband who gives it to his mistress, Mrs. Modern, whose bankrupt husband, Mr. Modern, asks it of her. For Richly this conquest is the straightforward consequence of the business law governing his newly acquired property right in Mrs. Bellamant, his "mortgage." Mr. Modern likewise understands the sexual economy as financial, insisting—in the face of his dwindling share of profits from his wife's relationship with Lord Richly—that she "shall not drive a separate Trade at my Expence" and tells her:

> Your Person is mine; I bought it lawfully in the Church, and unless I am to profit by the Disposal I shall keep it all for my own Use . . . had I felt the Sweets of your Pleasures, as at first, I had never once upbraided you with them; but as I must more than share the Dishonour, it is surely reasonable I should share the profit.[109]

Modern's speech here reflects the relational, property-like right to his wife's fidelity that had motivated the law of adultery as far back as the medieval wife abduction cases. Even Mr. Gaywit, whose love for Emilia is one of the few genuine attachments in the play, describes his romantic predicament in the language of the property law that requires him to marry Lady Charlotte or else forfeit his entire inheritance: "I will leave my Case to your own Determination when you know it. Suppose me oblig'd to marry the Woman I don't like, debarr'd for ever from her I love." (In the legal context, to be "debarred" is to be excluded from possession—which Gaywit must choose to be with regard to either his inheritance or his preferred partner.)

Yet the play describes more than a private economy, as evidenced by its treatment of the expenses Mrs. Modern incurs to keep herself attired attractively enough to engage in her extra-marital flirtations. She unintentionally reinforces the idea that the social economics of upper-class society reveal something about the national character when she receives a bill from her dressmaker and exclaims, "Bills! Bills! Bills! I wonder, in a civilized Nation, there are no Laws against Duns."[110] Turner notes the importance of the concept of "civility" to post-Restoration society; the phrase was used to "distinguish between 'civilised' Christian nations and more 'barbarous' or heathen peoples," as well as "good manners . . . cultivated in mixed company, in the developing sphere of urban social life."[111] Here Mrs. Modern conflates the meanings, implying that England risks degeneration as a civilization in the absence of complete freedom to participate in drawing room flirtations without regard to the physical costs of the necessary accoutrements. Fielding thereby critiques the usurpation of the British subject as a construct of territorial identity and static principles by the relativistic system embodied in the new economy.

The link between adultery and nationalist discourse becomes explicit when Mr. Modern, frustrated that his wife will not agree to his plan that she be discovered with Lord Richly and thereby allow him a cause of action for criminal conversation, exclaims "[w]hy had I not been born a *Turk*, that I might have enslaved my Wife, or a *Chinese*, that I might have sold her?"[112] Fielding's use of orientalism here does not merely establish the comfortable zone of otherness writers typically create in order to normalize the center. Mrs. Modern in fact explicitly suggests that her husband is worse than the eastern caricatures he resorts to:

> [t]hat would have been only the Custom of the Country. You have done more, you have sold her in *England*, in a Country where Women are as backward to be sold to a Lover as to refuse him; and where Cuckold is almost the only Title of Honor that can't be bought.[113]

Despite the inherent racism in suggesting that English women, unlike their eastern counterparts, have the moral capacity at least to dislike being prostituted, Fielding condemns English couples even more severely for intentionally preferring financial benefit to honor. Furthermore, Mrs. Modern's comparison underscores that there is something particularly perverse about, as Mr. Modern puts it, "*the Law* . . . giv[ing] you more in one moment than [Lord Richly's] Love for many Years."[114] Mrs. Modern points out that it is not "the Custom of the Country" in England to sell wives, yet this practice is facilitated by precisely the formal authority intended to preserve custom: the English common law, which had come to recognize this tort.

Ironically, however, the full value of Modern's cuckoldry is a product of the law itself; when he declares his intent to sue Mr. Bellamant, his wife's other lover, for criminal conversation, he exclaims, "I shall take the strictest Satisfaction which the Law will give me: so I shall leave you at present to give Satisfaction to your Wife."[115] Here "the Law" stands in, alternately, for the sort of moral satisfaction traditionally secured by a duel, and the sexual satisfaction normally associated with matrimony. And later, disingenuously sympathetic to Mr. Modern who has "discovered" his wife with Mr. Bellamant,

Lord Richly exclaims, "[l]aws cannot be too rigorous against Offences of this Nature: Juries cannot give too great Damages."[116] This line contains perhaps the central legal paradox of the play: even if the first sentence were true the latter would not necessarily follow. To the extent that one believes adultery to be as grievous a harm as Modern claims it to be, it belongs less to the world of tort than to that of criminal law. The allusion to civil juries giving "damages" immediately undermines the inherent claim that an act of adultery violates natural law in such a way that makes it a universal, rather than a particularized, wrong. Were laws truly so rigorous the conduct would be criminalized. This speech, too, echoes the testimony of Lord Abergavenny's servant Osman, that he had told Lydell that his conduct with Lady Abergavenny was a "crime" for which he could give the Lord "no satisfaction"—an implication used to similarly contradictory purposes by Abergavenny's counsel.

Much of this blurring, of course, comes from the basic historical fact that debtors and felons inhabited the same physical space in eighteenth-century London. Mr. Modern fears, at the start of the play, that he is "in a fair way to go to Jail the next Morning" for debt.[117] And, after Mr. Modern's dishonorable behavior comes to light, Mr. Gaywit chides Lord Richly for bringing him into society, saying, "you have increased [the company] by one who should only grace the Keeper of Newgate's Levee."[118] The Moderns further illuminate this connection when Mrs. Modern describes the idea of moving to the country to save money as "Racks and Tortures" and her husband replies that "many more are in that of a Prison," implying that debtor's prison would be physically the same as a felon's prison with the torturous punishments the latter could entail.[119]

The threat of imprisonment as a consequence for the profligate spending of the social circle in which the characters move therefore lends a criminal light to the sexual-commercial exchanges being made. At the end of the play, when Mr. Gaywit points out that, with respect to Mr. Modern's claim against Mr. Bellamant, "the Damages will not be very great, which are given to a voluntary Cuckold," Emilia replies, "I see not why; for it is surely as much a Robbery to take away a Picture unpaid for, from the Painter who would sell it, as from the Gentleman who would keep it."[120] In other words, she makes the point that adultery, like robbery, is of sufficiently universal odium that no showing of relational wrong should be necessary for it to be prosecuted. Fielding throws light onto the unnatural moral order governing the tort of criminal conversation by comparing it to the normal arrangement of culpability in a criminal context. The shadow discourse of criminal culpability is, then, the second legal framework within which the play operates, and through it Fielding resuscitates the formal authority of state punishment as a more transcendent form of bodily control.

The audience apprehends this duality when the adulteress Mrs. Heron, acting as chorus, says in her epilogue that she offers advice in the same way "[a]s Malefactors, on their dying Day,/ Have always something at the Tree, to say."[121] The primary characters too, particularly in their more scrupulous moments, describe their conduct in the language of criminal culpability. Mr. Bellamant accuses his lover Mrs. Modern of inducing him to behave criminally in betraying his virtuous wife: "if to rob a Woman who brought me Beauty, Fortune, Love and Virtue: if to hazard the making her miserable be no Breach of Honour, Robbers and Murderers may be honourable men."[122] When he subsequently refuses to introduce her to Mrs. Bellamant, Mrs. Modern says "[t]his is too plain an Evidence of your Contempt of me; you will not introduce a Woman of stain'd Virtue to your Wife" and asks "[c]an you, who caused my Crime, be the first to contemn me for it?"[123] In this exchange, Mrs. Modern suggests that Mr. Bellamant's opinion of her has been derived from a form of criminal adjudication, with evidentiary fact-gathering and eventual condemnation.

When Mr. Modern first approaches his wife with the scheme to reveal her affair with Richly, she is outraged, telling him that "at thy base Intreaties I gave up my Innocence" and that she "had sooner see thee starve in Prison." Modern explicitly blurs the line between the prospect of debtor's prison and the morally criminal nature of his proposal, saying, "I own myself in the wrong. I ask ten thousand Pardons. I will submit to any Punishment . . . I never will be guilty of the like again."[124] Furthermore, Lord Richly compares the Bellamants to co-criminals as he hatches a plan to seduce Mrs. Bellamant, impugning her husband's fidelity, observing that "persuading a Thief that his Companion is false, is the surest way to make him so."[125]

Continuing the metaphors of criminality, when Mr. Bellamant, at the end of the play, confesses to his wife his misbehavior with Mrs. Modern he states, "[w]hen the Criminal turns his own Accuser, the merciful Judge becomes his Advocate: Guilt is too plainly written in my Face to admit of a Denial, and I stand prepar'd to receive what Sentence you lease."[126] Mrs. Bellamant forces the role of adjudicator back upon her husband, replying "[a]s you are your own Accuser, be your own Judge; you can inflict no Punishment on yourself equal to what I feel."[127] And Mr. Bellamant, concerned about his son's marital prospects in light of his misconduct, laments, "[S]hall I not see my children suffer for their father's Crime?"[128] Finally, when Bellamant confronts Lord Richly about his designs on Mrs. Bellamant he states, "yours was the Presumption, mine is only Justice, nay, and mild too; unequal to your Crime which requires a Punishment from my Hand, not from my Tongue."[129] From all of these exchanges, it is clear that—while one of the play's running jokes is the ease with which wives may cheat with no real social consequence and their husbands routinely profit from it—the conduct at stake is nonetheless culpable in a manner deserving of formal sanction by the criminal law. Criminality haunts the play, rendering the social triviality it lampoons culturally non-trivial.

Furthermore, Fielding proposes that the law's deflection of this entire criminal enterprise into the realm of business law is a broader problem for the political identity of England as a sovereign entity. Even in a comic satire with farcical characters, he touches on the same anxieties over territorial stability implicated by the very different trials of Catherine Howard and Queen Caroline. The play's worthy emblem of British military might abroad, Captain Merit, voices this anxiety most brutally, exclaiming, "How happy is that Country, where pimping and whoring are esteemed publick Services, and where Grandeur, and the Gallows lie on the same road."[130] That Captain Merit himself is unemployed and looking for Lord Richly's assistance in securing a new post suggests that the very independence of English nation-hood is vulnerable, with its swords subservient to the quasi-criminal sexual market dramatized in the play.

The play proposes, nonetheless, that we publicly adjudicate the latent criminality of adultery. By combining the tort law's functional reliance on the "discovery" of criminal conversation with the adjudicatory function of the theatrical spectacle itself, the play—like the trial compendium discussed above—proposes itself as a punitive agent. At multiple points throughout the play, Fielding emphasizes the extent to which evidence of adultery is a key element to a successful cause of action. In her very first lines, Mrs. Heron warns potential adulterers that if they would like to continue in their misconduct, they must "keep wide of proof."[131] When Mr. Modern bribes Mr. Bellamant's servant John to claim he had witnessed the affair, John describes it as "double perjury," enforcing the idea that participating in the public outcry constitutes a form of evidentiary testimony of the same sort that would be collected in a court of law. And Mrs. Heron's closing epilogue puts the finest point on the precise relationship between formal proof and the adultery economy:

They fail not at th' Unfortunate to Flout,
Not because Naughty but because found out.
Why, faith if these Discoveries succeed,
Marriage will soon become a Trade, indeed!
This Trade, I'm sure, will flourish in the Nation,
'Twill be esteem'd below no Man of Fashion
To be a Member of the Cuckold's Corporation!
. . . Money alone Men will no more importune,
When ev'ry Beauty makes her Husband's Fortune!

While Juries value Vertue at this Rate,
Each Wife is (when discover'd) an Estate![132]

Business law can, therefore, only transform an adulterous wife into a legal "estate" with her virtue valued at a particular dollar figure when she is "discover'd." This process of commoditization remains divorced from questions of morality; the issue is not whether a woman has been "naughty" but whether she has been "found out."

Earla Wilputte argues that

> Fielding's unflinching depiction of sordid social fact forces the audience to realize that everyone in society is an actor and that contemporary life has become an immoral farce. Fielding's characters talk of plays they attend to show the play-attending audience that they are watching themselves.[133]

Wilputte is correct that the audience are players in the sense that they are susceptible to surveillance, yet I would make a stronger claim: the players on the stage participate in the punishment of the audience, and the play imagines its own staging as a form of criminal adjudication. As Mrs. Heron tells us at the outset, "ever was the Stage's true Intent,/ To give Reward to Virtue, Vice its Punishment."[134] She further emphasizes the possibility of reciprocal punishment between the criminals represented on the stage and those occupying the seats by admonishing the audience not to judge the characters on the stage for being unrealistic, saying "[f]rom whatever Clime the Creatures come,/ Condemn 'em not because not found at home."[135] As it becomes obvious that the social situations on the stage are exactly those comprising society at large—that the "Creatures" are indeed found at home —the consequence is the need for punishment. While, Fielding suggests, the task of criminal punishment for adultery may indeed have transferred from the state itself to the panopticon of a theater house, it remains justified by the same concerns over sovereignty that haunted the pre-modern understanding.

The Modern Husband may have been the most explicit literary critique of the tort of criminal conversation, but it was not the only one. Wilputte notes that Richardson's *Pamela* (1740) and Fielding's novels *Tom Jones* (1749) and *Amelia* (1751) "each employ wife-selling to illustrate the decaying sense of shame and honor in society while alluding to the corruption filtering down from the governors through the family."[136] And Wollstonecraft's Maria eventually defends, against Venables' suit, the lover she meets in the very asylum in which he places her after she refuses to be prostituted to Mr. S___. Wollstonecraft highlights the ways in which the cause of action itself constitutes a denial of female agency:

> Such are the partial laws enacted by men; for, only to lay a stress on the
> dependent state of a woman in the grand question of the comforts arising
> from the possession of property, she is . . . much more injured by the loss
> of the husband's affection, than he by that of his wife; yet where is she,
> condemned to the solitude of a deserted home, to look for a compensation
> from the woman who seduces him from her?[137]

As Adam Komisaruk points out, however, Maria's objection to the tort
appears to have less to do with the possibility for commoditization of human
relations that Fielding condemns than with the gender asymmetry characterizing such commoditization.[138]

Adultery Discourse and Feminist Resistance

Fielding uses the theater punitively, to undermine the formal legal discourse
constructing an adulterous woman as a commercial asset to her husband,
and in doing so to re-establish the male British subject as an idealized servant of empire rather than a rapacious contractual party. After this move,
however, the adulteress remains an object incidental to masculine goals. No
longer a token of exchange, she becomes, like Mrs. Heron imagines herself,
a criminal at the Tyburn tree who must die to right the wrongs to public
and nation occasioned by the adultery. By contrast Wollstonecraft seems to
imagine a world in which criminal conversation claims would exist yet be
available to both parties. In writing of the female legal subject as a potential
claimant under the common law (and the adulterous husband as a potential
means to financial recovery), Wollstonecraft anticipates Nancy Hartsock's
call for women to engage in the "historical, political, and theoretical process
of constituting ourselves as subjects as well as objects of history."[139] Indeed,
reading Wollstonecraft against Fielding illuminates the dangers, identified by
some of Foucault's feminist critics such as Hartsock and Barbara Christian, of
rejecting the possibility of a constitutive subject due to the role of discourse in
forming an individual's self-conception. In any case, while Wollstonecraft's
reformulation of legal subjects remained hypothetical, the nineteenth century
would see similar discursive resistance gain traction in the real world.

The highly personal aspects of adultery and its proofs yet again entered
the public discourse as implicating sovereign-subject relations during
Queen Caroline's 1820 trial for divorce on the grounds of adultery. Susan
Heinzelman notes that the trial "was a traumatic event that must have raised
historical anxieties about the fragility of the monarchy," particularly because
"[n]o English citizen could think of Caroline on trial without recalling other
sovereigns or queens [such as Charles I and Anne Boleyn] who had stood
in Parliament or other politico-legal spaces to defend themselves."[140] In her

public letter to King George, read aloud at her trial, Caroline conflates the rhetoric of oppressed subject and wronged wife.

On the one hand, she relies upon the legal understanding of the procedural rights due to any English citizen—the right to confront witnesses against her, the right to a public trial as opposed to a secret tribunal, the right to due process defined by the laws of Great Britain, rather than those of foreign nations—to establish herself as one with the average citizen in the face of an inappropriate state exercise of power. She says:

> I have always demanded a *fair trial* . . . Instead of a fair trial, I am to be subjected to a sentence by the Parliament, passed in the shape of *a law* . . . The injustice of refusing me a clear and distinct charge, of refusing me the names of the witnesses, of refusing me the names of the places where the illegal acts have been committed; these are sufficiently flagrant and revolting; but it is against the *constitution of the Court itself* that I particularly object, and against that I most solemnly protest . . . I demand a trial in a Court where the Jurors are taken impartially from amongst the people, and where the proceedings are open and fair.[141]

On the other hand, Caroline invokes a highly personal account of her expulsion from her marriage and her separation from her child: personal grievances that would, to be sure, have universal resonance with female subjects but grievances that acknowledge that her gender is at the forefront of the judicial proceeding.[142] The double standard of George's extramarital activities in comparison to hers became a matter of public debate in an age when Wollstonecraft and other writers were making claims against essentialist views of gender. Caroline presents her case with recognition of the inherent problem of a legal order increasingly defined in terms of universal right, as applied to a female body. The tension between her use of Enlightenment-era rights language and the gendered nature of her specific wrongs belies the ostensible universality of the abstract values of British justice. She offers her own truths not by rejecting the common law concept of rule of law but by demonstrating how it has been violated—a failure on her part, Foucault might have said, to wholly reject the "great stories of continuity" that have facilitated coercive power couched as reason and natural justice.[143] Yet, as Nancy Hartsock has observed, Western women's narratives of subjugation within patriarchal structures make it "far more difficult . . . to imagine ourselves as isolated and abstract individuals," thereby challenging some of the core assumptions of Enlightenment-era reasoning.[144] As Hartsock concludes, "[a]s an aspect of being situated these knowledges represent a response to and an expression of a specific embodiment,"[145] which means that narratives like Queen Caroline's present valuable resistance to unjust power structures without having to blow up the mere possibility of knowledge (and admit total powerlessness as a result). In aligning herself with the potentially abused English subject, Caroline not only co-opted Enlightenment rights-speak to her cause but harnessed the English cultural trauma surrounding royal adultery into a common law narrative not about threatened Kingship but violated Queenship.

Notes

1. Smeeton ed., *Trial of Queen Caroline*, p. 11.
2. Robins, *Rebel Queen*, pp. 192–3.
3. Ibid. pp. 200–10.
4. Ibid. pp. 310–11.
5. Blackstone, *Commentaries*, vol. 4, p. 2.
6. The relationship between crime and tort has never been quite as simple as Blackstone suggests. Contemporary legal scholars argue over whether it is appropriate for the tort law to allow, as it does, so-called "punitive damages" for particularly egregious conduct, and corporations may be criminally fined for regulatory offenses that fall short of the *mens rea* requirements generally associated with criminal law. Owen, "A Punitive Damages Overview," pp. 373–413
7. Goldberg & Zipursky, "Torts as Wrongs," p. 949.
8. Foucault, *History of Sexuality*, p. 144.
9. Ibid. p. 144.
10. Pollock & Maitland, *English Law Before the Time of Edward*, vol. 2, p. 470.
11. Ibid. p. 470.
12. Foucault, "Discipline and Punish," p. 1669.
13. This discussion also has considerable importance in the ongoing legal debate about the appropriate understanding of tort law. Contemporary tort scholars are divided between the view of torts as compensation for losses and the view that tort law should be understood to provide civil recourse for formal wrongs. For examples of the compensation model see Fleming, *Law of Torts*, p. 1; Atiyah, *Accidents*, p. 239 (describing tort law as primarily the rules governing compensation for "road accidents and industrial accidents"); Calabresi, *The Costs of Accidents*, p. 312. For articulations of the wrongs-based conception see, for example, Smith, "The Critics and the 'Crisis,'" p. 778; Weinrib, *Private Law*, pp. 134–5; Goldberg & Zipursky, "Torts as Wrongs," pp. 918–20.
14. Dunn, *Stolen Women*, pp. 238–80.
15. Ibid. p. 120.
16. *Statutes*, vol. 2, pp. 87–8.
17. Ibid. p. 87.
18. Dunn, *Stolen Women*, pp. 124–5.
19. Ibid. p. 150.

20. Jointure was the part of a husband's property a wife received in freehold after his death, as opposed to dower, which was a specific sum set aside for the wife which the husband could not access during his lifetime. See generally the Statute of Uses 1536.
21. Dunn, *Stolen Women*, p. 131.
22. Hartsock, "Postmodernism," p. 21.
23. Turner, *Fashioning Adultery*, p. 6.
24. Ibid. p. 4.
25. Ibid. p. 5.
26. Ibid. pp. 1–2.
27. Blackstone noted that at the Restoration (when the Cavalier Parliament had repealed most of the constitutional changes adopted during the Interregnum) "it was not thought proper to renew a law of such unfashionable rigour." Blackstone, *Commentaries*, vol. 4, p. 42 and that "the temporal courts therefore take no cognizance of the crime of adultery, otherwise than as a private injury." A similar legal situation existed in Scotland during the same periods. In his *Commentaries* Baron David Hume writes that while adultery was technically a statutory crime—"heinous and in some cases capital" it had not "for many years been the subject of a criminal prosecution." Hume, *Commentaries*, vol. 1, p. 449.
28. McIlwain, *Political Works of James I*, p. 272.
29. Norton, *Founding Mothers and Fathers*, p. 6.
30. Locke, *Two Treatises on Government*, Ch. 5.
31. Turner, *Fashioning Adultery*, p. 8.
32. Lawrence Stone has described, as an eighteenth-century development, the concept of the "affective marriage," based on the premise that "the pursuit of happiness, best achieved by domestic affection, was the prime legitimate goal in life." Stone, *Family, Sex*, p. 180.
33. Turner, *Fashioning Adultery*, p. 8.
34. Foucault, "Governmentality," p. 10.
35. Blackstone, *Commentaries*, vol. 4, pp. 74. Historian David Turner also notes several cultural developments that complicate any narrative of adultery's "privatization," notably the newly flourishing public sphere of the theater, in which depictions of adultery became fashionable, and the tendency of the newly valorized cult of domestic bliss to result in middle class attacks on aristocratic sexual vice. Turner, *Fashioning Adultery*, p. 8.
36. For more on the relationship between murder pamphlets and the novel, see Bell, *Literature and Crime*; Lincoln Faller, *Turned to Account*, and Rawlings, *Drunks, Whores, and Idle Apprentices*.
37. Turner, *Fashioning Adultery*, p. 132.
38. Ibid. p. 123.

39. Ibid. p. 125.
40. Ibid. p. 127.
41. Ibid. p. 128–9. See also Horder, *Provocation and Responsibility*, pp. 87–8; Andrew, "The Code of Honour and its Critics," pp. 409–34.
42. Gowing, *Domestic Dangers*, p. 132.
43. Turner, *Fashioning Adultery*, p. 172. In *Road to Divorce: England 1530–1987* (1990), Lawrence Stone collects the empirical data on the explosion in criminal conversation cases between 1680 and the 1790s. Stone, *Road to Divorce*, p. 246.
44. Edwards, *Female Sexuality and the Law*, pp. 54–5.
45. Turner, *Fashioning Adultery*, p. 179.
46. Ibid. p. 183.
47. See for example *Abergavenny* v. *Lydell,* where Abergavenny's servant Osman testified that "he never knew of greater Friendship and Intimacy" than that shared by his master and the defendant, and another witness' observation of the "mutual Respect" between the two. *Trials for Adultery*, pp. 15–19.
48. Turner, *Fashioning Adultery*, p. 193.
49. Marilyn Morris provides a detailed analysis of the representations of criminal conversation suits in tabloid journalism in the late eighteenth century. She argues that "[a]nalysis of the *Bon Ton's* virtual recreation of the sort of social policing found in small communities for a national readership demonstrates the tabloid's paradoxical nature. Although outwardly subversive, trading in scandalous secrets and flouting taboo, its message was essentially conservative." Morris, "Marital Litigation," pp. 33–4.
50. The term "history" likewise echoes the typical eighteenth-century novel title as it describes a protagonist, such as Richardson's *Clarissa, or the History of a Young Lady* (1747–1748) or Fielding's *The History of Tom Jones, a Foundling* (1749).
51. *Trials for Adultery*, vol. 1, p. ii.
52. Jane Austen dramatizes this effect in *Mansfield Park* (1814) when published gossip about Maria Rushworth's affair with Henry Crawford entertains Mr. Price. Upon reading that "the beautiful Mrs. R., whose name had not long been enrolled in the lists of Hymen, and who had promised to become so brilliant a leader in the fashionable world" had "quitted her husband's roof in company with the well–known and captivating Mr. C.," he remarks that "[a] little flogging for man and woman too, would be the best way of preventing such things." Austen, *Mansfield Park*, pp. 408–9.
53. *Trials for Adultery*, vol. 1, p. iii.
54. Ibid. p. iii.
55. Ibid. p. iii.
56. Ibid. p. iv.

57. Ibid. p. iv.
58. Ibid. p. 13.
59. Ibid. p. 15.
60. Ibid. p. 21.
61. Ibid. p. 21.
62. Ibid. p. 22.
63. This logic is similar to that which motivated the use of pardons subsequent to the conviction of juveniles, as will be discussed in the next Part.
64. *Trials for Adultery*, vol. 1, p. 22.
65. Ibid. p. 23.
66. Ibid. p. 23.
67. Ibid. p. 20.
68. Ibid. p. 2.
69. Ibid. pp. 2–3.
70. Ibid. p. 24.
71. *New and Complete Trials for Adultery*, vol. 1, p. iii.
72. Ibid. p. 14.
73. Ibid. p. 17. Indeed, no monarch is more associated with the interrelationship between the definition of adultery and the security of the English kingship than Henry VIII. Henry established the Church of England explicitly to render a marriage with Anne Boleyn legitimate and indeed the taint of potentially being a bastard never entirely disappeared from his heir Elizabeth I. (A good account can be found in Judith M. Richards, *Elizabeth I* (2011).) He effected the subsequent execution of Anne on trumped-up charges of adultery because his attempts to render that marriage illegitimate failed; by divorcing her shortly before she died the King aimed, according to historian Antonia Fraser, "to brand Princess Elizabeth a bastard." Fraser, *The Wives of Henry VIII*, p. 254.
74. *New and Complete Trials for Adultery*, vol. 1, p. 15.
75. Ibid. p. 23.
76. Ibid. p. 14.
77. Ibid. p. 15.
78. Ibid. p. 21.
79. Ibid. p. 22.
80. Ibid. p. 24.
81. Nineteenth-century historian Eliakim Littell gives a detailed account in *Littell's Living Age* (1847).
82. *New and Complete Trials for Adultery*, vol. 1, p. 24.
83. Ibid. p. 25.
84. Ibid. pp. 24–5.
85. Ibid. p. 27.
86. Ibid. p. 28.

87. Littell, *Littell's Living Age*, p. 124.

88. *New and Complete Trials for Adultery*, vol. 1, p. 29.

89. Littell, *Littell's Living Age*, p. 124.

90. *New and Complete Trials for Adultery*, vol. 1, p. 29.

91. Radzinowicz, *A History of English Criminal Law*, pp. 11–12.

92. The Act, resulting from First Lord of the Treasury Robert Walpole's frustration with humorous theatrical attacks from Whig and Tory writers alike, required that the Lord Chamberlain approve any play before it was staged. Hume, *London Theater*, p. 132.

93. Ibid. pp. 54–6.

94. Barrett & Harrison, *Crime and Punishment in England*, pp. 147–50.

95. Fielding was not the first to use the criminal element to mock the political elite generally or Walpole specifically. In *The Beggar's Opera* (1728) John Gay mocks the aristocratic fascination with Italian opera by making criminals and prostitutes his protagonists and lampooning both Walpole and Wild.

96. Foucault, "Human Nature," p. 187.

97. Wilputte, "Wife Pandering," p. 458.

98. Hume, *London Theater*, p. 125.

99. Ibid. p. 22.

100. Fielding, *Modern Husband*, p. 23.

101. Wollstonecraft, *Maria*, p. 62

102. Ibid. p. 62.

103. Ibid. p. 83.

104. Ibid. p. 78.

105. Ibid. p. 78.

106. Foucault, "Governmentality," p. 11.

107. Fielding, *Modern Husband*, p. 23.

108. Ibid. p. 49.

109. Ibid. p. 45.

110. Ibid. p. 2.

111. Turner, *Fashioning Adultery*, p. 11.

112. Fielding, *Modern Husband*, p. 46.

113. Ibid. pp. 46–7.

114. Ibid. p. 47 (emphasis added).

115. Ibid. p. 60.

116. Ibid. p. 71.

117. Ibid. p. 3.

118. Ibid. p. 78.

119. Ibid. p. 47.

120. Ibid. p. 79.

121. Ibid. p. vii.

122. Ibid. p. 40.
123. Ibid.
124. Fielding, *Modern Husband*, p. 13.
125. Ibid. p. 34.
126. Ibid. p. 60.
127. Ibid. p. 60.
128. Ibid. p. 61.
129. Ibid. p. 67.
130. Ibid. p. 8.
131. Ibid. p. viii.
132. Ibid. p. 82.
133. Wilputte, "Wife Pandering," p. 461.
134. Fielding, *Modern Husband*, p. viii.
135. Ibid. p. viii.
136. Wilputte, "Wife Pandering," p. 462.
137. Wollstonecraft, *Maria*, pp. 76–7.
138. Komisaruk, "The Privatization of Pleasure," p. 41.
139. Hartsock, "Foucault on Power," p. 171.
140. Heinzelman, *Riding the Black Ram*, pp. 92–3.
141. Smeeton ed., *Trial of Queen Caroline*, pp. 12–14.
142. Ibid. p. 9.
143. Foucault, *Language*, p. 152.
144. Hartsock, "Postmodernism and Political Change," p. 29.
145. Ibid. p. 29.

2

The Gothic Law of Marriage

Adultery remained quasi-criminal in the legal imagination in various ways over the eighteenth and early nineteenth centuries. Irish legal writer Sollom Emlyn alludes to this in his preface to the second edition of the popular *State Trials* (1742)—a compilation of significant criminal trials, which continued through multiple editions into the nineteenth century. While he acknowledges "the general opinion" that adultery is no longer criminal he adds, referring to the dormant yet still-existent Interregnum statutory authority, "I must confess, I see not but that Adultery is indictable by our Law"[1] More to the point, in 1800 Lord Auckland made an unsuccessful attempt to formally re-criminalize adultery as a misdemeanor punishable by a fine and imprisonment.[2] In a speech to the House of Lords Auckland echoes the language of empire Henry Fielding deployed seventy years earlier in *The Modern Husband,* declaring that "Great Britain had preserved her existence amidst the paroxysms and convulsions, and downfalls of nations by the effect of or being a little less irreligious and less immoral than others."[3] As in the eighteenth-century examples described in Chapter 1, Auckland makes the discursive link between marital fidelity and British sovereignty.

Yet just 30 years later, even the tort of criminal conversation met its official demise after the public trial of another woman named Caroline. In 1836 Tory MP George Norton made a poorly-calculated attempt at political gain by suing incumbent Prime Minister Lord Melbourne for criminal conversation with his wife, the beautiful society hostess, poet, and feminist writer Caroline Norton. While Norton's evidence was so thin that the jury did not even retire before delivering its verdict against him, it was still an occasion of humiliation for Caroline, who stated that she was made to "appear a painted prostitute in a Public Court."[4] While the defendant in tort, Lord Melbourne, not only won the verdict but if anything "relished," as Ian Ward puts it, "his depiction in court as an ageing roué, one that was capable of seducing the beautiful young wives of political opponents,"[5] the proceeding effectively functioned as a criminal adjudication for Caroline. As she describes it, she was "condemned . . . to remain perfectly neuter; perfectly helpless; excluded, by the principles of our jurisprudence, from all possibility of defence."[6] Caroline's experience of the tort action as a "condemnation" shows that, in being the object of such a trial and rendered, by the procedural rules and the fact that she was not formally a party, incompetent to defend herself, she had in fact been the object of state-sponsored punishment. Ward has pointed out that Caroline was also helpless outside the courtroom, unable to control whether "her husband decided to furnish eager journal editors with salacious details of her alleged affairs."[7] The quasi-criminal status threatening Caroline was, therefore, a product of the interaction between formal torts jurisprudence and narratives generated in the public sphere.

In this chapter, I argue that nineteenth-century reforms to divorce law, and their accompanying cultural discourse, demonstrate both the oppressive and progressive functions of adultery trauma as aspects of English legal development. The Matrimonial Causes Act of 1857 officially created more gender balance by formally recognizing the wrong of male adultery and removing adultery, categorically, from even the theoretical reach of the criminal law. Caroline Norton influenced this development through public advocacy, in which she deployed the language of failed history as a form of traumatic violence toward women, using the structure of common law thinking about the historical life of adultery against the legal status quo. I further argue that Norton's rhetoric suggests, perhaps intentionally, the Gothic function of divorce law in Charlotte Brontë's *Jane Eyre* (1847), which used the oppressive legal operation of marriage to explore anxieties and aspirations over the possibility of legal change. I also show, however, that even after the Act's passage, the discursive link between adultery and the trauma of failed kingship remained: both in the old ecclesiastical court precedents imported into the new statute and in literary texts such as the poet laureate Alfred, Lord Tennyson's *Idylls of the King* (1859–1885). I conclude by suggesting that Robert Browning's *The Ring and the Book* (1868) explicitly recognizes the danger of a culture constructing adultery as a quasi-crime and the latent violence attached to this persistent discursive ambiguity.

The Matrimonial Causes Act and Victorian Adultery

Caroline Norton's legal ordeal prompted her to write a lengthy letter to Queen Victoria protesting the divorce laws as they existed at the time of her husband's suit against Lord Melbourne. Divorce entailed a two-step process: a plaintiff could bring a petition for a so-called divorce *a mensa et thoro* ("from bread and board") in the ecclesiastical courts.[8] Then he or she had to petition Parliament for a private bill dissolving the marriage: a *divorce a vinculo matrimonii* ("from the bonds of matrimony"). The only ground for divorce was adultery and a husband could prevail solely by showing that his wife had been unfaithful.[9] For a wife to prevail, however, she needed to show that her husband had committed "aggravated" adultery—adultery accompanied by bigamy, incest, bestiality, sodomy, desertion, cruelty, or rape.[10] A divorce *a mensa et thoro* did not allow the parties to remarry; for that a private bill was required and, prior to 1857, only four women had successfully petitioned Parliament for such a bill.[11] The upshot of this state of affairs, combined with the laws governing married women's property, was that a wife lost legal identity upon entering marriage and yet, unlike a husband, could not escape it no matter how abusive or adulterous her husband proved to be.

In her letter to the Queen, Norton protests this asymmetry in social contractarian language:

> [t]here are bad, wanton, irreclaimable women, as there are vicious, profli-
> gate, tyrannical men: but the difference is *this*: that to punish and restrain
> bad wives, there are laws, and very severe laws (to say nothing of social
> condemnation); while to punish or restrain bad husbands, there is, in
> England no adequate law whatever.[12]

She suggests that the adultery laws should properly function as a guard against the predations inherent in a sexual state of nature and disrupts the Burkean view of English identity as one of ordered liberty by linking it to "tyranny." To further this point she explicitly compares the English divorce laws to those more equitable systems in Scotland and France, asking "[w]hy is England the only country obliged to confess that she cannot contrive to administer justice to women?"[13] She answers by showing how England has reified the state of nature into the law itself through the

> legal fiction that women are "non-existent," and man and wife are still
> "one," in cases of alienation, separation, and enmity, when they are about as
> much "one" as those ingenious twisted groups of animal death we sometimes
> see in sculpture; one creature wild to resist, and the other fierce to destroy.[14]

Like the metaphorical sculpture, the law is the product of civilized artifice, yet it sustains and preserves a state of beastliness.

Furthermore, like Queen Caroline before her, Norton explicitly subverts the legal narrative, discussed in Chapter 1, of female adultery as a quasi-criminal threat to kingship. She uses the very same history in support of an alternative legal story: one in which the threat to English identity comes less from adultery generally than from the legal double standard kings may use both to commit it and punish it. Throughout her letter she compares potentially adulterous husbands to male monarchs, protesting that a wife must remain married to a cheating husband "even if . . . he were the father of as many natural children as Charles II"[15] and notes that the very concept of divorce was "contrived" for the "passions" of King Henry VIII.[16] She then resorts to the same project of historical narratizing typical to common law reasoning as it produces a rule of law from a series of stories. Her attempts, as she puts it, to "[put] a spine to history" to connect "the various events of different reigns" reveal "how widely different has been the measure dealt to sinful Kings and erring Queens."[17] She concludes that "[w]e trace the incontinence of the former by successive creations in the peerage; and the faults of the latter, by records of imprisonment and death on the scaffold."[18] In dealing with the afterlife of legal history Norton deploys cultural memory in a manner similar to Walter Scott and the Tolbooth gallows: our point of access to this deep past and the rule of law it has generated comes through physical artifacts: in this case records (presumably those in *Burke's Peerage* and those produced by the criminal law).

She further notes the epistemological problem at the heart of both legal and historical truth-production, which is that it will always be the product of discourse. "What the truth was," she says, "respecting all or any of these dead Queens,—over whose senseless dust contending historians still do battle,— we can never know."[19] Yet she correctly identifies the existing divorce law as a site of collective trauma

> *this* we *do* know; that the punishment, here, of those sins which have no distinction in Divine law, was meted out very differently to them and their royal helpmates: that history describes the tyrant husband of Anne Boleyn, as one 'who never spared man in his wrath, or woman in his lust.'[20]

Here she renders explicit the cultural trauma that had been implicit in Queen Caroline's trial and also noted in the Katherine Howard chapter of the 1780 *Trials for Adultery*: Henry VIII used divorce as a weapon of violence against women, and in so doing did violence to the body politic as a tyrant. She compresses all of these anxieties—political, legal, and sexual—into one story when she observes

> The "Defender of the Faith and Father of the Reformation" had cut off the head of his adored Anne Boleyn, and was dressed in white and silver as an exultant bridegroom, to marry a fresher love; declaring the children of his former marriage (our Queen Mary and Queen Elizabeth), to be both bastards.[21]

Unlike in the traditional common law narrative, in which female adultery itself is the threat to the health of the state, Norton links the asymmetrical criminalization of adultery to the hypocrisy of the Church of England and the unnecessary illegitimacy of female English monarchs.

Insofar as the common law provides the historical logic Norton uses to expose the repressed collective trauma of the status quo, it functions as what Foucault called *Parrēsia*—the "form of speech which will exercise power in the framework of the city."[22] In Foucault's conception, despite its official power, *Parrēsia* allowed "the freedom of other speeches,"[23] including the discourse of "the weak reproaching the strong for his injustice,"[24] as Norton does here. Norton's lobbying can also be understood as an operation of cultural trauma, in which she belongs to what Jeffrey Alexander would call a "carrier group"[25] due to her talent, despite her marginalized status, for "meaning making,"[26] in the public sphere. However one understands it, Norton's participation in the legal ferment surrounding adultery and divorce reveals the generative potential of the trauma embedded into the collective memory of the common law.

In 1857, due in large part to Norton's lobbying efforts, Parliament passed the Matrimonial Causes Act, transferring jurisdiction over divorces to the common law courts. Because private bills of divorce had been so expensive, the Matrimonial Causes Act effectively expanded access to divorce beyond the realm of the very wealthy. It likewise abolished the tort of criminal conversation at common law, collapsing such claims into divorce proceedings and thereby removing the particularly one-sided legal theater of the crim-con action which Norton had so strenuously protested.[27] As Kelly Hager notes, the Act also made an important semantic advance: it moved divorce into the actual framework of the law, rather than requiring legislative action to make an exception to the law.[28]

Despite the significance of these developments, the Act managed to retain many of the structural injustices of the old system: Parliament imported all of the canon law precedent on divorce *a mensa et thoro* directly into the Act as the official basis for statutory construction. This meant, among other things, that the lop-sided requirement that a wife, and not a husband, prove aggravated adultery made it into the new statutory regime (and would not be abolished until the Matrimonial Causes Act of 1923).[29] Regardless of the new Victorian vogue for legal positivism and statutory innovation, the long, historical arch of natural law thinking—and all of its accompanying mythologies—would remain alive even in the process of statutory interpretation. Indeed, the hybrid state of affairs in which ancient canon law divorce precedents informed a wholly new legislative creation created conflict around the question of legal continuity during the Parliamentary debates on the Act. Lord Chancellor Cranworth downplayed the significance of the proposed new law, stating that "for 200 years the principle of the Bill had been in operation." By contrast, the Early of Malmesbury asserted that the proposed Bill was "opposed to the existing law of the land."[30] As Hager notes, these two opposing views make it clear that while divorces had been granted by Private Act of Parliament for almost two hundred years . . . until the passage of the 1857 Act, the British could at least pay lip service to the indissolubility of marriage.[31]

Both sides struggled to describe a legally contested concept in the language of English historical legitimacy. The history of the permanence of marriage, then, remained in something of a discursive flux.

After the Act passed and divorces proliferated, so too did the supply of legal proceedings to provide entertaining adultery narratives for the general public. The demand for such materials became so great that the newspaper *The Divorce Court Reporter* was founded in 1857. As Barbara Leckie argues, "[t]he divorce court publications, in their exposure of the perpetrators of adultery, made it clear to a population for whom privacy was a personal right, that their sexual crimes were always being watched."[32] Leckie further observes that the popular press coverage of divorce proceedings served a similar role to that I identified as more intentionally undertaken in the eighteenth-century divorce compendiums, and by literary works such as Fielding's: "[a]s the law retreated, the visibility of the 'criminal' and, in these cases, the specifically domestic crime of adultery, became a central mechanism through which the law discreetly operated."[33] Unlike the openly dialectical relationship between eighteenth-century trial narratives and literary products, however, by the time the novel form had evolved into its nineteenth-century incarnation, there was a disconnect between English literary representations of adultery and those circulating in the cultural milieu through periodicals and legal news.

When cheap periodicals replaced the novelistic eighteenth-century divorce compendiums, the gap between middle and low culture surrounding the topic of adultery became much greater. Nonetheless, it is still easy to discern the discursive connection between early and later conceptions of adultery as criminal, most particularly concerning its inevitable connection to actual crimes of violence. In 1857 the young Scotswoman Madeleine Smith was tried for the poisoning of her former lover Emile L'Angelier, with whom it was alleged she had been continuing an affair despite her engagement to another man. After Smith's acquittal, the *Saturday Review* declared, "[w]hether Madeleine Smith poisoned L'Angelier or not, her parallel correspondence with him and with Minnoch in March is established; and this is the moral anomaly in presence of which the fact of murder is a mere sequence."[34] Once more the discursive criminalization of adultery turns in large part upon the narrative construction linking it to inevitable violence.

At the same time these events were unfolding in Britain, during the second half of the nineteenth century continental Europe and America were seeing the emergence of a literary sub-genre that would produce a large number of canonical texts: the "adultery novel." This era produced Flaubert's *Madame Bovary* (1857), Queirós's *O primo Basilio* (1878), Tolstoy's *Anna Karenina* (1878), Clarín's *La Regenta* (1884), Fontane's *Effi Briest* (1896), and Chopin's *The Awakening* (1899). The critical literature on these texts has identified a number of thematic commonalities, which show the struggle between the new philosophies of romantic individualism and timeless anxieties over the preservation of social order. Maria Rippon, who has made a study of the function of adultery in this time period, points out that "all six novels deal with adulteresses who have faithful husbands whom they do not love, who believe that they have found happiness in their extramarital affairs, and who either die or suffer degradation due to their affair(s)."[35] She notes that "very often, the conflict arises in these novels between wives who crave novelty, excitement, and undying passion and husbands who live by the code of conduct prescribed by their societies to the detriment of their seemingly happy marriages."[36] Adulterous love is punished in all of these texts, though the narrator's sympathies lie, to varying extents, with the adulteress protagonists. Yet, Rippon suggests that Nietzsche's theory of the ethics of *ressentiment* can explain the downfall of the heroines in these texts, who must fall in part due to the petty-mindedness and jealousy of the secondary characters by which they are surrounded. She also observes that, interestingly, in most of these texts "deviating from the herd comes not with the act of infidelity and deception but with the adulteresses' refusal or inability to keep that act a secret."[37] In other words, that particular eighteenth-century concern over the public harm of "discovery" remains legible in the nineteenth-century literary representations of adultery.

In *Adultery in the Novel* Tony Tanner argues that the very structure of the novel form facilitates the narratization of adultery, even as it formally condemns it. While the nineteenth-century novel was conservative in its centering of the importance of family and domestic affairs, thereby creating a "strictness that works to maintain the law,"[38] the novel also "always contained potential feelings for that which breaks up the family—departure, disruption, and other various modes of disintegration."[39] For Tanner, the novel is drawn to presenting adultery because the real interest in a narrative about a family comes from the possible fissures the family contains.[40] The dichotomy he dismantles between whole and broken families is somewhat similar to the ways in which the need for a legal order is dependent upon the possibility of wrongs occurring in the first place; rather than "a simple *contest* between marital fidelity and adultery," Tanner says, "contracts and transgressions are inseparable, the one generating the other."[41] Referring to Foucault's characterization of transgression as affirmative, Tanner concludes that "[f]or the social world of the novel in [the nineteenth century] adultery is . . . a leap into limitlessness, with the result that the whole ambiguous problematics of limits are brought into the open."[42]

Rippon and Tanner both suggest that the uses of adultery in the nineteenth-century novel were not entirely punitive but opened, at least to some extent, the possibility of resistance. On the one hand, this literary phenomenon would seem well-timed with the liberalizing of the legal framework governing marital relations, marked by the Matrimonial Causes Act. Yet most of the texts they discuss in their treatments are Continental or American. Indeed, scholars have noted a general absence of a great tradition of adultery in the nineteenth-century English novel.[43] One reason often given for this absence is a general Victorian aversion to the improper. Indeed, when *Madame Bovary* was being prosecuted as an obscenity in France, Fitzjames Stephen noted that English literature would be free of such French "contamination" because English writers' "weaknesses forbid such dangerous eccentricity quite as much as their virtues."[44] Robert Buchanan agreed, declaring "[t]here is no danger of our writers indulging in indecencies. Whatever our private life may be, our literature is singularly alive to the proprieties."[45]

If one understands this anomaly, however, with regard to my claim that the quasi-criminality of adultery carries a particular traumatic narrative about British sovereignty, an explanation more complex than prudery arises. In a world still reeling from the effects of the French Revolution, the importance of distinguishing French from English nationhood became deeply important.[46] Relegating adultery to the category of "French literature" protected not only English morals from obscenity but English sovereignty from overthrow.[47] The following sections will consider the forms in which adultery nonetheless manifested itself in Victorian literature, against this backdrop of concerns. First, I look at *Jane Eyre*, written ten years before the Matrimonial Causes Act, and claim its importance to the discourse of failed history that contributed to that reform. I then read *Idylls of the King* and *The Ring and the Book* as very different meditations on the quasi-criminality of adultery in its relationship to sovereign authority and British common law evolution.

Jane Eyre and the Matrimonial Causes Act

In *Culture and Adultery,* Barbara Leckie takes issue with the notion that England lacked a nineteenth-century literary discourse on adultery, arguing that the very censorship that sought to suppress it was itself discursively productive. She concludes that "the only legitimate way to discuss adultery was to translate it as a domestic detective story in the service of the law,"[48] and argues that texts such as Caroline Norton's *Lost and Found* (1863) and Mary Elizabeth Bradon's *The Doctor's Wife* (1864) have what she describes as a "detective function," focused on the deceived party in the adulterous triangle, much like a divorce court did, to create an epistemological question about the evidence of adultery. I suggest that an even more prominent novel which, by virtue of the mystery that drives it, shares a similar detective function, should be considered in the canon of Victorian adultery texts: *Jane Eyre* (1847).

Due to its implicit treatment of adultery and divorce, *Jane Eyre* has a viable and hitherto overlooked claim to a role in the legal ferment over the Matrimonial Causes Act. In an 1848 letter to Lady Dacre, Caroline Norton praised the book, speculated as to its author, and noted "it is a very remarkable book, whoever wrote it, and made a very deep impression on me."[49] A close reading of Brontë's text shows this effect, revealing structures of thinking about and within the law of divorce and adultery that appear in Norton's influential letter to the Queen a decade later and can thus fairly be speculated to have contributed, at least sub-textually, to those ideas. Charlotte Brontë's Jane is neither the "deceived party" in the traditional sense nor the momentarily liberated adulterous heroine of the Continental and American texts mentioned earlier; she is a combination of the two. This section will consider the function of marriage in *Jane Eyre* as a juridical form of traumatic repression. Initially, by establishing marriage as an engine of violence and illegitimate punishment, the text opens a space for Jane and Rochester's adulterous coupling as an alternative. Subsequently, however, this space itself eventually collapses into yet another iteration of despotism until it can be reconstituted on legally legitimate grounds. Brontë imagines the Gothic operations of both inescapable marriage and adultery, in the particular context of the English legal order, in a way that anticipates some of Norton's arguments ten years later.

The Despotism of Marriage

Far more subtly than in any of the texts discussed previously, Brontë rejects both marital indissolubility and bigamy/adultery and thereby appears to endorse the sort of middle-of-the-road liberal legal order that would eventually inform the Matrimonial Causes Act. Unlike authors such as Tennyson, however, Brontë remains preoccupied with the threat presented by marriage itself to the woman as a rights-bearing citizen. The Gothic lends itself well to dramatizing any sort of legal anxiety because—like the common law itself—the impact of the genre comes in part through how it depicts the inevitable power of the past operating on the present. Furthermore, other scholars have shown how Gothic spaces function to recover women's experiences from the historical and legal records that would elide them.

Diana Wallace has asked how we can re-imagine women's recorded experiences if historical and political events are seen as more important than domestic. She concludes that, where women are legally dead, the gothic genre expresses their past existence as a kind of haunting:

> To say something is "Gothic" is at once to imply that it is obsessed with the return of the past, and to define it as unhistorical, not "proper history," fantasy rather than fact. Conversely, historical fiction proper is defined partly by its eschewing of the fantastic, the supernatural, and (ironically) the "fictional" sense of the invented or imaginary.[50]

Where Sir Walter Scott's historical novels emphasized realism and historical specificity, as opposed to the "feminized," supernatural Gothic genre associated with authors such as Ann Radcliffe (famously parodied by Jane Austen in *Northanger Abbey* (1817)), the Gothic historical novel yokes them together. Wallace argues that the Gothic works as a "mode of history"—obsessions with inheritance, lost heirs, and illegitimate offspring "explore the ways in which the 'female line' has been erased in 'History'."[51] Working on the legal question specifically, Kathryn Temple argues for a "representational bond between law and the Gothic novel," pointing to similarities between the work of Wollstonecraft and Radcliffe who both "avoided a direct onslaught on the monolithically imagined legal system yet commented obliquely on their exclusion."[52] Temple says that—in Radcliffe and Wollstonecraft, as in Blackstone himself—one finds that "sites of struggle over the gendered juridical are literalized as legal spaces that invite, deny, or resist entry to variously gendered bodies."[53] *Jane Eyre* is rife with such spaces—at times explicitly gendered, at others more universal.[54] In the chapters of the text concerning Jane's adult life, Brontë continues to blend the legal and the seemingly supernatural forces that characterized the sufferings of the child Jane into a form of Gothic repression, which she eventually organizes around the ambiguous nature of marriage as an institution.[55]

Charlotte Brontë herself was apparently deeply in love with the married master of the boarding school she attended in Brussels, sending him letters notable for the sadomasochistic language in which she describes her longing. On one occasion she describes him as "the only master I have ever had", and on another she laments:

> Day or night I find neither rest nor peace. If I sleep I have tortured dreams in which I see you always severe, always gloomy and annoyed with me. I do not seek to justify myself, I submit to every kind of reproach—all that I know—is that I cannot—that I will not resign myself to losing the friendship of my master completely—I would rather undergo the greatest physical sufferings. If my master withdraws his friendship entirely from me I will be completely without hope . . . I cling on to preserving that little interest—I cling on to it as I cling on to life.[56]

It may, then, be unsurprising that most of the novel's potential marital pairings which threaten to separate Jane and Rochester seem similarly sadistic. Setting aside, for the moment, the relationship between the protagonists, each of the text's other three actual or potential marriages presents a unique horror, born of vaguely-suppressed violence premised on and mandated by background legal realities requiring and sustaining matrimony.

To start with the mildest of the three, Blanche Ingram's campaign to win Rochester's hand arises from the legal fact that her father's estates were entailed away and her eldest brother would inherit almost everything.[57] We see in Blanche how the accepted, misogynistic use of English property law has decidedly illiberal effects: due to her own desperation, Blanche's efforts to secure Rochester mimic a tyrant's violent suppression of a subjugated population. It appears to be a war of all against all, as Thomas Hobbes would have it, with the spoils going solely to the strongest. Jane notes how Blanche is "vivaciously accosting him"[58] and Blanche's own view of marriage is that of a despot: "[w]henever I marry . . . I am resolved my husband shall not be a rival, but a foil to me. I will suffer no competitor near the throne; I shall exact an undivided homage."[59] While she is impoverished by the feudal-style entailment that passed her father's estate, undivided, to her brother, she seeks the same categorical ownership.

The game of charades the Thornfield party plays on a rainy day extends the comparison between marriage and legal oppression: in acting out the first part of the word "Bridewell," the London prison, Rochester and Blanche portray a bridal couple on their wedding day, and—to portray the "*tableau* of the whole"—Rochester portrays a prisoner. As Joanne Rea has perceptively noticed, the name "Bridewell" has even more specific historical connotations of "adultery and of frustrated attempts to dissolve a marriage": Henry VIII lived in Bridewell Palace while waiting for the dispensation to wed Anne Boleyn, and in 1553 Edward VI gave the Palace to the city of London as a jail for loose women and derelicts. This moment resurrects the familiar cultural trauma of English sovereignty associated with the Boleyn marriage and execution, which Norton later resurrects in her Letter. Rea astutely points out the significance of the fact that "[b]y binding himself to a profligate, whose excesses had 'prematurely developed into insanity,' Rochester is dragged through a matrimonial 'dungeon' worse than any in Bridewell."[60]

The potential pairing of Blanche and Rochester also operates as an unjust criminal condemnation of Jane's feelings, which the reader has come to identify with and intuit that Rochester reciprocates. Forced to compare her attractions and situation to Blanche's, Jane puts her hopes on metaphorical trial: "Arraigned at my own bar, Memory having given her evidence of the hopes, wishes, sentiments I had been cherishing since last night . . . Reason having come forward and told in her own quiet way, a plain, unvarnished tail ... I pronounced judgment."[61] Brontë thus illustrates the dangers of "Reason"—and the Enlightenment legalism the concept represents—serving as the sole arbiter of the good.

Jane's potential marriage to St. John Rivers provides a second rendition of marriage as both legal subjugation and physical violence. When St. John describes missionary work as a calling, he also presents his release from the ennui of being a parish minister as an escape from slavery: "[f]rom that moment my state of mind changed; the fetters dissolved and dropped from every faculty, leaving nothing of the bondage but its galling soreness."[62] Indeed, though ostensibly obeying a call from God, St. John aggrandizes his authority by rejecting earthly codes entirely: "I am the servant of an infallible Master. I am not going out under human guidance, subject to the defective laws and erring control of my feeble fellow-worms: my king, my lawgiver, my captain, is the All-perfect."[63] St. John's imagining of himself as a newly freed, rights-bearing individual translates almost immediately into the need to assert his unfettered sovereign autonomy over Jane. Of her obedience to St. John's desire that she learn Hindi Jane says

> [i]n his presence every effort to sustain or follow any other became vain: I fell under a freezing spell. When he said "go," I went, "come," I came, "do this," I did it. But I did not love my servitude.[64]

The imagery of slavery—echoing as it does her abject childhood situation at the mercy of John Reed's tyranny—becomes increasingly violent the closer St. John approaches to demanding matrimonial union. She shudders at his "hardness and despotism."[65] When he first kisses her before retiring to bed she says "[p]erhaps I might have turned a little pale, for I felt as if this kiss were a seal affixed to my fetters."[66]

That both St. John and Jane use the phrase "absolutely" to describe his potential possession of her suggests the legal distinction between "absolute" and "qualified" property—the latter of which applies to wild animals, which only remain property so long as their owner can contain them.[67] Absolute property, by contrast, is owned without qualification and includes domestic animals which are considered never to have had natural liberty in a wild state. The "iron shroud" Jane fears, therefore, signifies both an impending physical and legal annihilation. It is precisely the legal annihilation Caroline Norton refers to when she notes that "a married woman in England has no *legal existence*: her being is absorbed in that of her husband ... the legal fiction holds her to be "*one*" with her husband, even though she may never see or hear of him."[68] Norton's repeated references to a husband as "tyrant" likewise echo Jane's visceral reaction to St. John, who would categorically isolate her—legally, spiritually, and geographically—from everything but his dominion. The existence of formal laws barring women from escaping marriage effectively reconstitute the pre-liberal legal order premised on absolute power.

The text's most dramatic example of marriage as Gothic horror is, of course, the union between Rochester and Bertha Mason. According to Mrs. Fairfax, Rochester's father "did not like to diminish the property by division, and yet he was anxious that Mr. Edward should have wealth, too, to keep up the consequence of the name" and thus "[o]ld Mr. Rochester and Mr. Rowland combined to bring Mr. Edward into what he considered a painful position, for the sake of making his fortune."[69] From the start, Rochester was entrapped—physically and painfully, in a manner described by Mrs. Fairfax as "trials"—by property laws.[70] Rochester himself describes his downfall in the language of bankruptcy:

> I started, or rather (for like other defaulters, I like to lay half the blame on ill fortune and adverse circumstances) was thrust on to a wrong tack at the age of one-and-twenty, and have never recovered the right course since.[71]

One of the particular oppressions inherent in Rochester's situation is how the laws forbid him from the course they are generally—and particularly in the nineteenth-century age of penology from which Brontë was writing —considered to promote: reformation. "I could reform," Rochester says, "if—but where is the use of thinking of it, hampered, burdened, cursed as I am?"[72] Thornfield is therefore unique amongst Gothic literary estates insofar as it not only physically conscribes horrors of the flesh but, by virtue of its significance as a piece of property, delimits the legal personhood of its owner.

Rochester attempts to come to terms with his entrapment by redefining criminality. While discussing his intentions with Jane in vague terms, he declares, "I know what my aim is, what my motives are; and at this moment I pass a law, unalterable as that of the Medes and the Persians, that both are right."[73] He breaks down his intended bigamy into constituent parts: his "motive" is clearly pure (reformation), and he has unilaterally adopted the role of absolute lawmaker to redefine the *actus reus* as legal.

While Jane responds, echoing the traditional common law view of bills of attainder, that "[t]hey cannot be, sir, if they require a new statute to legalise them," yet he counters that "unheard-of combinations of circumstances demand unheard-of rules."[74] This debate is a fairly standard rehearsal of the age-old positions in favor of and opposition to legislative innovation. Jane argues that "[t]he human and fallible should not arrogate a power with which the divine and perfect alone can safely be trusted . . . [t]hat of saying of any strange, unsanctioned line of action 'Let it be right'."[75] The fallacy in Jane's argument is, of course, that if the "line of action" is unsanctioned only in an earthly sense, then only the "human and fallible" forbad it in the first place. The problem with which most of the balance of the text will be occupied is whether the crimes of bigamy and adultery fall into the former or latter category. In arguing for precisely the sort of legislative amendment Rochester would accomplish by personal fiat, Caroline Norton dwells on the importance of the distinction between Divine and positive law in the Parliamentary debates. She quotes the Irish Peer Lord Clancarty's description of marriage as a "divine ordinance" and paraphrases the Scotch Lord Campbell's counter-argument that "marriage was held indissoluble *in times of Popery,* but is not held so now; and on that very account a judicial instead of an ecclesiastical jurisdiction ought now to be established."[76] The chaos, Norton suggests, urges us to abandon the byzantine path of the old law and its repressions in favor of new legislation. Brontë, however, lingers on the costs, respectively, of either following or abandoning long-recognized prohibitions, however confusing and oppressive their quasi-criminal status has made them.

Indeed, Rochester describes his participation in the marriage to Bertha with particular care to emphasize the fact that his conduct was not criminal. It was "a capital error . . . Mind, I don't say a *crime,* I am not speaking of shedding blood or any other guilty act, which might make the perpetrator amenable to the law: my word is *error.*"[77] Again, when he alludes to his departure to England and imprisonment of Bertha at Thornfield, he recurs to the concept of culpability as the touchstone for criminality, and rejects it: "You take measures to obtain relief: unusual measures, but neither unlawful nor culpable."[78] Despite this studied avoidance of claiming criminal guilt, Rochester describes his life in the formal terms of criminal punishment (similarly to the young Jane's contemplation of her undeserved punishments at the hands of the Reeds). He describes his condition as carceral, in which "hope has quitted you on the very confines of life."[79] Alternatively, he emphasizes that his punishment was self-imposed, as "seeking rest in exile" and "voluntary banishment."[80] He recharacterizes the criminal prohibition on bigamy as merely an unjustified social prohibition, asking "[t]o attain this end, are you justified in overleaping an obstacle of custom—a mere conventional impediment, which neither your conscience sanctifies nor your judgment approves?" and wants the unwitting Jane to tell him whether he is "justified" in "daring the world's opinion" by marrying her.[81] Justification is a particular legal concept mitigating criminal liability, yet he omits to tell her he contemplates a legal crime; on the other side of the scale, he places only social reprobation.

After Jane tells him she is happy after their engagement he further characterizes the illegality of his decision as socially constructed, not the product of divine or natural law: "It will atone—it will atone . . . It will expiate at God's tribunal. I know my Maker sanctions what I do. For the world's judgment—I wash my hands thereof. For man's opinion—I defy it."[82] Even this rationalization is problematic, suggesting at once that he has God's "sanction" for proceeding but must "atone" for the decision based on the happiness it will bring an innocent third party. (That we will subsequently see Rochester's language echoed by the monomaniacal St. John Rivers' rejection of the legal codes of his "feeble fellow-worms" in going off to his death in India reemphasizes that Rochester's position was dangerously unmoored from moral reality in a way that would likely victimize Jane.) As we have seen so many times before, the language of legality breaks down around the concept of adultery; through Rochester's internal contradictions we sense that what he proposes is in fact criminal, yet perhaps ought not be.

Brontë's descriptions of Bertha repeatedly emphasize her physical and moral monstrousness.[83] They likewise complicate the meaning of the parson's words calling for objections to Rochester's union with Jane: "So many as are coupled together otherwise than God's word doth allow, are not joined together by God, neither is their matrimony lawful."[84] Rochester asks the objecting solicitor Briggs: "would you thrust on me a wife?" to which the man replies, "I would remind you of your lady's existence, sir; which the law recognizes, if you do not."[85] The proximity of this declaration to the discovery of Bertha's debased physical existence suggests that the law's "recognition" may not, in fact, be the same as "God's word." Indeed Rochester's confession, as self-condemnatory as it is, invites competing accounts of the crime he had attempted to commit:

> Bigamy is an ugly word!—I meant, however, to be a bigamist; but fate has out-manoeuvred me, or Providence has checked me,—perhaps the last. I am little better than a devil at this moment, and, as my pastor there would tell me, deserve no doubt the sternest judgments of God, even to the quenchless fire and deathless worm ... She thought all was fair and legal and never dreamt she was going to entrapped into a feigned union with a defrauded wretch, already bound to a bad, mad, and embruted partner![86]

Though Rochester concedes that "Providence" may have intervened, the secular alternative of random chance remains a possibility. Indeed the mention of "bigamy" as simply a legal term of art, a "word," lessens its severity alongside the description of Jane's potential fate that is really a description of his own as Bertha's husband: "entrapped" in "a feigned union."

Once Rochester establishes the physical horror of Bertha's existence in his domestic space, however, he moves on to render the legal horror of the formal ties that bind him to her, which implicitly negates the possibility of cabining the former. "You shall yet be my wife," he tells Jane, for "I am not married," going on to mention "all the hideous and degrading agonies which must attend a man bound to a wife at once intemperate and unchaste."[87] His insistence that legal truth cannot be reconciled with moral truth (and therefore should not prevent their living morally in adultery) turns on the uncanny fact that "a nature the most gross, impure, depraved I ever saw, was associated with mine, and called by the law and by society a part of me."[88] He relegates the formal requirements of the law to the Foucauldian control of the social world: both operate against "nature" to effect the grotesque combination of Bertha and Rochester. Rochester even goes so far as to characterize Bertha herself as unlawful, in asserting that "to the last I repudiated the contamination of her crimes, and wrenched myself from connection with her mental defects. Still, society associated my name and person with hers."[89] Against the image of his unfair imprisonment in a union with a criminal, Rochester says of Jane, "[y]ou are my sympathy—my better self—my good angel. I am bound to you with strong attachment . . . to tell me I had already a wife is empty mockery: you know now that I had but a hideous demon."[90] Rochester's marriage to Bertha—only amplified by the two lesser horrific pairings discussed earlier—thus seems the worst sort of abomination: a physical, legal, and moral containment, made worse by the paradox of its legal requirement (that he remain married to an insane spouse)[91] supporting rather than subverting legal wrongs.

It is worth noting that in her letter Caroline Norton also alluded to the ways in which the old divorce laws victimized husbands as well: both due to the impossibility of divorce for any but the rich and to the requirement of adultery as the sole grounds. She gives, as an example, a case with many parallels to Rochester's plight:

> A respectable tradesman was tried for bigamy, and convicted. The second wife deposed, that he had courted her for six years; had no money with her; on the contrary, supplied her with money since his apprehension; had always been very kind; and that they had a child of his, residing with them. The undivorced wife was living with an omnibus man, and had been in a lunatic asylum.[92]

Norton used that particular example to demonstrate that, had the parties been wealthy, "we should simply have had 'Grayton's Divorce Bill' going quietly through the House of Lords."[93] Yet it also demonstrates the juridical horror of the laws binding not only the husband but the second wife and his child—like Rochester, Jane, and Adele—to an allegedly mentally incompetent spouse.

The Rehabilitation of English Law

From what I have discussed thus far, it becomes clear that *Jane Eyre*, in many ways, challenges the definition of adultery—even bigamy—as a genuinely criminal act and characterizes the institution of legally binding marriage as a possible source of grave oppression and violence. It is certainly due in part to these reasons that such contemporary critics as Matthew Arnold objected to the novel's morality.[94] And in this sense, *Jane Eyre* participates in the tradition of "adultery novel" within which critics have not frequently read it. Despite all of this, however, Rochester's attempt to subvert the legal strictures defining marriage actually end up transfiguring his partnership with Jane into precisely the oppressive tyranny associated with the legal but inappropriate marriages considered in the text.

He proposes to her on the fairy holiday of Midsummer Eve and subsequently tells Adele the story of the "fairy from Elf-land come to make me happy" by taking him to the moon, and describes her ring as "a talisman that will remove all the difficulties" in getting there.[95] In cautioning Rochester over his excessive enthusiasm after their engagement, Jane says, "[h]uman beings never enjoy complete happiness in this world. I was not born for a different destiny to the rest of my species: to imagine such a lot befalling me is a fairy tale."[96] With this admonition, she breaks down the otherworldly language he uses to subvert legal reality: she was not indeed born in the world of the dead and is therefore not exempt from the laws—the English laws—that prevent Rochester from re-marrying. Caroline Norton likewise opens her Letter by similarly rejecting the logic of the fairy tale as a plausible substitute for the operation of positive law. She states

> I know those pleasant tales of an earlier and simpler time, when oppressed
> subjects travelled to the presence of some glorious prince or princess, who
> instantly set their affairs to rights without reference to the law, are quaint
> old histories, or fairy fables, fit only for the amusement of children.[97]

Laws, for both Brontë and Norton, must be dealt with on their own terms.

From almost the very moment Jane accepts Rochester's proposal, their shared means of imaginative self-fashioning shifts from the discourse of the otherworldly back into that of the despotic, which is otherwise associated with John Reed and the other corrupted romantic pairings in the text. As part of his ruse about planning to marry Blanche, which he uses to segue into proposing to Jane, Rochester assumes the role of law-giver, attempting to banish Jane away from England (as he had once been banished) to the colonial peripheries in Ireland where he has found her a new place as a governess. When she contemplates this fate and decides to adopt it, she makes it clear that her actions are not those of a subject but a rights-bearing individual: "I am no bird; and no net ensnares me; I am a free human being with an independent will, which I now exert to leave you."[98] In echoing an earlier episode in which the young Jane had no "will" in her response to Mrs. Reed's tyrannical parenting, Brontë suggests, in Wollstonecraftian language, not only that Jane has matured into full-fledged independent adulthood, but also a disturbing parallel between Rochester and the tyrannical Reeds themselves.

Indeed, the engagement begins a period in the text in which Rochester and Jane view their relationship largely through an orientalist lens in which he figures as an Eastern despot, perhaps due in part to his unilateral creation (like the "Medes and Persians" he had earlier mentioned) of a legal order permitting their union. Immediately upon their engagement, Rochester mutters a claim of absolute possession: "God pardon me . . . and man meddle not with me. I have her, and will hold her."[99] Jane herself then forcibly shifts the imaginative landscape of their operations from the fairy-like to the Biblical,[100] shutting down Rochester's romantic effusions by saying

> I was thinking of Hercules and Samson with their charmers . . . You don't talk very wisely just now; any more than those gentlemen acted very wisely. However, had they been married, they would no doubt by their severity as husbands have made up for their softness as suitors.[101]

She then proceeds to elicit severity by exercising curiosity—a dynamic far earlier foreshadowed during her first days at Thornfield during which she first noted a hallway "looking, with its two rows of small black doors all shut, like a corridor in some Bluebeard's castle."[102] This tale of the quintessentially brutal *Arabian Nights* husband recurs when Jane seeks to ask Rochester about his pretended engagement to Blanche, and he responds, "[c]uriosity is a dangerous petition: it is well I have not taken a vow to accord every request."[103]

While the particular dangers of marital curiosity in this case turn, of course, on the specific fact of Bertha's concealment, Jane's ignorance of that fact means that her accusations of despotism arise from the power structures of marriage generally. When Rochester offers to give her, in lieu of information, "half his estate," she calls him "King Ahasuerus," referring to the Biblical Persian king whose absolute power his wife Esther was able, through her marital subordination, to channel away from violence against the Jews.[104] After Jane admits that what she is after is knowledge and Rochester fears that she will "turn out a downright Eve on my hands!" she notes, "you have just been telling me how much you liked to be conquered . . . Don't you think I had better take advantage of the confession?"[105] That these suggestions of conquest and tyranny derive from the married state itself, and not something particular to Jane's curiosity seems clear when she exclaims "[h]ow stern you look now! That will be your married look, sir, I suppose?"[106] Indeed, from this point on, according to Jane, "He had no such honeyed terms as 'love' and 'darling' on his lips: the best words at my service were 'provoking puppet,' 'malicious elf,' 'sprite,' 'changeling,' &c."[107] Even the words of endearment Rochester does offer during this portion of the novel take on the cast of despotic authority. Jane "thought his smile was such as a sultan might, in a blissful and fond moment, bestow on a slave his gold and gems had enriched."[108] When Rochester himself says he would not exchange her for "the Grand Turk's whole seraglio" she responds that she'll "go out as a missionary to preach liberty to them that are enslaved—your harem inmates amongst the rest."[109] In other words, her orientation towards Rochester has come to echo her childhood stand against the enslavement by John Reed. Rochester views the absolutism as reciprocal, saying, "[i]t is your time now, little tyrant, but it will be mine presently, and when once I have fairly seized you, to have and to hold, I'll just . . . attach you to a chain like this."[110]

To understand exactly what is going on in these passages, it is helpful to look to Alain Grosrichard's theoretical work on the fantasy of the seraglio in the seventeenth and eighteenth centuries. Grosrichard starts from the premise that, in the Enlightenment era of reason-based political authority, the concept of "despotism" had come to haunt the European imagination as the ultimate threat.[111] His central psychoanalytical claim, based upon his analysis of Enlightenment-era writers such as Rousseau and Voltaire, is that the figure of the Eastern despot is a site for the Western, Enlightenment mind to outsource repressed fantasies of domination and unlicensed pleasure.[112] The sudden despotic turn in the Jane-Rochester relationship, then, has two functions in the text. The first is, of course, sexual, as a means of simultaneously condemning and inviting fantasies of sexual subjection and decadence. But the second is political. Grosrichard points to the origins of the despot fantasy as explicitly linked to the new liberal legal order; its role in Brontë's text is to support that order even while questioning it. In other words, while Jane confronts the potential Gothic oppressions of even legal, English marriage, and asserts her independent political identity against the potential subjugation attendant to such marriage, she nonetheless participates in a fantasy that displaces those terrors away from the legal order in which she participates. English fairyland may not, in the end, be entirely realistic, but the basic bundle of rights provided by English law can be made to serve both romantic and feminist ends, with a little bit of effort.

Norton's *Letter* seems to take these very tensions as its starting point. She opens with an appeal to Queen Victoria as a woman, describing an evening gala in the library of Lincoln's Inn, on the occasion of Prince Albert's invitation to become a Barrister. She notes how the treasurer of Lincoln's Inn thanked the Queen for her "gracious regard for the profession of the law," congratulated her "on the great amendments of the law effected since [her] accession," and affirmed that "the pure glory of those labours must be dear to [her] heart."[113] Norton describes the aesthetic juxtaposition between the "young beloved queen, with ladies in waiting" and the "dingy law courts" and declares:

> It was the very poetry of allegiance, when the Lord Chancellor and the other great law officers did obeisance in that Hall to their Queen, and the Treasurer knelt at a woman's feet, to read of the amendments in that great stern science by which governments themselves are governed; whose thrall all nations must submit to; whose value even the savage acknowledges,— and checks by its means the wild liberty he enjoys, with some rude form of polity and order.[114]

Norton appears to relish the paradox of the law kneeling to a woman before she begins her taxonomy of the ways in which it does violence to womankind. Yet the episode underscores the fact that Victoria's assent to legislative change is required (as does the fact that Norton directs her pamphlet to the Queen in the first place). Though the content of the law is tyrannical in its operation against women generally, Norton concedes that the process of legal amendment is preferable to the wild liberty of the state of nature.

Like Norton's *Letter, Jane Eyre* complicates the cultural discourse of adultery as it stood in the mid-nineteenth century. On the one hand the text troubles the cultural identification of adultery as quasi-criminal, in part by developing the law of marriage as a Gothic bugbear in and of itself, and presenting adultery and bigamy in the most relational light possible: if the "hellish" Bertha is the sole victim, the text suggests, can it be a wrong at all, much less a public one? Yet the Jane-Rochester adulterous relationship becomes symbolically aligned with the classic threat to all of the western legal order: the Eastern despot. While, Brontë suggests, marriage can create horrifying spaces of Gothic imprisonment, so can adultery—particularly for the female party. The text then returns to a position that—if not exactly conservative—does endorse the basic project of English law, as a buttress against the limitless authority of the despot.[115] In that sense, Brontë participates in the problematic imperialist discourse that uses the concept of Eastern tyranny to subjugate it discursively. At the same time, however, she deploys a concept of legal evolution that puts pressure on the presumed stasis of the existing marriage laws.

We can understand *Jane Eyre* as a particularly complex entry into the cultural narrative of adultery as a quasi-crime, with potential real-world influence. Brontë's treatment of adultery—as, by turns, an escape from the juridical entombment of oppressive marriage and a site for the exercise of illegitimate (and highly un-"English") absolute power—suggests a schizo-phrenic, traumatic legal concept which she seems almost to invite the positive law to address through legal change. Certainly, the echoes of *Jane Eyre* in Caroline Norton's writing urge that conclusion. While Brontë ultimately sublimates such tensions through the *deus-ex-machina* of the Thornfield fire, it will disappear entirely in the next text this chapter will consider, in which adultery retains an air of static criminality.

Idylls of the King as English Adultery Text

As Tennyson was Poet Laureate for most of Victoria's reign, his work is par-ticularly significant in any survey of the cultural representations of an official, legal phenomenon of the period. Simon Petch has identified at least one specific nineteenth-century legal discourse in which Tennyson participated: the debate over the Judicature Act of 1873, which proposed the merger of the courts of law and equity.[116] Equity, as Petch notes, was once understood as a synonym for "natural justice," and courts of equity provided a separate forum from the common law courts for certain types of cases to be decided according "to the Lord Chancellor's conscience," instead of on the basis of the more rigid common law rules.[117] The individualistic, discretionary moral-ity represented by equity was, therefore, always a threat to the prerogatives of common lawyers. In the Victorian age, furthermore, the spread of the Darwinian concept of the "law of nature" as bloody and random cast doubt on the possibility or desirability of a "natural justice" with moral priority to the common law.[118] One Victorian treatise-writer noted that equity "for exactly 500 years since the reign of Richard II has been like a branch dissoci-ated from its parent stock" but is now to "be grated back into the Common Law of the land" due to the Judicature Act, thereby giving Victorian lawyers "the pleasanter and more profitable task of finding points of contact between [law and equity] and illustrating the one by the other."[119] Another effect of the Judicature Act was that the less-than-two-decade old Court of Divorce and Matrimonial Causes became subsumed into the new Probate, Divorce, and Admiralty Division. Increasingly, therefore, the project of the common law was coming to be one of homogenization, including with respect to adultery.

Petch, however, argues that Tennyson's knights' oaths, in *Idylls*, to "rev-erence the King as if he were/ Their conscience, and their conscience as their King," suggests that "Arthurian society in Tennyson's poem is based on the radical, original meaning of Equity in England as the conscience of the King."[120] Perhaps because this concept of Equity highlights the particular importance, for the body politic, of the King as an embodied individual,

Tennyson's use of the Camelot myth depicts Guinevere's adultery as a cultural trauma. Her adultery is part of the collective textual memory Tennyson incorporates—via several intermediaries, most notably *Mort d'Arthur*—into a tribute to nineteenth-century English royal authority and law-giving.[121] The unmaking of sovereignty through adultery has registered as a collective trauma throughout the life of the doctrine as a tort, a crime, and—by 1857—grounds for divorce. This section considers *Idylls* as an explication of this trauma, and the relationships between sovereign and subject that contribute to the discourse of adultery as quasi-criminal, even after its formal legal identity, at the time of the poem, had been de-emphasized and enfolded into the common law of divorce.

Idylls of the King has been heavily studied in the context of Victorian "Anglo-Saxonism," which had both racial and philological strains.[122] Aaron Heisler describes as "anachronistically archaic" Tennyson's self-conscious imitation of the thirteenth-century Middle-English text *Brut* by Layamon who was, himself, using Anglo-Saxon forms to versify the twelfth-century Norman text *Roman de Brut* which was, in turn, based upon Geoffrey of Monmouth's *History of the Kings of Britain*. While Heisler points out that Anglo-Saxon would have been foreign to the Celtic ancient Britons, Tennyson's resort to it nonetheless locates the *Idylls* in a self-consciously historicized tradition of English kingship.[123] Tennyson's effort is thus structurally similar to that of Victorian legal treatise-writers like Pollock and Maitland, who fashioned "bridges" between medieval and contemporary law. (Indeed, on the specific question of the indissolubility of marriage they note "[t]he nature of the ancient Germanic marriage has in our own day been the theme of lively debates" and that "[p]hrases and ceremonies which belong to this old time will long be preserved in that curious cabinet of antiquities, the marriage ritual of the English Church.")[124] As treatise writers sought to reinforce the legitimacy of nineteenth-century law by demonstrating both its continuity with and evolution beyond its medieval incarnation, so does Tennyson connect Victoria's sovereignty to the initial glory of Arthur's, while distinguishing it through the crucial element of marital fidelity. The text likewise models the logic of the common law in its implicit capacity for, and even mandate of, evolution over time.[125]

At the time of *The Idylls'* publication, Tennyson drew criticism for his emasculation of Malory's highly masculine Arthur by depicting him as a cuckold. Swinburne complained that Tennyson had "lowered the note and deformed the outline of the Arthurian story, by reducing Arthur to the level of a wittol, Guinevere to the level of a woman of intrigue, and Launcelot to the level of a 'co-respondent,'" an allusion to the trivial culture of cuckoldry so well parodied by Fielding a century earlier and currently providing entertainment in the tabloids via divorce trials.[126] Nonetheless, in dedicating the epic to the late Prince Consort Albert, Tennyson designates the poem as a tribute to marital fidelity, idealized as a component of sovereignty. He compares Albert to Arthur, re-imagined as both a loyal husband and obedient subject to his conscience. While Arthur (and Albert) "loved one only and . . . clave to her" he also "reverenced his conscience as his king."[127] The dissolution, through death, of the marriage of Victoria and Albert becomes a threat to the cohesion of the former's empire, over which "commingled with the gloom of imminent war,/ The shadow of His loss drew like eclipse,/ Darkening the world."[128] Victoria's sovereignty appears destabilized by the loss of a partner who cleaved to her as if marital completeness were a necessary condition for hegemonic political authority.

It is similarly clear that both political order and humanity depend upon the purity of the union between Arthur and Guinevere. Tennyson suggests that unification of husband and wife into one legal entity is a pre-condition for the consolidation of warring factions into one political entity. As Arthur says at the start of the poem:

> . . . for saving I be joined
> To her that is the fairest under heaven,
> I seem as nothing in the mighty world,
> And cannot will my will, nor work my work
> Wholly, nor make myself in mine own realm
> Victor and lord. But were I joined with her
> Then might we live together as one life,
> And reigning with one will in everything
> Have power on this dark land to lighten it,
> And power on this dead world to make it live.[129]

These lines establish the central problem of the text: much like Victoria's empire, which is "eclipsed" by the darkness of her consort's death, the unification of England as a political state depends upon a conjugal "joining" of its king with his wife. His "will"—both as an individual man and as a source of political legitimacy—is impotent without collapse into the will of another, to form "one," either as a unified legal entity under his direction or as an example of companionate leadership, with both parties working together. The priest who marries the royal couple reiterates this charge: "Reign ye,/ and live and love, and make the world/ Other, and may thy queen be one with thee,/ And all of this Order of thy Table Round/ Fulfill the boundless purpose of their King!"[130] Again, Tennyson conflates Arthur's "purpose" of "making the world other" into being "one" with Guinevere.

This language reflects a particular common law understanding of marriage, as reflected in Victorian attorney M. C. Merttins Swabey's 1857 treatise on the relevance of canon law precedent for interpreting the Matrimonial Causes Act. Quoting the jurist Lord Stowell, Swabey states

> a marriage, in its origin, is a contract of natural law; it may exist between two individuals of different sexes, although no third person existed in the world, as happened in the case of the common ancestors of mankind. It is the parent, not the child, of civil society.[131]

He thereby links the concept of natural justice, typically associated with social contract theory, to the institution of marriage itself. As in Tennyson's depiction of the creation of Camelot, marriage is necessary to the creation of a social contract, and all of the liberal legal order that follows it. (Swabey further notes that religion only comes into play secondarily:

> [marriage] then becomes a religious as well as a natural and civil contract . . . Heaven itself is made a party to the contract, and the consent of the individuals pledged to each other, is ratified and consecrated by a vow to god.)[132]

In *Idylls,* too, the religious component to marriage follows soon after the creation of the social contract: the wedding scene gives way immediately to a confrontation with the "heathen" Roman lords who demand tribute from Arthur. After the marriage is solemnized the knights immediately join together to sing in defiance of the Romans:

> Blow trumpet! He will lift us from the dust
> Blow trumpet! Live the strength and die the lust!
> Clang battleaxe, and clash brand! Let the King reign![133]

The refrain sublimates the King's marriage into—at once—an image of the Christian resurrection symbolized by the trumpet and the dust, an assertion of political autonomy, and an end to sexual license, represented by Rome —"the slowly-fading mistress of the world." The feminization of Rome as "mistress" bears the double connotations of proprietress and kept woman. The latter definition—particularly when combined with Tennyson's frequent references to "Idolaters" and "Heathens"—taps into a long anti-Catholic tradition of personifying Rome as a prostitute.[134] The wedding itself, therefore, facilitates English political independence by supplanting the debauched relationship to Rome with the monogamy of Arthur and Guinevere's new marriage. With marriage thus established as the backbone of the idyll of Camelot, most of the remaining books in the poem present various challenges to this order. Most of the Arthurian vignettes Tennyson selects to incorporate into the text presage, in some way, the ultimate dissolution of sovereignty resulting from Guinevere's eventual betrayal of Arthur.

In the chapter "The Marriage of Geraint," Tennyson foregrounds a lesser-known Arthurian figure whose story reinforces the conflict between sovereignty and adultery.[135] Unlike most of the other characters in the *Idylls,* Geraint does not figure in the primary French and English Arthurian texts but is known mostly from the collection of medieval Welsh manuscripts known as the *Mabinogion.*[136] Tennyson's Geraint marries the beautiful Enid, a favorite of Guinevere's who in turn "with true heart,/ Adored her, as the stateliest and the best/ And the loveliest of all women upon earth."[137] The text's first direct reference to Guinevere's affair with Lancelot comes indirectly through Geraint's observations of his wife's relationship with the Queen:

> Long in their common love rejoiced Geraint
> But when a rumour rose about the Queen,
> Touching her guilty love for Lancelot,
> Though yet there lived no proof, nor yet was heard
> The world's loud whisper breaking into storm,
> Not less Geraint believed it, and there fell
> A horror on him, lest his gentle wife,
> Through that great tenderness for Guinevere,
> Had suffered or should suffer any taint
> In nature . . .[138]

Geraint's views on the potential effects of the Queen's rumored affair on his own wife's chastity reflect the same concern, expressed in the eighteenth-century adultery trial compendiums, of the particular dangers of upper-class adulteresses corrupting through example. Furthermore, the moment the hint of adultery enters the text, the action immediately shifts to the peripheries of the legal order established by Arthur. Geraint makes the excuse that he needs to leave Camelot because his princedom is "Close on the borders of a territory,/ Wherein were bandit earls, and caitiff knights,/ Assassins, and all flyers from the hand/ Of Justice and whatever loathes a law."[139] Geraint thereby establishes himself as an iteration of Arthur, intending to impose a system of justice on another pre-legal state of nature. Upon arriving in his own lands, however, Geraint instead spends his time on romantic pleasures with Enid, who laments that he is "forgetful of his promise to the King." While she is berating herself for being the cause of his infidelity toward Arthur, Geraint overhears her say she is "no true wife," from which incorrectly he concludes that she, like Guinevere, has committed adultery.[140]

Just as the first rumors of adultery lead to the unraveling of the Arthurian legal order, however, the reinforcement of fidelity begins to restore it, at least for a time. Geraint is wounded in a fight with some of the very lawless knights he had returned to his lands to subdue. He is taken—assumed dead—to the hall of the "brute Earl" Doorm, who attempts to force Enid to eat and drink with him. After her many refusals out of loyalty to Geraint, he shouts "I compel all creatures to my will"[141] and "unknightley with his flat hand" slapped her.[142] It is only upon hearing Enid's many professions of loyalty to her fallen husband that Geraint is able to rise, take his sword, and "shore through the swarthy neck" of Earl Doorm, whose "russet-bearded head rolled on the floor."[143] The "brute" lord who rules over "creatures" rather than men has been removed as head of authority by the restoration of a monogamous marriage.

Indeed, after the pair escape Doorm's castle, they immediately reunite with Arthur, who had taken it upon himself to visit the lawless lands Geraint had mentioned and "cleanse this common sewer" of the realm. As Geraint's wounds healed physically, Arthur "rooted out the slothful officer/ Or guilty, which for bribe had winked at wrong,/ And in their chairs set up a stronger race"[144] and "cleared the dark places and let in the law,/ And broke the bandit holds and cleansed the land."[145] With the threat of adultery cleared away the legal order in this part of the kingdom can evolve out of the state of nature, away from the "darkness" that seems to recur throughout the text whenever a marriage is disrupted.

Eventually, Tennyson structures the start of the decline of Camelot around the second-most famous adulterers in Arthurian legend, Tristain and Isolde. The "Last Tournament" unfolds at the same time that Arthur rides north to confront the brutish Red Knight who had been attacking the local peasantry. The wounded peasant who had come to court to beg the king's assistance said that when the knight was slaughtering his pigs "I called upon thy name as one/ That doest right by gentle and by churl."[146] This exchange parallels an earlier scene in which Arthur, sitting as jurist, dispenses justice to his several wronged subjects. Yet unlike the successful knightly adventures that result from his earlier session of lawgiving, Arthur's defeat of the Red Knight results in his first awareness of his own decline. The Red Knight tells the king that he has founded his own northern Round Table, consisting of knights better than Arthur's: "My knights are all adulterers like his own,/ But mine are truer, seeing they profess/ To be no other."[147] This boast crystallizes the central fallacy of Arthur's regime: England's break from the Roman "mistress" under a new sovereignty was dependent upon the joining of Arthur and Guinevere. With this union compromised by adultery, "his hour is come,/ The heathen are upon him, his long lance/ Broken, and his Excalibur a straw."[148]

While Arthur faces these prognostications in the north, Sir Tristain—

whose love for Isolde betrays not only his liege lord, her husband, Mark of Cornwall, but his new wife, the French Isolde of the White hands—wins the "last tournament." Upon receiving the tournament's prize, a ruby necklace, Isolde at first scorned it, asking if it was merely "The collar of some order,/ Which our King hath newly founded."[149] As he put it around her neck, Tristain replied to the contrary: "Thine order, oh my Queen!"—an instant before King Mark materialized out of nowhere and "clove him through the brain."[150] This episode is an inversion of the earlier scene in which Geraint's removal of the lawless Earl of Doorm's head restored both his marital unity and the legal order of the surrounding territory. Here Tristain explicates the fact that Arthur's legal "order" has been supplanted by the adulterous order of Isolde's hold over him. At the moment this replacement is complete Tristain, too, loses his head, marking (in a way this episode does not in the source material), the unmaking of the Round Table and English sovereignty.

Later, when Arthur visits Guinevere at the convent during Modred's uprising, he tells her that "The children born of thee are sword and fire,/ Red ruin, and the breaking up of laws, . . ." declaring that:

> [w]hen the Roman left us, and their law
> Relaxed its hold upon us, and the ways
> Were filled with rapine, here and there a deed
> Of prowess done redressed a random wrong
> But I was first of all the kings who drew
> The knighthood-errant of this realm and all
> The realms together under me, their Head.[151]

Here Arthur links the possibility of systemic redress for legal wrongs to his singular royal body, represented through synecdoche as a Head. Guinevere herself had earlier connected the fact of her own adultery to Arthur's loss of control over his kingdom, calling Arthur "a moral child without the craft to rule/ Else had he not lost me." This language supports Petch's argument as to the significance, for nineteenth-century debates over equity courts, of the King's conscience as an arbiter of justice. Guinevere does not suggest that being a cuckold has affected Arthur's military might, but, rather, moral sophistication and "craft"—precisely the qualities necessary to function as a just law-giver. This reading, then, helps to explain why the adulterous violation of the king's marital bond functioned as a serious, rather than purely symbolic, crime against the entire legal order upon which Camelot's existence depends. The text thereby illustrates how the persistent construction of adultery as quasi-criminal in the legal discourse may relate to the threat it poses to that discourse itself.

Finally, Tennyson's selection of source material so deeply linked to the

English originary story suggests that this preoccupation with sovereignty traces a particular historical vector. Arthur's cuckolded identity was—as George IV had suggested of his own—a wrong to the people, as whose head and conscience he was supposed to serve. With the faithful marital bodies of Tennyson's own sovereign and her late spouse so vividly invoked at the start of the poem, the temporal remove to the Arthurian period necessarily implicates the various historical queens whose alleged adulteries complicated and re-constituted English sovereignty in the centuries between Guinevere and Victoria. Furthermore, the proliferation of adultery throughout the text, with non-royal couples moving in a kind of network with Guinevere and Arthur, suggests the same anxiety over contagion seen in the eighteenth-century compendiums and Fielding. *Idylls of the King* may, therefore, be considered to function as a uniquely English adultery text. Far from avoiding the subject, Tennyson narrates it as inextricably interwoven with—while destructive of—the English legal order. The poem reflects the ambiguities of an era that saw, on the one hand, Queen Victoria's royal assent to the Matrimonial Causes Act and, on the other, Effie Gray's famous social banishment by the same monarch after she annulled her unconsummated marriage to John Ruskin and remarried John Everett Millais. Even in an era of legal ferment the centuries-old conception of adultery as subverting English royal authority remained.

Legal Ambiguity and Violence in *The Ring and the Book*

Tennyson's rival Robert Browning would also take up the fraught status of adultery as a legally destabilizing transgression. In June of 1860, Browning discovered, while browsing in a second-hand market in the Piazza di San Lorenzo in Florence, an old book containing a collection of documents relating to a 1698 Roman murder trial.[152] The "Old Yellow Book," as he referred to it, contained fourteen pamphlets related to the trial of Count Guido Franchesini for the honor killing of his seventeen-year-old wife Pompilia: six summarizing points of law in his favor, five against him, and three presenting evidence such as witness affidavits. It also contained two pamphlets relating to a petition, filed after Guido's conviction, to clear Pompilia's reputation and prevent her estate from falling into the hands of the convent where she had been temporarily imprisoned. Finally, it contained two pamphlets giving popular accounts of the affair; one taking the Count's side and the other Pompilia's.

The complexity of these documents parallels the complexity of the underlying web of legal and factual circumstances surrounding the case, which require a brief summary. Because Pompilia's father Pietro held only a life estate in his property, Pompilia's mother Violante secretly adopted Pompilia from a prostitute, holding her out as her own so the estate would pass to the child after Pietro's death. Years later, she arranged a marriage between then-thirteen-year-old Pompilia and the secretly impoverished Count Guido; both parties to the bargain had expected a better financial windfall from the alliance than turned out to be the case. Guido became abusive to Pompilia's parents, who fled his decrepit castle in Arezzo and returned to Rome, where they immediately initiated a civil lawsuit seeking to divest Guido of Pompilia's inheritance based on the fact that she was not, in fact, their daughter. The courts decided to split the difference. On the one hand they held Pompilia to be a bastard and invalidated Pietro's transfer of his estate to Guido. They nonetheless allowed Guido to retain Pompilia's dowry, on the theory that he should be compensated for Violante's deception. Pompilia herself then attempted to escape from Guido, fleeing from Arezzo to Rome with the aid of a young priest, Giuseppe Carponsacchi. Guido apprehended the pair with the help of the authorities, and they stood criminal trial for adultery. The courts responded to the two parties' competing, and equally plausible, tales of ill-use at the hands of the other by again splitting the difference and imposing relatively mild punishments: temporarily banishing Carponsacchi to Civitas and imprisoning Pompilia in a convent, which she was almost immediately allowed to quit, on plea of ill health, for the home of her adoptive parents. Only after these two trials, and the revelation of Pompilia's pregnancy, did Guido commit the murder that was the basis for the trial in the Old Yellow Book; he rounded up a band of toughs and brutally stabbed Pompilia and her parents to death in their home.

In *The Ring and the Book,* Browning uses these three trials, and the various points of view presented by the conflicting documents in the book, to develop a complex rendition of the inherent epistemological problem of law. The reader experiences these events over and over again, from the perspectives of eleven different narrators, but the inaccessibility of objective truth at the center of the "ring" presents an implicit indictment of the judicial process of truth creation (as well as a depiction of the problems of subjectivity more generally).[153] Furthermore, in the first book, Browning makes a Foucauldian acknowledgment of the authority of public discourse in generating official "truth." He describes the book as "A book in shape but, really, pure crude fact"[154] and "the truth,/ The untempered gold, the fact untampered with,/ The mere ring-metal ere the ring be made!"[155] The movement from book to ring requires the action of reading and interpretation; his narrator invites his listeners (in the frame of the story) and, by proxy, Browning's readers to "[l]et this old woe step on the stage again!/ Act itself o'er anew for men to judge."[156] By the end of the book, however, we see that discursive truth and legal truth are equally slippery, that the "ring" created is, of course, circular and empty.

More particularly, Browning problematizes the specific legal disposition of adultery. The text presents a classic account of the networks of causation that so frequently link adultery and violence in the cultural imagination, yet foregrounds the official ambivalence as to its legal standing. The first narrator presents, as the legal question at the heart of Guido's trial, "if, and when/ Husbands may kill adulterous wives, yet 'scape/ The customary forfeit"[157] and notes that the task of the court would be to study "all authority/ And precedent for putting wives to death,/ Or letting wives live, sinful as they seem."[158] Browning thereby creates a slippage between the question of whether legal precedent supports Guido's execution despite his honor-based provocation defense, and whether it supports Pompilia's execution, for an act for which she had already been officially imprisoned.[159] (Guido's prosecutor, too, took his task to be "to prove Pompilia pure.")[160] This shift in the characterization of Guido's adjudication points directly to the dangers of quasi-criminality. In holding Pompilia to be guilty of something, the prior court had created a legal truth about her criminality. Yet it had not punished her as a criminal, with flogging or worse, leaving Guido to fill in the vacuum of punishment with his own lawlessness. Browning has shifted the threat of violence discursively linked to adultery from its popular eighteenth-century form—the cuckold's duel with a male seducer—to direct retribution against the sinning wife.

Browning repeatedly dwells on the fundamental legal uncertainty as to whether Pompilia and Giuseppe had been guilty of a crime or a tort. The book told from the perspective of "Half-Rome," which sides with Guido, declares of Pompilia that "[t]his morning she confessed her crime, we know."[161] That side also describes Violante's deception as "treason," casting Guido in the role of a betrayed sovereign whose symbolic relational wronging has so frequently justified the criminalization of adultery.[162] Guido speaks of the importance of marital fidelity to nationhood, suggesting that he slaughtered the trio, while "trusting God and Law," in service of the potential "Utopia" of a "Rome rife with honest women and strong men,/ Manners reformed, old habits back once more."[163] Making the classic argument in favor of criminalization, he says he believes his wife's alleged transgression needed to be punished because of the public harm it occasioned. On the other hand, Pompilia, on her deathbed, refers to herself as "the chattel that had caused a crime," suggesting that, as a piece of property, she was legally connected to criminality yet not capable of the intent necessary to participate in it herself.[164] The court describes the facts as supporting a form of civil wrong, short of criminality: "Here's plenty of fault to find, no absolute crime/ Let each side own its fault and make amends!"[165] In this view of events, the harms were purely relational, susceptible of civil recourse between the parties but not requiring

criminalization. The public opinion of this outcome reveals the explicit conflict between the tort and criminal conceptions; the citizens of Arezzo believe
the maybe-lovers to be "in limbo each and [criminally] punished for their
pains," and yet summarize the situation to "the inquiring neighborhood"
with the assurance that "[i]n Rome no wrong but has its remedy."[166] This line
rephrases the classic maxim of equity courts, *nullu recedat e curia cancellariae
sine remedio*, or "Equity will not suffer a wrong to be without a remedy."[167]
The blending of this principle of private law into a statement about criminal
punishment is yet another example of the legal schizophrenia surrounding
the idea of adultery as a criminal act.

The narrator speaking for Half-Rome, therefore, parodies the resulting
illogic of the court's ultimate decision to send Carponsacchi to Civitas, suggesting the court viewed it as "nowise an exile—that were punishment."[168]
Guido himself later points out that such a sentence was, in fact, a punishment, asking "why should law banish innocence an inch?" and concluding
"Law has pronounced there's punishment, less or more."[169] It is on the basis
of the criminal understanding of adultery, which he thereby claims was formally adjudicated but insufficiently punished, particularly in light of the new
"proof" of Pompilia's child, that he took action:

> I do kill the offending ones indeed,-
> When crime of theirs, only surmised before,
> Is patent, proved indisputably now,-
> When remedy for wrong, untried at the time,
> Which law professes shall not fail a friend,
> Is thrice tried now, thrice found worse than null . . .
> Then, when I claim and take revenge- "So rash?"
> They cry- "so little reverence for the law?"[170]

From Guido's point of view, his murders "Blackened again, made legible
once more/ Your own decree, not permanently writ."[171] From the other
side, Caponsacchi likewise holds the court's adjudication partially responsible
for Pompilia's death, condemning them for the paradox of finding "guilt
enough/ To be compatible with innocence" and therefore "punish[ing] best
a little and not too much."[172] In addition, Half-Rome critiques the court's
still-earlier adjudication of the civil claim brought by Pietro for the return
of Pompilia's dowry, which it holds to be as harmfully incoherent as the
criminal:

> Was justice ever ridiculed in Rome:
> Such be the double verdicts favoured here
> Which send away both parties to a suit

Nor puffed up nor cast down,—for each a crumb
Of right, for neither of them the whole loaf.[173]

By finding neither wholly for Pietro nor wholly for Guido, the court sets into motion a chain of lawlessness that culminates in the murders. In connecting the civil trial with the criminal the text further emphasizes how the question of adultery straddles both, as well as the extent to which the court's authority to generate consistent legal truths is hampered by the existence of competing, yet internally coherent, narratives that pull it in opposite directions and lead to violence.

Apart from the nature of adultery itself, the poem's second great legal question is the relationship between adultery and Guido's *mens rea*. His guilt turns in part on whether the "provocation" defense, recognized for cuckolded husbands as described in Chapter 1, is available to him. With this plot, Browning contributes to a nineteenth-century legal misnomer: the idea that the law had long-allowed a cuckolded husband to have his sentence reduced from murder to manslaughter on the basis of provocation. As discussed in Chapter 1, this was a defense known to the common law when the jealous spouse killed his partner's lover. However, as Krista Kesselring notes, the reports from the Old Bailey reveal almost no seventeenth- or eighteenth-century cases of husbands receiving leniency for killing their adulterous wives. She shows that husbands appeared only to use that argument successfully for about thirty years. Specifically, in a set of seventeen cases decided between 1841 to 1870 in which the adultery was proven, two men were found not guilty, ten received manslaughter verdicts, and five received murder verdicts (four of which were later reprieved).[174] By contrast, in a set of twenty-five cases from 1871 to 1900, one man was deemed not guilty, five were convicted of manslaughter, and nineteen were convicted of murder (six of them ultimately executed).[175] Despite the seeming lack of any well-established rule about this form of provocation argument, however, Kesselring gives examples of mid-nineteenth century litigants referring to a so-called "long tradition" and "unwritten law" allowing a reduction in charge in such cases.[176] She argues that, in the Victorian era,

> as marriage became romanticized as the site of consolation and comfort and as women became idealized as the chaste guardians of virtue, the provocative quality of adultery inhered more in the wife's unfaithfulness than in the other man's "invasion" of a husband's rights, as it had been in the eighteenth century and earlier.[177]

If Kesselring correctly identifies a false nineteenth-century myth about a long-standing provocation defense premised on adultery, Browning participates in it with *The Ring and the Book*. 'Half-Rome' asks of his listener, as they crowd into church to view the bodies, "[w]as it enough to make a wise man mad?/ Oh, but I'll have your verdict at the end!"[178] Guido himself characterizes this question, which he has apparently been repeatedly asked, as "Pricked you to punish now if not before?—Did not the harshness double itself, the hate/ Harden?"[179] The concept of hate "hardening" relates to the formation of intent through premeditation. Unlike the purely honor-based justification for killing unfaithful spouses, the heat-of-passion defense requires that the defendant's will be temporarily overborne by the shock of his discovery. The passage of time necessarily nullifies this defense. Guido, however, attempts to obscure the question of his *mens rea* with the question of Pompilia's criminality. Again, this move turns on the inadequacy of the court's initial adultery judgment. Guido claims he "called in the law to act and help,"[180] which at the time resulted in accusations that he was a "coward" who "shrank from gallant readiness and risk"[181] and that his current situation amounts to being "convicted of having been afraid."[182] Having already started with the proposition that the law has determined his wife to be a criminal, he argues that his will was not overborne at the moment of actual discovery due to his respect for the law:

> comprehend
> How one brought up at the very feet of law
> As I, awaits the grave Gamaliel's nod
> Ere he clench fist at outrage—much less stab![183]

This logic is, of course, backwards insofar as it treats Pompilia's murder not as an act that might have been mitigated by his failure to form will, but as an entitlement invested at the moment of his discovery and deferred. As a legal defense, Guido's speech is a failure, but his resort to it is yet another example of the cultural image of adultery as implicating and undermining sovereignty.

At both the start and end of the text, Browning makes clear that one piece of the discursive ring he creates is the relationship between the Roman story he narrates and the contemporary England from which he writes. The narrator in the introduction speaks of beginning the process of truth generation in the nation where the events took place: "[w]ell, British Public," he declares, "[f]ar from beginning with you London folk, I took my book to Rome first, tried truth's power/ On likely people."[184] After asking the Italians where he might find the actual court records chronicling the trial, their supposed response was "Records, quotha?/ Why, the French burned them," referring to the 1796 invasion by the French republic and the Napoleonic invasion of 1808.[185] This allusion links the longstanding vulnerability of the Papal States and the absence of unified Italian nationhood directly to the textual and theoretical instability of the legal conclusions dramatized by the poem. At the end of the text, however, he reminds us of the specific domestic relevance of the unstable Rome he depicts, as his final narrator describes the work as "Thy rare gold ring of verse (the poet praised)/ Linking our England to his Italy."[186]

The text can, therefore, be understood as part of the same tradition as Norton and Brontë, critical of the quasi-criminalization of adultery. Pompilia's criminal adjudication—even in the absence of significant punishment—caused her eventual murder.[187] Furthermore, Browning makes it clear that this quasi-criminal standing is the product of both formal legal and informal social discourses. By ending the text on the relationship between Italy and the United Kingdom, he invites the reader to consider the implications of this problem in their own contemporary context. Here, the challenge to sovereignty comes not from adultery itself but from the instability of its legal identity and the abuses that can result. Also, like Norton and Brontë, Browning critiques the failed history Tennyson glorifies and suggests that the law must learn from, rather than re-embed, the criminal traumas of the past.

Notes

1. Emlyn, *State Trials*, pp. xxxiii–xxxiv.
2. Radzinowicz, *History of English Criminal Law*, p. 196.
3. Debate Respecting Divorce Bills, cols. 1552–62. His speech was met with a "general cry of hear, hear!"
4. Chase & Levenson, *The Spectacle of Intimacy*, p. 38.
5. Ward, *Sex, Crime and Literature*, p. 30.
6. Norton, *A Letter to the Queen*, pp. 9–10.
7. Ward, *Sex, Crime and Literature*, p. 31.
8. Hager, "Chipping Away at Coverture," p. 1.
9. Ibid. p. 1.
10. Ibid. p. 1.
11. Ibid. p. 1.
12. Norton, *A Letter to the Queen*, p. 13.
13. Ibid. p. 28.
14. Ibid. p. 28.
15. Ibid. p. 41.
16. Ibid. p. 14.
17. Ibid. p. 48.
18. Ibid. pp. 48–9.
19. Ibid. p. 50.
20. Ibid. p. 50.
21. Ibid. p. 54.
22. Foucault, *Government of Self and Others*, p. 105.
23. Ibid.

24. Ibid. p. 135.

25. Alexander, *Toward a Theory of Cultural Trauma*, p. 11.

26. Ibid.

27. 20 & 21. Vict. c. 85. Though subsequently amended in the 1930s, in its original form the Act allowed a husband to sue for divorce on the grounds of simple adultery, while requiring that a wife show adultery in combination with incest, bigamy, cruelty or else rape or sodomy.

28. Hager, "Chipping Away at Coverture," p. 2.

29. Ibid. p. 1 n4.

30. *Hansard's Parliamentary Debates*, vol. 146, col. 204.

31. Hager, "Chipping Away at Coverture," p. 3.

32. Leckie, *Culture and Adultery*, p. 68.

33. Ibid. p. 68.

34. Cited in ibid. p. 53.

35. Rippon, *Judgment and Justification*, p. xviii.

36. Ibid. p. xi.

37. Ibid. p. xiii.

38. Tanner, *Adultery in the Novel*, p. 4.

39. Ibid. p. 369.

40. Ibid. p. 371.

41. Ibid. p. 376.

42. Ibid. p. 376. Foucault says "Transgression contains nothing negative but affirms limited being—affirms the limitlessness into which it leaps as it opens this zone to existence for the first time." *Language*, p. 35.

43. See for example Armstrong, *Novel of Adultery*, in which she points to the greater freedoms enjoyed by English women as an explanation for the absence, and Moretti, *Way of the World*, stating "Every great narrative tradition has dealt with the theme of adultery . . . In England nothing—absolutely nothing" Ibid. p. 188.

44. Stephen, "Madame Bovary," p. 40

45. Buchanan, "Immorality in Authorship," p. 25.

46. Nancy Johnson has argued that "[t]he 'new philosophy,' which is associated with revolutionary France in these narratives, thrives on families weakened by wayward individuals who are enticed by thoughts of self-determination and advancement." Johnson, "The 'French Threat'," pp. 181–3.

47. British royalist Edmund Burke had famously captured the horrors of the overthrow of French monarchy with reference to the particular, physical violation of Marie Antoinette, who had been falsely accused—among many other crimes—of adultery. Burke, *Revolution in France*, p. 71.

48. Leckie, *Culture and Adultery*, p. 14.

49. Norton, "Letter to Lady Dacre," p. 3.

50. Wallace, *Female Gothic Histories*, p. 4.

51. Ibid. p. 5.

52. Temple, "Imagining Justice," pp. 69, 71.

53. Ibid. p. 71.

54. In a very influential reading of the novel in their book *The Madwoman in the Attic*, Sandra Gilbert and Susan Gubar argue that Bertha Mason functions as an "avatar" of Jane, with the two characters linked by the dual imprisonments and repressions they have suffered as women living in their time period. Gilbert & Gubar, *Madwoman in the Attic*, p. 359. Julia Miele Rodas has offered the qualification—with which I agree and implicitly build on in this section—that "the madwoman is manifest in outlets other than the heroine, and most significantly, perhaps, in the person of her husband, Edward Fairfax Rochester." Rodas, "Brontë's *Jane Eyre*," p. 149.

55. In its standard incarnation the gothic repression is often a physical manifestation of a form of psychological imprisonment or entombment. Eve Sedgwick has observed that in gothic fiction the self is "massively blocked off from something to which it ought normally to have access," Sedgwick, *Coherence of Gothic Conventions*, p. 12, and critics have used this notion to account for the pervasive anxieties over burial and imprisonment that permeate the gothic genre. In her survey of the gothic tradition in fiction, Elizabeth MacAndrew points out the commonly recurring "structure that makes a closed-off region within an outer world" in relation to which the reader is carefully positioned. MacAndrew, *Gothic Tradition in Fiction*, p. 110. With respect to *Jane Eyre* specifically, Laurence Talairach-Vielmas contends that the Gothic figure of the ghost allows Jane to escape Rochester's grasp and, in so doing, male authority. Talairach-Vielmas, "Portrait of a Governess," p. 127.

56. Brontë, *Letters*, vol. 1, pp. 379–80.

57. Brontë, *Jane Eyre*, p. 182.

58. Ibid. p. 212.

59. Ibid. p. 203.

60. Rea, "Brontë's *Jane Eyre*," p. 77,

61. Brontë, *Jane Eyre*, pp. 182–3.

62. Ibid. p. 405.

63. Ibid. p. 447.

64. Ibid. p. 443.

65. Ibid. p. 452.

66. Ibid. p. 444.

67.

> Property in possession is divided into two sorts, an absolute and qualified property . . . [P]roperty in possession absolute . . . is where a man has, solely and exclusively, the right, and also the occupation, of any moveable chattels.

... [A]nimals ... that are not of a tame and domestic nature, are either not
the objects of property at all, or else fall under our other division, namely,
that of qualified, limited, or special property.

Blackstone, *Commentaries*, vol. 2, p. 389.

68. Norton, *A Letter to the Queen*, p. 8.
69. Brontë, *Jane Eyre*, p. 145.
70. Ibid. p. 145.
71. Ibid. p. 154.
72. Ibid. p. 155.
73. Ibid. p. 156–7.
74. Ibid. p. 157.
75. Ibid. p. 157.
76. Norton, *A Letter to the Queen*, p. 27.
77. Brontë, *Jane Eyre*, p. 245.
78. Ibid. p. 245.
79. Ibid. p. 245.
80. Ibid. p. 245.
81. Ibid. pp. 245–6.
82. Ibid. p. 287.
83. Bertha's character has been much-studied as a symbol of Victorian suppression
    and silencing of feminine sexuality. As Ian Ward, who has written on the
    relevance to the text of nineteenth-century lunacy laws, puts it,

    [a]ll the prejudices are written in: that madness in a woman is peculiarly
    bestial, and threatening and downright odd; that it is rooted in a moral or
    sexual deficiency; that the desire to domesticate its constraints was powerful,
    and preferred by many contemporaries; that the necessary form of constraint
    would be mental rather than physical, the gaze directed towards internal as
    much as external strategies of surveillance; that such a strategy might well
    lead to catastrophic results; and that lunacy can creep up, or indeed arrive
    abruptly, and destroy any family, no matter how watchful it might be

    Ward, *Law and the Brontës*, p. 89. Furthermore, the publication of Jean Rhys's
    novel *Wide Sargasso Sea* (1966) and Giyatri Spivak's post-colonial criticism
    have shed light on Brontë's latent imperialist narrative. Due to its focus on the
    operation of divorce and adultery laws on Jane as a narrating protagonist, this
    chapter gives regrettably short shrift to Bertha and her own legal context. But
    the neglect also reflects the depth and breadth of existing scholarship on the
    topic.
84. Brontë, *Jane Eyre*, p. 323.
85. Ibid. p. 324.

86. Ibid. pp. 326–7.
87. Ibid. p. 345.
88. Ibid. p. 345.
89. Ibid. pp. 345–6.
90. Ibid. p. 354.
91. Rochester implies that, in addition to being insane, Bertha committed adultery prior to their departure from the West Indies: "Bertha Mason,—the true daughter of an infamous mother—dragged me through all the hideous and degrading agonies which must attend a man bound to a wife at once intemperate and unchaste" Ibid. p. 345. Under the Matrimonial Causes Act he could have sued for divorce on that ground alone; even in 1847.
92. Ibid. p. 43.
93. Ibid. p. 43.
94. In Arnold's view,

> Miss Brontë has written a hideous, undelightful, convulsed, constricted novel . . . one of the most utterly disagreeable books I've ever read . . . [because] the writer's mind contains nothing but hunger, rebellion, and rage and therefore that is all she can, in fact, put in her book.

Arnold, "Letter to Arthur Hugh Clough," p. 258.
95. Ibid. p. 300.
96. Ibid. p. 290.
97. Norton, *A Letter to the Queen*, p. 4.
98. Brontë, *Jane Eyre*, p. 139.
99. Ibid. p. 294.
100. Marilyn Nickelsberg offers a more precise Biblical reading of the adulterous relationship, premised on Jane's blasphemous allusions to Rochester, of who she had "made an idol," and her ultimate decision to sever relations with him by leaving Thornfield after the aborted wedding. Nickelsberg contends, despite the text's outraged reception by the devout, that these two episodes were direct allusions, respectively, to II Corinthians 6: 14–18 and Matthew 5: 29–30. Nickelsberg, "Rending the Veil of Sin," p. 292.
101. Brontë, *Jane Eyre*, p. 293.
102. Ibid. p. 122.
103. Ibid. p. 293.
104. Ibid. p. 294.
105. Ibid. p. 294.
106. Ibid. p. 294.
107. Ibid. p. 307.
108. Ibid. p. 301.
109. Ibid. pp. 301–2.

110. Ibid. p. 303.
111. Grosrichard, *The Sultan's Court*, p. 3.
112. Ibid. pp. 77–90.
113. Norton, *A Letter to the Queen*, pp. 5–6.
114. Ibid. pp. 7–8.
115. This legal reading of the text contextualizes Nancy Armstrong's claim that *Jane Eyre* participated in the effort of the Victorian novel—sustained across a range of innovations to the genre and historical developments—to "sustain the Lockean fantasy" by killing off the characters "outside the gender binary," such as Helen Burns, Bertha Mason, and St. John Rivers. Armstrong contends that in the text "gender . . . renders those imagined as beyond its disciplinary reach and thus ineligible for the rights and protections of a liberal society." Armstrong, "Gender Must Be Defended," p. 546. While this claim, in my view, proves too much, Brontë's feminist use of the discourse of adultery does tend to normalize the Lockean legal order as Armstrong suggests.
116. 36 & 37 Vict. c. 66.
117. Petch, "Law, Equity, and Conscience," p. 124.
118. Ibid. p. 131.
119. Chute, "Equity Under the Judicature Act," p. 3.
120. Petch, "Law, Equity, and Conscience," p. 133.
121. The genealogy of literary British kingship Tennyson compresses into the text is not exclusively Arthurian; Jane Wright has noted his allusion to Henry V's speech to the Governor of Harfleur in Shakespeare's text. Wright, "An Unnoticed Allusion," p. 109.
122. Heisler, "English Destiny of Tennyson's Camelot," p. 152.
123. J. M. Gray and Gerry Turcotte have both explored the considerable influence of Monmouth's *History of the Kings of England* and *British History* on Tennyson's epic.
124. Pollock & Maitland, *English Law Before the Time of Edward I*, vol. 2, p. 382.
125. For example Jeffrey Jackson has explored Tennyson's use of the eventually discarded sword Excalibur as a metaphor for the violence and materiality the poet would like to see excluded from the project of contemporary British empire-building. Excalibur, Jackson concludes, "furnishes us with an additional means of appreciating how necessary it is that the old order 'changeth, / Yielding place to new'." Jackson, "The Once and Future Sword," p. 225.
126. Swinburne, "A. C. Swinburne on the Idylls," p. 319.
127. Tennyson, "Idylls of the King," pp. 8–10.
128. Ibid. pp. 12–14.
129. Ibid. pp. 84–93.
130. Ibid. pp. 471–4.

131. Swabey, *The Act to Amend the Law Relating to Divorce and Matrimonial Causes*, p. xxii.

132. Ibid. p. 17.

133. Tennyson, "Idylls of the King," pp. 499–501.

134. In his study of Victorian concerns about idolatry Dominic Janes traces the origins of the idea of Rome as a female prostitute. Janes, *Victorian Reformation*, p. 22.

135. Paul Zietlow argues that in telling the story of this marriage Tennyson "explores the psychology of a human relationship in ways that contribute to a general movement in *Idylls of the King* running counter to the idealistic desire for moral certainty and spiritual transcendence, a progression of increasing complexity and darkness." Zietlow, "The Case of Geraint and Enid," p. 734.

136. For a summary of the Geraint legend in the *Mabinogion* see Thomson, "Owain: Chwedl Iarlles y Ffynnon," p. 159.

137. Tennyson, "Idylls of the King," pp. 19–21.

138. Ibid. pp. 23–33.

139. Ibid. pp. 34–37.

140. Ibid. p. 108.

141. Ibid. p. 628.

142. Ibid. p. 717.

143. Ibid. p. 728.

144. Ibid. p. 939.

145. Ibid. p. 943.

146. Ibid. pp. 73–4.

147. Ibid. pp. 84–5.

148. Ibid. pp. 87–8.

149. Ibid. pp. 735–6.

150. Ibid. pp. 744–8.

151. Ibid. pp. 453–9.

152. Altick, "Introduction," p. 12.

153. Laura Sturve has made a convincing argument that Browning used such fragmented narratives in *The Ring and the Book* to critique the "narrative procedures" of the nineteenth-century adversarial criminal justice system. Sturve, "Browning's Attack on the Law," p. 424.

154. Browning, *The Ring and the Book*, 1.86.

155. Ibid. 1.364–6.

156. Ibid. 1.824–5.

157. Ibid. 1.130–1.

158. Ibid. 1.218–19.

159. Adultery was one of the "nineteenth-century four"—the four motives an accused could argue should reduce his murder sentence to manslaughter under

the provocation defense. Gruber, "A Provocative Defense," p. 280.

160. Browning, *The Ring and the Book*, 1.1218–19.

161. Ibid. 2.164.

162. Ibid. 2.641.

163. Ibid. 5.2038–40.

164. Ibid. 7.520. Legal scholars such as Alafair Burke have frequently noted that provocation law reflected norms about women as male property. Burke, "Equality, Objectivity, and Neutrality," p. 1062.

165. Browning, *The Ring and the Book*, 2.1171–2.

166. Ibid. 2.1210–12.

167. Simon Petch has argued that *The Ring and the Book*, like *Idylls of the King*, reflects Victorian anxieties over the disappearance of courts of equity. For Petch the Pope's justifications for under-punishing Pompilia's decision to flee her husband's home with another man may have contravened the "'standing ordinance' of God to obey her parents and her husband," but "fulfilled the natural law, the obligation of a mother to protect her child, which is also the law of God." Petch, "Equity and Natural Law," p. 108. Petch concludes that much of the moral instability of the poem comes from the fact that "the language of equity, which the Pope uses with such confidence, would undergo institutionally determined changes in meaning that rendered it as unstable as the poem's several appeals to natural law." Ibid. p. 110.

168. Browning, *The Ring and the Book*, 2.1183.

169. Ibid. 5.1285–92.

170. Ibid. 5.1077–86.

171. Ibid. 5.1998–9.

172. Ibid. 6.1736–8.

173. Ibid. 2.747–52.

174. Kesselring, "No Greater Provocation," p. 219.

175. Ibid. p. 219.

176. Ibid. p. 220.

177. Ibid. p. 223.

178. Browning, *The Ring and the Book*, 2.1263.

179. Ibid. 5.650–2.

180. Ibid. 5.1088.

181. Ibid. 5.1090.

182. Ibid. 5.1095.

183. Ibid. 5.1105–8.

184. Ibid. 1.422–4.

185. Ibid. 1.431–2.

186. Ibid. 12.869–70.

187. Scholars of the poem generally agree that, regardless of the truth about her rela-

tionship with Carponsacchi, Pompilia functions as what Adam Potkay calls an "authoritatively privileged figure of purity and sanctity." Potkay, "The Problem of Identity," p. 143. Thus, one moral certainty that emerges from the morass of subjectivities presented by the text is that her murder was a crime and a sin.

Part II

Child Criminality as *Mens Rea*

3

The "Faerie Court" of Child Punishment

Foucault identifies as "the birth of the prison" the 1840 opening of Mettray, the French prison farm for juvenile offenders.[1] In its effort to regularize child punishment, Foucault notes, Mettray collapsed the discourses of moral, man-made, and scientific law into a materialist, hybrid "science" of punishment based in large part upon perpetual surveillance: "the entire parapenal institution . . . culminates in a cell, on the walls of which are written in black letters: 'God sees you.'" The camp "was related to other forms of supervision, on which it was based: medicine, general education, religious direction."[2] Foucault concludes that this "birth" eventually led to a "great carceral continuum that diffused penitentiary techniques into the most innocent disciplines, transmitting disciplinary norms into the very heart of the penal system and placing over . . . the smallest irregularity, deviation or anomaly, the threat of delinquency."[3] Mettray certainly played a significant discursive role for nineteenth-century British reformists who, newly preoccupied with the problem of urban crime—and in particular child criminals—looked to it as an example of a successful juvenile reformatory.[4] Reformists in this historical moment focused on child criminality as simultaneously distinct from and emblematic of adult criminality, with mixed results for the child criminal himself. Yet in blurring the science, pedagogy, and religion of child punishment into one conceptual "continuum," Foucault misses the fact that this penological development was the product of two distinct public discourses with corresponding legal ramifications.

On the one hand, as Foucault indicates, the forces of social reform—ostensibly concerned with protecting children—eventually proceduralized juvenile punishment en masse, fueled by a cultural fetish around the figure of the child criminal as an object for rehabilitation. Yet at the same time, the nineteenth century also produced what I will call the "evolutionary" moment in the representation of child development. The Victorian era is famous for creating the idea of childhood as sacred and distinct from adulthood. In this rendition, paradoxically—and specifically because they are closer to divinity and therefore pre-fallen—children lack the knowledge of good and evil, making them less capable of acting according to fixed moral principles. Because the basic requirement for criminal liability is that a malfeasor knows the difference between right and wrong and still choose to do wrong, the new Romantic idea of childhood implicitly troubles the basic possibility of child criminality as a logical proposition. Accompanying this view one can discern an anxiety over the child's maturation in the wrong direction, a concern which (as I will describe in greater detail in the section on Charles Kingsley, below) reflects a broader post-Darwinian fascination with imagined processes of human evolution and devolution. As a legal matter, the Crown frequently resolved this tension in individual cases through the royal pardon: the narrative of punishment took place through the formal adjudication of guilt and sentencing, with the consequences removed (or at least mitigated) by the Crown acting as *deus ex machina* in granting mercy.

This chapter will take up a very specific source of imagery of the punishable child in which the structure of the pardon resolves the chronic trauma inherent in the conflict between the two legal views of childhood I have identified: the increasingly popular genre of fairy tale. I will argue that the fairy tale's temporal and material malleability enables it, first, to place children in an idealized, Edenic world prior to the knowledge of good and evil that allows them to form *mens rea;* second, to rehabilitate them through punishment fantasy; and third, to spare them from the consequences of earlier misconduct through a form of royal pardon. This narrative translates into the popular imagination the very impulse toward pardoning that the legal treatise writers of the eighteenth century had begun to propose as the proper common law outcome for juvenile transgressions—yet within the heavily procedural discourse of the nineteenth-century reformers. At the same time, however, the make-believe framing of the fairy tale format allows children's authors to make very real criticisms of the potential violent injustice imposed by earthly legal systems recently created to manage these processes.

This chapter will first trace the judicial development of the idea of child criminality to demonstrate how one eighteenth-century murder, *Yorke's Case* (1748), became a traumatic image of juvenile crime in the English legal imagination, and how this contradictory image of the child criminal continued to appear in nineteenth-century debates about juvenile justice reform. I will examine the political discourse of the juvenile justice crusaders to demonstrate that, contrary to the traditional narrative in which Victorian reforms constituted a sea change in thinking about child criminality, reformers in that era animated a previously-repressed common law trauma legible in the eighteenth century. The legal artifacts of both centuries reflect the ongoing cultural anxiety surrounding the English law's capacity to make the choice between potentially illegitimate state violence exercised against the morally incompetent child or the unknowable degree of potential violence exercised by the morally incompetent child against society. With these debates in mind, I will turn to the subsequent renditions of juvenile moral development and culpability in the work of two of the best-known nineteenth-century fairy tale writers, George MacDonald and Charles Kingsley. Both iconoclastic clerics who used the magical genre to negotiate complicated syntheses of biblical typology and nineteenth-century science, they presented child readers with very different depictions of the relationship between their pre-fallen natures and the problems of earthly punishment. MacDonald's child protagonists demonstrate the spiritual importance of discipline in refining and protecting the pre-lapsarian moral qualities unique to children. Kingsley, on the other hand, uses the case of child criminality and punishment to both critique and rehabilitate the English common law system generally. Both bodies of work reveal a discursive tension between the attractive and morally narratable drive toward child punishment and fear over the potentially illegitimate earthly procedures for inflicting it. These works reify a central paradox in juvenile jurisprudence, which they resolve by implying the singular importance of the royal pardon. The chapter will conclude with an examination of the relationship between law and fairy tale in Dickens's *Great Expectations* and *David Copperfield*, to demonstrate the cultural importance of child punishment as a mode of imagining adult criminality and its systemic responses.

The Parish Children and the Devil

Before the eighteenth century, the statutory law made very few distinctions between youthful and adult defendants, and those it made were somewhat arbitrary. As of 1581, children younger than six could not be punished for failing to wear woolen caps on Sundays and holidays, nor males younger than seven for failure to own the mandatory longbow with two shafts (for serving in the militia).[5] A statute dating from the time of Henry VIII stipulated leniency for servants and apprentices under the age of eighteen who stole from their masters.[6] Apart from cases involving specific statutory provisions such as these, age had little to do with the disposition of criminal trials in the sixteenth and early seventeenth centuries. Virtually no surviving records from any of the thirty-one assize judges riding circuit during that period make mention of the age of a defendant, and rarely in a way that suggests that it was a factor in mitigation of a sentence.[7]

Despite the absence of historical record, several of the great reformation-minded legal treatise writers of the Restoration Era attempted to articulate a "tradition" of age-related mitigation in criminal punishment. Due to his commitment to the idea of culturally-driven change in the common law, it is no surprise that Matthew Hale was one of the first legal thinkers to "find" precedent in the traditions of the common law for age-based mitigation in criminal punishment. He starts from the basic principle that *mens rea*—or "bad intent"—is a prerequisite for criminal guilt under the common law. As Hale puts it:

> Man is naturally endowed with these two great faculties, understanding and liberty of will, and therefore is a subject properly capable of a law properly so called . . . The consent of the will is that, which renders human actions either commendable or culpable; as where there is no law, there is no transgression, so regularly where there is no will to commit an offence, there can be no transgression, or just reason to incur the penalty or sanction of that law instituted for the punishment of crimes.[8]

Within this framework, he claims infancy as a factor weighing against the existence of *mens rea* in defining whether a crime has been committed at all. Tellingly, in light of so little actual precedent, he resorts to pre-common law jurisprudence to make this case, noting that in the reign of the First Century Anglo-Saxon King Athelstan, the minimum age at which a minor could be executed for a capital offense was twelve.[9] More recently, Hale states, "men grew to greater learning, judgment and experience, and rectified the mistakes of former ages and judgments," and the law of juvenile *mens rea* had changed by the eighteenth century.[10] It is also worth noting that, while other writers such as Michael Dalton (1564–1644)[11] and Coke had stipulated the "knowledge" of the difference between good and evil as a touchstone for criminality, Hale took up the more rigorous requirement of "understanding" the same.[12]

In Hale's summation, due to this teleological progression in the legal meaning of "understanding," it is "clear" that youths between ages fourteen and twenty-one are equally subject to capital punishment because they can "discern between good and evil" and "if the law should not animadvert upon such offenders by reason of their nonage, the kingdom would come to confusion."[13] Hale's expansion on this claim reflects a general anxiety about the juvenile capacity for evil:

> Experience makes us know that every day murders, bloodsheds, burglaries, larcenies, burning of houses, rapes, clipping and counterfeiting of money, are committed by youths above fourteen and under twenty-one; and if they should have impunity by the privilege of such their minority *no man's life or estate could be safe.*[14]

The idea that no one could be safe in the absence of juvenile punishment evinces the belief that not only do juveniles between these ages commit violent crimes, but they commit them in such quantities as to render the polity unstable and every person's life in jeopardy. (Hale's nineteenth-century editors, Stokes and Ingersoll, writing from the context of their own era's various innovations in prison technology, point out that Hale misses the idea that "there is no necessity that if they be not capitally punished they must therefore go unpunished . . . in the common instances of larceny and stealing, some other punishment might be found, which might leave room for the reformation of young offenders.")[15]

According to Hale, however, between the ages of twelve and fourteen, a minor is not, under the common law, to be presumed prima facie capable of forming the adequate intent necessary to be found criminal.[16] In cases where no presumption of capacity exists, the judge may decide on a case by case basis and thus children between these years may escape capital punishment. In other words, as Hale puts it,

> [b]y the law as it now stands, and has stood at least since the time of *Edward* the Third, the capacity of doing ill, or contracting guilt, is not so much measured by years and days, as by the strength of the delinquent's understanding and judgment.[17]

Hale makes a deft rhetorical move here: by emphasizing the general *mens rea* requirement ("understanding") of a very specific, distant moment in time, he establishes the historical precedent for the idea that children must be treated differently by the law due to the lack thereof. Hale further contends that even in cases below age twelve—where child defendants enjoy a presumption of incapacity—they can nonetheless be executed if the court determines enough evidence of "understanding and judgment" exists to rebut that presumption. Again, the test depends on whether the youth can "discern between good and evil at the time of the offence committed."[18] In such cases, Hale notes, the judge can reprieve him for a time after the judgment in order to allow the crown to offer a pardon.[19]

Hale's truth claims—though based on a partially fictitious history of judicial deference to youth—took little time to become fully incorporated into the law's actual treatment of juvenile offenders. Subsequent treatise writers cite Hale himself for the proposition that children are treated differently; notable texts following Hale include William Hawkin's *Summary of the Crown-Law* (1728); Thomas Wood's *Institute of the Laws of England* (1738), and, most significantly, Blackstone's *Commentaries* (1765–1769). Court records indicate that, by the late eighteenth century, judges were increasingly taking a defendant's age into account in determining liability and punishment.[20] It seems that changing cultural attitudes about the capacity of children to form criminal intent may have prompted individual treatise writers and judges to effect a collective change in the law while nonetheless espousing a coherent account of historical continuity.[21]

One of the cases relying upon the new understanding of child intent claimed by the treatise writers becomes, itself, a particularly significant part of that history. From Blackstone's *Commentaries* up through nineteenth-century case law and treatises (including Stokes' and Ingersoll's 1847 notes on Hale's *History* itself), jurisprudential discussion of child criminality dwells on the 1748 *Yorke's Case,* in which ten-year-old William York is found guilty of murdering a five-year-old girl. The court report of this case highlights a number of features that remained legible in cultural anxieties over child criminality into the nineteenth century. Both the defendant and the victim are "parish children," whose guardians leave them in their shared bed before going out into the fields to work. Upon their return, the girl is missing and, eventually, the husband finds a shallow grave containing the child's body "cut and mangled in a most barbarous manner."[22] Upon interrogation, the boy explains that the little girl had the habit of wetting the bed and that she had done so that morning. He says he then took her out of the bed, carried her to the dung heap, and, using a large knife he had found in the house, stabbed her to death. Afterwards he buried her in the dung heap, placing the bloody dung and straw under the body and covering it all with clean straw, then washed himself with water as cleanly as he could.[23]

It is significant that the archetypical common law precedent cited in the late-eighteenth and early-nineteenth centuries to typify child criminality as a separate legal status begins, like so many literary representations of the same phenomenon, as an orphan story. Both children are wards of the state, and the murder takes place beyond the supervision of adults. It is a crime that occurs in a closed, child-specific world, where the story begins with accusations of the childish transgression of bed-wetting. As Perry Nodelman notes, adult authors depict children in children's literature as "the *unheimlich* in the home" who "don't appreciate the safety of the safe places that more responsible beings have created for them."[24] The power this case would come to hold as a classic representation of the otherly criminality theorized by Hale can be explained by Nodelman's observation of children's literature in general: "texts written specifically for children in order to create safe literary experiences for them almost inevitably focus on the *unheimlich*—on ways in which children lack safe homes or . . . have the safety of their homes disrupted."[25] Nodelman's theory suggests the psychoanalytic mechanism for the importance of *Yorke's Case* in common law memory: the child becomes a distinct cultural preoccupation when deprived of parentage and located in a somehow grotesque domestic space. There is no suggestion that York's field-laboring guardians provided him and his sister with a domestic space any less safe than typical for children of that social class, yet the fact of their solitude underscores the quality of childhood vulnerability Nodelman identifies as uniquely culturally compelling.

Indeed, the case report notes that when William York repeats his confession shortly before his trial, the boy adds that "the devil put him upon committing the fact."[26] The task for the justices presiding over York's trial is to determine whether he has adequate understanding to distinguish between good and evil; York's "devil" defense highlights the extent to which a child's moral ambiguity can take fantastical, embodied forms, like the supernatural creatures that test children left to their own devices in fairy tales. In the case of York himself, the Chief Justice concludes that there are tokens of "mischievous discretion"—essentially premeditation, as evidenced by the boy's efforts to hide the body—such that he is a proper subject for capital punishment. The court reasons that "it would be of very dangerous consequence to have it thought that children may commit such atrocious crimes with impunity" and contemplates the specific risks of children murdering younger children or "poisoning parents or masters, burning houses, &c, which children are very capable of committing."[27] Note the slippage in the court's logic at this moment: from concern over the question of the child's actual possession of post-lapsarian knowledge, it moves into a more utilitarian calculus: the "dangerous consequence" of children running amok if the system fails to deter by example and the fear that everyone would, therefore, be at risk. The internal logic of this opinion contains the basic contradiction with which this chapter opened: children may not be criminal, but their formal criminalization serves a culturally important purpose. This contradiction functions as a chronic crisis across the common law imagination of the eighteenth and nineteenth centuries: both the possibility of child killers like William York and the state's violent response to that possibility contribute to the crisis, as they have to the cycle between crime waves and over-incarceration in our own day. Eventually, the court finds York guilty but—exactly as urged by Hale years before—pardons him on condition of "entering immediately into the sea service."[28] The narrative of his evil-doing unfolds as an official matter, with a conviction, but the Crown intervenes to avoid the traumatic question of punishment itself.

In her comprehensive work on the evolving understanding of a child's capacity to function as a legal subject, historian Holly Brewer notes, "the eighteenth and early nineteenth centuries witnessed a struggle between intent and threat, between sparing the child and seeking to make the child an example."[29] In other words, the court report reflects a great discomfort surrounding the question of whether William York's "devil" qualifies as *mens rea* for the purposes of imposing capital punishment on him. But at the same time, the specter of a world in which children lawlessly burn barns and poison masters is too terrifying to acquit him formally. As Brewer puts it, "All children were criminals in their understanding, in that they need to be reformed and educated. On the other hand, they could not be criminally responsible."[30] *Yorke's Case* also challenges what has become a sort of conventional wisdom about juvenile punishment: that prior to the nineteenth century, children were regularly hanged for capital offenses. In his *History of Capital Punishment* John Laurence holds that

> [i]n the reign of George II it was no uncommon thing for children under the age of ten years to be hanged, and on one occasion ten of them were strung up together, as a warning to men and a spectacle for the angels.[31]

B. E. F. Knell disputes this generalization, however, noting that while occasional examples of eighteenth-century child executions exist, the fact that the court took nine full years to pass sentence on William York—and that he was eventually pardoned—suggests that such condemnations were likely infrequent.[32]

We know that the government used the pardon power frequently in the late eighteenth century to quell public outcry over the Bloody Code's soaring and apparently ineffectual levels of capital punishment for theft crimes (discussed as a cultural trauma in its own right in the Introduction to this book). William Pitt and his ministers realized they needed to apply capital punishment with, as Simon Devereaux puts it, "as much restraint as would be necessary for the hanging spectacle to communicate its message without overwhelming its audience's moral senses and thereby defeating the ritual's deterrent purposes."[33] *Yorke's Case* reveals the pardon power's particular potential to assuage common law ambivalence over the possibility of child *mens rea* as early as the eighteenth century. This effect appears empirically well-established by the nineteenth. Between the years 1801 and 1836, Old Bailey records indicate that 103 children had been sentenced to death (unsurprising given the large number of capital offenses formally on the books— most of these cases involved theft).[34] Yet not one of these cases resulted in an execution, prompting the politician E. G. Wakefield to describe a death sentence imposed on a child as a "formal lie."[35]

Child Criminality and the Victorian Reformers

The forgoing has sought to demonstrate that common law ambivalence over child *mens rea* persisted across the eighteenth and into the nineteenth centuries. If there was a clear shift in the nineteenth-century discourse around child criminality, however, it was in the idea emerging mid-century that children should potentially be subject to a wholly separate criminal process from adults. Reformers began to argue that because children were so morally different from adults—particularly in their increased capacity for rehabilitation— the end goals of the adult criminal justice system (retribution and deterrence) were insufficient. Arguing for legislation enabling state-funded reformatory schools focused, instead, on rehabilitation, Mary Carpenter, founder of the Red Lodge Reformatory in Bristol, says that her students "would most certainly be leading a life of crime, if not cared for and trained to honest industry" and asserts that "surely it is worth no little expense and labour to rescue these poor young boys from vice and misery."[36] This instinct was part of a much larger movement towards social reform, much of which is beyond the scope of this project. The same wave of reformers interested in child labor and education—on the premise, in large part, that uneducated, working children became brutalized—produced a movement to create a separate system of juvenile justice.[37] Indeed, the episode of William York is given a new spin when translated into the nineteenth-century context: the author of York's entry in the 1825 compendium of *The Newgate Calendar* notes:

> If we were not well aware of the frequent negligence of keepers of poor-houses we should say that this premeditated and deliberate murder could not have been effected. Several hours must have elapsed during the shocking transaction; where, then, was the care over the infant paupers? The overseers of the poor, in many instances, are extremely attentive to their parish dinners; but, were they to employ the time lost in this sensuality in care and attendance to the morality of the individuals placed under their control, such crimes might be voided, and the child of charity brought up in the paths of industry and virtue.[38]

Though the author attributes to York the damning legal characteristic of premeditation, he locates it in a more complex social context than evident in the eighteenth-century court report. York is no longer an individual juvenile evaluated solely according to his moral capacities. Rather, he is a "child of charity"—an emblem of a system in need of reform.

Historian Heather Shore argues that the concept of juvenile delinquency, as a discrete social problem, was "invented" in the nineteenth century in conjunction with three core legal concepts: legal process, institutions for juveniles, and conceptions of the family.[39] With respect to the first, it is worth noting that the nineteenth century also saw the creation of the first modern professionalized police force, spearheaded in London by Sir Robert Peel, and the proliferation of prisons.[40] Increasingly, incarceration became a substitute for capital punishment; Stokes's and Ingersoll's comment on Hale's draconian view of juvenile capital punishment reflects this new array of penal options. Shore argues that "juvenile delinquency" only became conceived as a social problem once named as such by various legislative initiatives.

The Juvenile Offenders Act of 1847 was the first of a series of attempts by Parliament to address this new problem, creating a separate category of criminality reserved for children, and specifying new procedures to cope with it. Additional Youthful Offenders Acts followed in 1845, 1857, 1861, and 1866. Such legislation gave judges additional sentencing options, such as imposing two-to-five-year terms in reformatories, as opposed to prison. Many of these reformers, however—like the proponents of the Matrimonial Causes Act discussed in the previous chapter—contextualized their efforts as part of an English legal tradition recognizing the distinct nature of childhood evil. Writing in 1887, magistrate Thomas Saunders echoed Matthew Hale's not-wholly-accurate account from two centuries before in an introduction to a treatise on the new laws governing child punishment:

> By the law of England, from time immemorial, the crimes of children have formed an exceptional feature in its criminal code, for it has never been lawful to inflict punishment upon them when from their immature age it is assumed they are incapable of properly distinguishing right from wrong; and although in the early stages of our history the distinction was by no means clearly marked, its principle was strictly recognized and acted upon.[41]

Yet in another treatise, not twenty years later, W. Clarke Hall declares the exact opposite: that "[o]nly by slow and painful degrees has it become recognized that the criminality of the child is a thing different, alike in kind and degree, from the criminality of the adult, and needing therefore different treatment."[42] In other words, for at least two hundred years, the common law's understanding of its treatment of child criminality was fractured. Like the Parliamentary debate over whether the Matrimonial Causes Act was a codification of ancient law or an abrupt legislative watershed, the inability of legal commentators to agree on even the historical arc of child criminality reveals the unresolved discursive trauma at the heart of this aspect of the criminal law.

In any case, Victorian rehabilitation-oriented efforts operationalized the concerns of reformers like Carpenter—or "child savers"—who believed children were more in need of care and guidance than punishment.[43] Other historians argue, however, that they created more criminal liability for children than existed before.[44] Additional legislation created new categories of crimes directed at young offenders—for example, the Vagrancy Act of 1824, which criminalized the status of being a "suspected Person or reputed Thief," including such youthful behaviors, common to urban environments, as gambling on the street. Similarly, the Malicious Trespass Act of 1827 made it illegal to enter a garden and steal fruit. As Susan Margery puts it, these acts had the effect of transforming the behavior of youths "from nuisances into criminal behavior."[45] They also subjected children—simply for being children in public places—to a high degree of the behavioral surveillance identified by Foucault. Due to this "creation" of juvenile delinquency, the number of youths under age seventeen in prison skyrocketed from around 9,500 in 1838 to around 14,000 just ten years later.[46]

This punitive strain in the discourse of child reformers incorporated new Darwinian understandings of evolution, which sought to characterize poor children and criminal children as altogether a different species from the ideal child who was, at the time, becoming a figure of Romantic inspiration. As Matthew Davenport Hill, the Recorder of Birmingham, puts it in a letter to Lord Brougham: "[a] child fed, clothed, and protected by his parents" is "indeed a child—a creature of promise" whereas "[t]he latter is a little stunted man already—he knows much, and a great deal too much, of what is called life . . . He consequently has much to unlearn—he has to be turned again into a child."[47] For such reformers

[t]he main object . . . is to reclaim these wanderers, to reverse their out-lawry, to bring them back into the brotherhood of society, to train them up so that they may be, in the expressive language of our old Common Law, *true men*.[48]

While ostensibly relying on the new science of evolution, such perspectives draw upon the old Puritan thread in early-modern discourse that saw children as, as Jacqueline Banerjee puts it, "already partaking of man's 'fallen' nature" and being "closer to the devil than to God."[49] For Banerjee "[t]he Victorians' willingness to adulate children conflicted not only with their behavior towards them, but, more deeply, with their suspicions about what children represent, and their desire to destroy it."[50]

The synthesis between evolutionary development and the development of the common law of child criminality becomes a theme for the literary authors of children's fairy tales during the same period. Eric Brown has demonstrated how the explosion of fairy stories during Victoria's reign—as in that of Elizabeth I before her—can be traced to the cultural interest in the idea of a "faery queen" on England's literal throne.[51] This cultural connection automatically renders feminized English sovereignty, as exercised over children, important in this new body of literature. However, due to the possibility of the idealized law-givers of fairyland dispatching a more perfect justice than their human counterpart and her Parliament, some literary fairy tale writers effectively critique the potential injustice of excessively punitive earthly laws and the illegitimacy of their operations on children. The works of George MacDonald and Charles Kingsley typify this genre. Both authors create narratives in which the competing desires for punishment and mercy allow more perfect rehabilitation for fictional William Yorks than does the operation of the real-life common law.

George MacDonald and the Problem of Eden

In his 1867 "unspoken" sermon "The Child in the Midst," George MacDonald explains one of his favorite theological premises: "to enter this kingdom [of heaven] we must become children."[52] He interprets Christ's words to his disciples at Capernaum[53] to mean "they could not enter into the kingdom save by becoming little children—by humbling themselves"[54] and in simple terms, affirms the Romantic idea that "the *childlike* is the divine."[55] In both his theology and his fairy tales, the goal of maturing into childhood is omnipresent: Lona, the Beatrice figure in *Lilith* (1895), is "one who, grow to what perfection she might, could only become the more a child";[56] his ever-present, eternal grandmothers seem younger in appearance as they grow older; and in a letter to his brother, MacDonald describes his children as "not little by any means now, but . . . growing more and more of children-as they grow bigger."[57] Roderick McGillis distinguishes MacDonald's divine child from Wordsworth's in that "for Wordsworth childhood is bound by time; it passes. For MacDonald, the opposite is true; childhood is a state of being which everyone must aspire to."[58]

In many of MacDonald's stories, as Lisa Hermine Makman has noted of Diamond in *At the Back of the North Wind* (1871), he preserves the moral value of the "eternal child" through his death and movement to heaven.[59] Yet existing in a pre-lapsarian state renders living children particularly vulnerable to evil even if, like Adam and Eve, they cannot yet be evil (or, to return to legal terms, cannot form *mens rea*). MacDonald notes this vulnerability in "The Child in the Midst," observing

> [o]ne of the saddest and not least common sights in the world is the face of a child whose mind is so brimful of worldly wisdom that the human childishness has vanished from it, as well as the divine childlikeness.[60]

The acquisition of "wisdom" alludes to the Tree of Knowledge and the Fall, yet MacDonald's belief in the infinite perfectibility of childhood suggests that Eden may yet be recoverable. He, therefore, asks whether Christ would "turn away from the child born in sin and taught iniquity, on whose pinched face hunger and courage and love of praise have combined to stamp the cunning of avaricious age?"[61] The answer, MacDonald says, is no: Christ would instead clasp to his bosom the "evil-faced child" specifically because "he needed it most."[62] A child may, it seems, wear the "face" of evil, but that evil is not yet intrinsic—the face may be removed. MacDonald's distinguishing children for this uniquely detached relationship with sin resonates powerfully with the legal concept, suggested by the treatise-writers cited above, of a child as pre-criminal:

No amount of evil can *be* the child. No amount of evil, not to say in the face, but in the habits, or even in the heart of the child, can make it cease to be a child, can annihilate the divine idea of childhood.[63]

Precisely because of this inherent perfectibility, however, the "evil-faced" child is an appealing object for reformation and instruction. In urging that seemingly evil children should be the dearest to Christ, MacDonald again draws the comparison between the role of divine and earthly fathers in dealing with a child's misbehavior:

How the earthly father would love a child who would creep into his room with angry, troubled face, and sit down at his feet, saying . . . "I feel so naughty, papa, and I want to get good!" Would he say to his child: "How dare you! Go away, and be good, and then come to me?"[64]

While rejecting the possibility of a child possessing intrinsic evil of the sort meriting irreversible punishment, then, MacDonald states the need for some form of intervention, the nature of which would become the theme of so many of his fantasy stories. This section will consider: first, how MacDonald uses the fairy tale genre to re-imagine and idealize children as Adam and Eve; second, how he builds that identification into a framework for juvenile punishment and pardon; and third, how he simultaneously aestheticizes such punishment and challenges the earthly procedures for inflicting it.

Elsewhere I have argued that in one of his most famous stories, "The Golden Key," MacDonald uses the adventures of his child protagonists Mossy and Tangle to reconcile Biblical claims about geological time in the Book of Genesis with the emerging geological knowledge about the age of the earth produced by Victorian science.[65] If Mossy and Tangle represent the idealized child's relationship to both Eden and Salvation, in other stories MacDonald presents the problem of imperfect children and the potential for Edenic fairylands to serve punitive functions, in service of the children's moral evolution. "Cross Purposes" is structurally similar to "The Golden Key": the fairies lure the child protagonists, Alice and Richard, from their village "somewhere on the Borders of Fairyland."[66] MacDonald tells us that "No mortal, or fairy either, can tell where Fairyland begins and where it ends."[67] Unlike their counterparts in the more serious "The Golden Key," however, these children have been sought because the Queen of Fairyland has found "her own subjects far too well-behaved to be amusing."[68] The children are necessary, then, on the assumption that they will prove intractable enough to require the discipline of fairy authority. Also, unlike the divine landscape of "The Golden Key," this Fairyland is far more integrated with the earthly legal and moral order. The fairy, Peaseblossom, who volunteers to bring Alice, is "the daughter of the prime minister," suggesting that the political structure of Fairyland mirrors that of the British Commonwealth in more ways than just the existence of a "faery queen."[69] Nonetheless, Fairyland appears, at least, to trace the rough structure of the Edenic Fairyland of "The Golden Key." As Alice sets out to follow Peaseblossom, the fairy describes the magical realm as "the place out of which go the things that appear to children every night," and assures her "the farther you go, the nearer home you are."[70] This space is thus governed by the moral logic of "growing" into childhood origins with which MacDonald is so preoccupied. Forward motion through the unfamiliar terrain, which requires moral development, is actually a return to the originary well of child-ness.[71]

Unlike Tangle however, Alice begins her journey to Fairyland as a morally-flawed child whom "her friends called fairy-like, and others called silly."[72] Meanwhile, Richard is "so poor that he did not find himself generally welcome."[73] Like the "parish children" in the real-life episode of William York, the scene for the exploration of the child's moral capacity occurs here in part due to the removal, through poverty, of adult supervision. Higher powers select them to travel together but their cooperation requires surmounting Alice's superficial class snobbery. When their fairy guides—Peaseblossom and the goblin Toadstool—abandon them in a river they must figure out how to traverse on their own, Richard offers Alice his hand but "she repelled it with disdain . . . wondering how ever the poor widow's son could have found his way into Fairyland. She did not like it. It was an invasion of privilege."[74] As they grow more physically dependent upon one another, Alice follows him "not of her own will, which she gave him clearly to understand."[75] The reference to Alice's lack of will draws attention to the role of the fairy world in developing precisely that capacity, the lack of which had become such a basic factor in the nineteenth-century legal understanding of childhood. Throughout their adventures, Alice, of course, comes to soften towards Richard and eventually realize that she loves him. At the end, they achieve a lesser version of the spiritual transcendence obtained by the "Golden Key" protagonists: "they had," the narrator tells us, "grown quite man and woman in Fairyland."[76] It is important to note that while MacDonald echoes the language of child reformers like Matthew Davenport Hill—who emphasizes the role of punishment in turning bad children into "true men"—he self-consciously rejects Hill's idea that childhood naughtiness turns on class. It is Alice, the doted-on, upper-class child, who is in greater need of reformation than her poor, "unwelcome" counterpart Richard.

The process of character building requires a series of symbolic deaths: on their first night in Fairyland, the children must sink to the bottom of a river and sleep there, symbolically drowned. Later, when they become separated by a sorcerer who creates an illusion placing them on either side of a high, ramparted castle, they must step off their respective ledges to find themselves once again reunited safely on the ground. In this text, MacDonald raises the troubling possibility of penal illegitimacy. While the text itself contains a punitive logic, which suggests that flawed children must endure privations to become perfected, it also provides the example of illegitimate authority and the unique susceptibility of children to it. Unlike the benevolent Old Men and Women of "The Golden Key," the elders Alice and Richard encounter appear to take a voyeuristic pleasure in controlling and manipulating the children. When they find themselves in the sorcerer's house (after inadvertently climbing into his hearth from an underground passage) he proclaims that "such young people have no business to be out alone. It is against the rules" and claims that he "must take charge" of them.[77] The sorcerer's asserted legal authority over the children is apparently false: because they thwart him, the Queen grants them, "in reward of their courage," permission to return to Fairyland as often as they want. This reward for enduring seemingly arbitrary punishment suggests that the children, though imperfect (particularly Alice), were improperly subject to the discipline of Fairyland, despite the fact that the Queen had initially desired their presence to allow her to assert authority over more naughty subjects. Yet, at the same time, their suffering improved them. In any case, MacDonald transfers Alice and Richard's attractiveness as objects for punishment to their failed guides; Peaseblossom and Toadstool are "banished from court and compelled to live together, for seven years, in an old tree that had just one green leaf upon it. Toadstool did not mind it much, but Peaseblossom did."[78] Here, as in the real-life *York's Case*, the unilateral royal prerogative to pardon and banish intervenes to impose the actual justice that had been lost by following "the rules."

Nodelman has noted, as a unique characteristic of children's literature, a potential inversion of the expected moral order: "that it is adult desires for children, attempts either to make them less innocent or to keep them from harm, that are dangerous and innocent childhood desires that are wise."[79] He argues that "in both celebrating and denigrating childhood desire and adult knowledge, the texts reveal the centrality of their ambivalence" which emerges from the interplay of opposites such as "home and away, safety and danger, desire and knowledge, adult and child."[80] "Cross Purposes," in its very title, suggests such a binary, one that might be described as "obedience and autonomy." Most of the stories considered in this chapter could not exist were it not for the attractiveness of the child as an object of perfectibility—an end that requires a narratable process of perfecting (with real-life nineteenth-century counterparts amongst the juvenile justice advocates). Yet these tales also belie an inherent skepticism about the potential trauma of punishment.

If the child-like is the divine, how do we trust earthly systems of law, executed by corruptible (and potentially literally corrupted) adults to police it?

While MacDonald never satisfactorily resolves this tension, in "The Lost Princess" (1874) he attempts to give a more complex model for appropriate child punishment. In this longer text, he takes up the rehabilitation of unambiguously "naughty" children through the gentle discipline of yet another magical wise woman. In this story, both children are girls—the violent Princess Rosamund and the shepherd's daughter Agnes, rendered self-absorbed and petulant through over-spoiling. Here MacDonald returns yet again to Edenic landscapes and themes of evolution. But the text is explicitly preoccupied with the fraught relationship between childhood and the discernment between good and evil—the crux of the legal *mens rea* requirement so central to the question of child criminality.

Both little girls are raised to believe that they are "Somebody" by overly indulgent parents.[81] Both girls are forcibly abducted by the Wise Woman, who puts them through a sort of magical moral boot camp designed to break them down, often through terror and self-abasement, only to help them grow more spiritually (and physically) beautiful. The Wise Woman, as I will discuss in greater detail below, has three primary functions. She criticizes the earthly systems of authority that have created these problem children prematurely into formal legal subjects ("Somebodys"). Yet she also aestheticizes for the reader—through the sheer beauty of her magical interventions—the proper process of child punishment. Finally, through displays of mercy and tenderness, she emphasizes the helplessness of children when faced with choices between good and evil, driving home the notion that evil does not need to be ingrained yet to be dangerous and that it may be simultaneously punished and pardoned.

With respect to the actual project of punishing children, MacDonald emphasizes that it should induce terror—an effect he dramatizes through the classic fairy tale trope of the dangerous woods. The Wise Woman forcibly carries off Rosamund—"struggling and screaming all the time"—through a forest filled with terrifying wolves and hyenas which, the narrator tells us, would be able to eat her alive were it not for the Woman's power over them.[82] "When people will be naughty," the narrator tells us, "they have to be frightened, and they are not expected to like it."[83] The terror, however, is not purely physical but psychological, as evidenced by Rosamund's nightmares of turning into the moon when she is left imprisoned in the cottage with chores she neglects to do.

Like the wardens of Mettray, the Wise Woman subjects Rosamund to constant surveillance; when Rosamund thinks she is alone, the woman is "watching over her from the little window" and food only magically appears for her to eat when chores have been completed, and she is actually hungry.[84] And, when the princess fails to clean the house during the day, her conscience begins to trouble her: "she had in the storehouse of her heart a whole harvest of agonies, reaped from the dun fields of the night!"[85] MacDonald also emphasizes that both Rosamund and Agnes have become corrupted precisely through a lack of punishment. Rosamund "was one of those who the more they are coaxed are the more disagreeable" and "[f]or such, the wise woman had an awful punishment, but she remembered that the princess had been very ill brought up, and therefore wished to try her with all gentleness first."[86]

Rosamund's moral education through fear has the desired effect, resulting in her first attempt to behave properly after the journey to the Woman's cottage:

> with the sufferings and terrors she had left outside, the new kind of tears she had shed, . . . and the trust she had begun to place in the wise woman, it seemed to her as if her soul had grown larger of a sudden, and she had left the days of childishness and naughtiness far behind her.[87]

Much later in the book, after having relapsed many, many times and eventually run away to find herself lost and physically injured in a peat marsh she believes to be full of Willow-the-Wisps, Rosamund "[sees] now that she was justly punished for her wickedness."[88] And once she is fully reformed, at the end of the book, the Wise Woman summarizes the relationship between nurturing and the terrors Rosamund suffered: "If I had not forgiven you, I would never have taken the trouble to punish you."[89] The straightforward didactic function of MacDonald's fanciful depiction of child punishment is most obvious. Nonetheless, the structure of Rosamund's moral evolution and its embodiment in the form of a network of fairy tale tropes implies some complex claims about the biological, as well as spiritual, nature of childhood, which formed the crux of the nineteenth-century legal debate about child criminality.

Most basically, MacDonald's "bad" children suffer from an inability to see the difference between right and wrong, the very moral uncertainty Hale identified in the eighteenth century, and worked to incorporate into the common law. With all "[Rosamund] knew of the world being derived from nursery tales, she concluded that the wise woman was an ogress, carrying her home to eat her."[90] Furthermore, the narrator notes that her frantic struggles to free herself from the woman's grip "will seem to those of my readers who are of the same sort as herself" to be "the right and natural thing to do." Yet uncontrolled nature is precisely the problem: "[t]he wrong in her was this—that she had led such a bad life, that she did not know a good woman when she saw her."[91] Later on, when the wind rustles through the bed of live heather the woman provides as a place for her to sleep, Rosamund takes the sound for "the hissing of serpents, for you know she had been naughty for so long that she could not in a great many things tell the good from the bad."[92] (It should be noted that this failure in perception also dulls the edge of the Wise Woman's apparent cruelty: Rosamund's terrors are largely the product of her lack of discernment and her inappropriate application of one fairy tale narrative to the very different one she inhabits.)

MacDonald explicitly and repeatedly situates this childish inability to distinguish good from evil in legal terms. When Agnes takes water from the Wise Woman (disguised as a beggar woman her parents had offered it to), the narrator notes, "[w]hoever is possessed by a devil, *judges* with the mind of that devil."[93] The idea of a child's possession by a devil external to herself as an explanation for her cruelty echoes William York's account of his crime, repeated in the official record of his conviction and subsequent pardoning. Similarly, in describing Rosamund's reformation MacDonald says, "The violence of which she had been *guilty* had vanished from her spirit."[94] In both cases, the process of adjudication—literal in York's case, figurative, through the language of "judging" and "guilt" in Rosamund's—results in condemnation. Yet the violence produced by Rosamund's devil "vanishes" in a moment of narrative pardoning.

The juridical overtones become more overt toward the end of the text. The Wise Woman devises a series of what she calls "trials" for Rosamund, which unfold in the many magical mood "chambers" of her cottage. (The word "chamber" strongly hints that the substance of what will be unfolding on each of these occasions is an act of judging.) In each room, Rosamund finds herself transported to some new otherworld where she is faced with temptations to resort to her bad behavior, and she fails multiple times before eventually triumphing. Before the trials commence, the Wise Woman tells her that the key to winning is to remember that "you must *not do* what is wrong, however much you are inclined to do it, and you must *do* what is right, however much you are disinclined to do it."[95] The princess responds "I understand that," demonstrating that she has arrived, ostensibly, to the phase of intellectual development compatible with discerning between right and wrong, upon which the test of legal competence turns.[96]

Yet once inside the chambers, this understanding appears fleeting and terrifyingly malleable. After failing multiple times, Rosamund reaches one chamber in which a beautiful girl creates flowers in her lap and tosses them onto the ground to make them grow. Despite longing to befriend the girl and earn her place in the garden, the princess is incensed when she cannot pick the flowers without killing them and suddenly "[s]he had forgotten all her past life up to the time when she first saw the child . . . she was now on the

very borders of hating her."[97] Rosamund's eventual victory over this struggle
—between the remembrance of right and wrong and the wholly disorienting
moral amnesia causing the desire to do the child violence—stages the basic
unsettled quality in a child's moral development. For MacDonald, this moral
fluidity is itself traumatic: it makes her a fraught and complex subject for the
exercise of punishment and an attractive object for pardon, which Rosamund
receives after her multiple failures in the mood chambers. Indeed, at the end
of the text, when the Wise Woman addresses the parents of Agnes (who has
not yet passed the various tests and entered into the realm of enlightenment
eventually reached by Rosamund) she states simply "[s]he is your crime and
your punishment." In other words, children cannot commit crimes but,
when improperly punished, are crimes, committed by their parents. For
MacDonald, then, a child may be subject to external devils for as long as
it takes for good moral education and discipline to take effect and become
innate. When that fails to occur, the crimes remain. (And will eventually,
one can assume logically, start to be the child's own once she has reached
maturity.)

For all of the text's preoccupation with punishment and pardon, however, MacDonald expands, rather than resolves, the ambivalence over appropriate penal authority developed in "Cross Purposes." Nodelman describes
as a "shadow text" the repertoire of knowledge that necessarily contextualizes
any piece of children's literature for a "hidden adult" reader. In the case of
the "Lost Princess," that knowledge includes an awareness of the impossibility of a magical old wise woman—or even the Church she represents in the
abstract—literally punishing naughty children into becoming better versions
of themselves. It also includes the unavailability of parents—even bad parents
like those in the story—to serve this role for many children. Therefore, when
the text crystallizes the ambivalence about authority discernible in "Cross
Purposes" into a specific critique of blackletter law—in this case represented
by the laws of Rosamund's father the King—it reveals a genuine discursive
conflict surrounding the project of juvenile punishment as an institution of
benign reformation.

In his effort to locate his abducted daughter, the King embodies all of
the petty tyrannies of legalism divorced from ethics or logic. Agnes—while
exploring a magical chamber of the Wise Woman, containing paintings that
serve as portals into the lands they depict—finds a painting of the royal palace
bearing a plaque that specifies execution for anyone who fails to bring all lost
children immediately to the palace. Agnes, exemplifying yet again the failure
to distinguish between good and evil, thinks "[i]t would serve [the Wise
Woman] right to tell the king and have her punished for not taking me to the
palace!"[98] Here the child's failure to make appropriate moral judgments about

desert and punishment underscores the fact that her sovereign—imposing draconian punishments for crimes of omission—likewise lacks that ability. Indeed, after Agnes has entered the painting and reached the palace, where she tells the king she believes Rosamund has been residing with her parents, "[a] band of soldiers, under a clever lawyer, was sent out to search every foot of the supposed region."[99] The king commanded them "not to return until they brought with them, bound hand and foot, such a shepherd pair as that of which they received a full description."[100] When the band locates the shepherd couple, they object that they cannot go back to the palace with them or else their house will be unguarded and their sheep lost. The lawyer answers, in paradoxical, *Wonderland*-like language, "You must learn, then, how both of you can go, and your sheep must take care of your cottage."[101] By setting the lawyer up as the head of this band of coercive authority, MacDonald emphasizes both the absurdity and the sheer dangerousness of black letter law—here parodied by the king's edicts—serving as the sole arbiter of human conduct.

The absurdities continue during the interrogation in the king's audience chamber. When the couple objects that they had no idea Rosamund was the princess, he notes, "[m]y proclamation left nothing to your judgment. It said *every* child."[102] When they object that they live far from the palace and could not have read the plaque bearing the proclamation, he responds: "[y]ou ought to have heard . . . It is enough that I make proclamations; it is for you to read them. Are they not written in letters of gold upon the brazen gates of this palace?"[103] The menace of the law being interpreted so literally and so categorically escalates into the unrestrained threat of physical violence without due process. The king declares: "You have murdered her! . . . You shall be tortured till you confess the truth; and then you shall be tortured to death."[104] While magical punishment has been the driving ethical imperative of the entire text, the sudden collapse of the narrative into a moment of earthly, adult punishment creates a tension surrounding the appropriate use of coercion in the defense of right.

This scene likewise echoes the unrestrained violence of the Queen of Hearts in *Alice in Wonderland*.[105] MacDonald alludes to Carroll's text earlier in the book, when Agnes looks about in her egg and observes that things have gone "drear and drearier." But the connections between the texts solidify in the audience chamber scene, where the king's casual threats of violence reorient on a child character. Upon realizing that Agnes is the shepherd's daughter he commands: "Take all three of them to the rack. Stretch them till their joints are torn asunder!"[106] A bit later, when Rosamund herself enters the chamber and attempts to greet her parents with kisses, her mother, not recognizing her, exclaims, "Get away you great rude child—will nobody take her to the rack?"[107] All of these moments—particularly situated, as they are, at the end of the text—suggest that the efforts to curtail actual crime through the engines of earthly law are likely to fail due to its inadequacy as a stand-in for divine law.

And yet, MacDonald nonetheless contributes to the discourse about juvenile reform simply by demonstrating the horrors of unpunished children. He even illuminates the connection between the unevolved (or devolved) children in this fairy tale and the threat of actual, urban child criminality when he compares Rosamund, excessively pleased with herself after her first attempt to obey the Wise Woman's orders, to a street urchin: "What honest boy would pride himself on not picking pockets?"[108] For MacDonald, this conflict seems caught up in the idealized children to which his texts are speaking. Because he would have them become like the evolved protagonists in his texts, and thereby serve as conduits to Salvation for the rest of us, he wants them to obey the "laws" he describes in his essay on magical world-building "The Fantastic Imagination" (1893)—his laws which allow Fairyland to provide aesthetically appealing punishments and the built-in pardon of a magical happily ever after. Yet, due to the shadow text and what it says about nineteenth-century juvenile delinquency, this question appears almost inseparable from that of the appropriate earthly agent for disciplining divine children. MacDonald's inability to fully resolve this problem reifies the trauma of potential state violence enacted upon the morally unknowable child subject. The identification of the "evil-faced" child as a desirable object for punishment despite the problems created by inadequate positive legal systems appear more explicitly in the work of Charles Kingsley. While MacDonald uses the laws he creates for his Fairy Land to punish his child characters right back into an abstracted Garden of Eden, however, Kingsley approaches this question by treating his child protagonists as, first and foremost, subjects of the British Crown here on Earth.

Charles Kingsley and the Fairy with the Birch Rod

"What next will be demanded of us by physical science?" asked Charles Kingsley, in an 1871 lecture at Sion College. "Belief, certainly . . . in the permanence of natural laws."[109] He went on to observe:

> I cannot see how our Lord's parables, drawn from the birds and the flowers, the seasons and the weather, have any logical weight . . . unless we look at them as instances of laws of the natural world, which find their analogues in the laws of the spiritual world, the kingdom of God.[110]

Kingsley's answer to his own question neatly summarizes a worldview in which his theological position as a clergyman of the Church of England can be reconciled with his belief in the theory of natural selection in which his university audience would have been interested. Indeed, his adherence to natural selection had led Darwin to include a version of Kingsley's remarks upon *On The Origin of Species* in the second edition of the book, and he was an important defender of the work.[111] Most famously, Kingsley dramatizes the processes of natural change in his children's novel *The Water-Babies* (1863), in which Tom, a degraded chimney sweep, "evolves" into a morally educated Christian man by first transforming into a magical "water-baby." Contemporary critics such as Gillian Beer and John Hawley have explored Kingsley's efforts to use the developing scientific discourses of the nineteenth century—particularly that of evolution—in service of Christian moral teaching through a kind of magical syncretism made possible by the fanciful world of the text.[112] As Immel, Knoepflmacher and Briggs have put it more recently, the text aspires "to harmonize laws of the natural world with the higher metaphysical laws of a world adumbrated by the imagination."[113]

However, to understand fully the relationship between science and religion and the structures of authority through which they act, one must also consider a third discursive framework which the text both critiques and legitimizes: that of earthly positive law. As I discussed in Chapter 2, Simon Petch has identified in other Victorian literature a general anxiety around the concept of natural law as embodied by the courts of equity that were abolished by the Judicature Act in 1873. Petch argues that Darwin's account of natural brutality amplified the growing preference for common law courts as a necessary bulwark against lawlessness.[114] This thread appears throughout Victorian debates over juvenile justice as well. In an 1855 speech to the Society of Arts, barrister and school inspector Jelinger Symons attacks the idea, attributed to skeptics of child punishment, that "the punishment with which the law visits juvenile crimes is arbitrary" because children, "exempted from the penalties of the law, may thieve, burn, or kill with impunity."[115] He describes such natural license as rife with "anti-social evils" and "at variance with all law, human and divine, and the experience and practice of mankind in all ages."[116] For Symons and his set, positive law appears necessary to constrain the terrors of the natural child in the same way that Hale had articulated centuries before.

Similarly, Kingsley's remarks at Sion College do not merely recast natural processes as manifestations of God's will. That he sees natural parables as embodied in "laws" implies the existence of interconnected systems of authority to create such laws and, as Kingsley's habitual usage makes clear, to enforce them through punishment, a process which necessarily implicates human, as well as evolutionary or divine, law-givers. Unlike MacDonald, for whom childhood is above all things unique and sacred, Kingsley uses the ambivalent figure of the child criminal as a special but prototypical human subject of earthly punishment in *The Water-Babies* (1863). In this children's fairy tale, the debased chimney sweep Tom flees from his earthly judges into a world in which physical and procedural trials and punishments mark his progress from "heathen" to Christian man of science. Kingsley utilizes the discourses of both science and earthly law to access what he believes to be a set of universal spiritual truths, but this triangulation breaks down into a perplexing multiplicity of authorities, all of whom seek to assert legal and penal control over Tom.

In this section, I will argue that Kingsley initially attempts to interpose an embodied Mother Nature in lieu of earthly systems of positive law as a more suitable mediator of divine laws. Yet, as in MacDonald's tales, there is confusion as to the appropriate authority. For Kingsley, in contrast to MacDonald, nature fails as a dispenser of divine justice and his fantasy world collapses into a return to reliance on earthly systems of legal authority. His effort to develop a principled reconciliation of evolution and God, then, fails to the extent of its pragmatic execution, leaving scientific discourses about the physical world somewhat morally suspect. Kingsley's simultaneous failure satisfactorily to rehabilitate the positive law framework he challenges early in the text leaves Tom—and the reader—uncertain as to the proper sources of authority best to mediate the all-important distinction between universal right and wrong. His eventual reliance on essentialist moral qualities of English common law underscores the discursive contingency of nineteenth-century conceptions of just punishment in general. Because Tom and Tom's readers are children, Kingsley may use the malleable magical landscape—and the pre-lapsarian potential for pardon—that allows for discursive experimentation with ideas about morality and authority. Yet, in stark contrast to MacDonald's protagonists, Tom is less important as an example of a punished child per se than as an example of a punished body generally, in the face of a number of conflicting sources of penal authority. Fear over the possibility that the child criminal is not distinct from his adult counterpart did motivate the more punitive side in the debate over juvenile justice. Symons declared that showing mercy to child criminals due to their incapacity for discerning good from evil

> must have still more weight in favour of the exemption of adult offenders, who, in the days of their childhood, had far less means of improveing their discernment . . . and whose age and long practice of crime will scarcely have quickened their moral sensibilities[117]

which would mean, if taken to its logical conclusion, that "the social equity of punishment is a mistake and penal justice is at an end."[118] The stakes of finding an acceptable mechanism for child punishment were, then, high indeed.[119]

While tensions over the legitimacy of punishment always complicate the standard liberal narrative of political bodies originating in pre-political social contracts never agreed to by present-day citizens, these tensions seem uniquely striking in Kingsley's strange text for children, in which he critiques both discipline and the lack thereof. In this sense, Tom's experiences in *The Water-Babies* resonate with Foucault's account of Mettray. In Kingsley's text, the frequent equivalence between the child Tom and adults like Mr. Grimes as proper objects for organized punishment belies any notion that the text speaks only to adult authority over children. Foucault notes that the architects of Mettray sought not only physical control over their inmates but to build a body of knowledge about the boys' "souls." In this process, they found support through new developments in medical and psychiatric discourses "that provided [Mettray] with a sort of 'scientificity'" and also by "a judicial apparatus which, directly or indirectly, gave it legal justification."[120] Kingsley's text, always searching for a "natural" material system for dispensing the punishment he takes as spiritually required for the "souls" of his characters, engages yet frequently rejects both the scientific and judicial discourses that support institutions like Mettray. In the end, I will argue that Kingsley chooses a fairly narrow earthly mediator as a gateway for spiritual natural law—the English common law system specifically—revealing a discomfort with the notion of punishment as either a purely physical science or a simple exercise of coercive power. His ultimate centering of the English common law—more easily accomplished in the simplistic language addressed to a child audience—is a largely unsatisfactory fusing of two discourses of the "natural." To the social contract origins story, which justifies a state's exercise of punishment against a background of spiritual right, Kingsley adds an evolution-based gloss of Anglo exceptionalism. The anxieties over legality and punishment that emerge in the text become subsumed in a final recursion to "Englishness" so self-consciously constructed as to undermine even the theoretical coherence of the idea of the "natural."

Tom is precisely the sort of child targeted by the "child-savers." He is a poor, working-class boy which in and of itself was likely sufficient to constitute a status crime under the new juvenile delinquency laws discussed above. To understand *The Water-Babies* as an embodiment of nineteenth-century penal discourse, one must note that, while Kingsley condemns the illegitimate abuse Tom suffers at the start of the text, he merely replaces it with the magical program of reformation he devises. Though before entering the magical otherworld in which most of the story takes place, Tom had not committed any actual crime so far as the reader can tell, the mere fact of his being a poor, dirty child creates the need for punishment. Kingsley has less to say about whether Tom should be punished at all than about who should do it.

Throughout *The Water-Babies*, Kingsley manifests ambivalence toward the structures of positive law created by men to distribute punishment; such law, he suggests, may at times be co-extensive with the law of nature, moral and physical, but a tension between the two permeates the tale. At the start of the story, Kingsley presents the legal authority to which the human Tom is initially subject as divided between two opposing male figures: the repugnant gamekeeper Mr. Grimes and the "grand old" Sir John.[121] The former, of course, represents the overtly illegitimate authority of the strong over the weak, authority which, Kingsley intimates, is all the more pernicious when its victim perceives it as the legitimate manifestation of a natural order. Tom took Grimes's beatings and other punishments "all for the way of the world, like the rain and snow and thunder, and stood manfully with his back to it till it was over, as his old donkey did to a hail-storm."[122] Kingsley's critique here seems to anticipate Foucault's observation that

> perhaps the most important effect of the carceral system and of its extension well beyond legal imprisonment is that it succeeds in making the power to punish natural and legitimate, in lowering at least the threshold of tolerance to penalty.[123]

This is, of course, exactly what was happening as reformists constructed juvenile delinquency as a category of offense. Kingsley further underscores the vast difference between Grimes's system of discipline and the natural forces to which Tom mistakenly compares it by noting that Grimes "knocked Tom down again, in order to teach him (as young gentlemen used to be taught at public schools) that he must be an extra good boy that day."[124] Grimes thus represents more than just the abusive authority of one tyrant, but the corrupt authority of an entire institutional and educational framework into which, as Foucault notes, the "carceral system" had extended, and which extracts only the false sort of "goodness" that results from the threat of violence.

Even more than Grimes, Sir John embodies the full weight of the man-made systems of legal and penal authority, introduced almost like the Old Testament God as ultimate dispenser of justice: "of all places upon earth, Harthover Place . . . was the most wonderful, and, of all men on earth, Sir John (whom [Tom] had seen, having been sent to gaol by him twice) was the most awful."[125] Yet Sir John is limited as a law-giver, by his own human appetites and concerns, to what he perceives as right and, consequently, separated by his self-interest from the ideal "right." Later on, we learn that "four days a week" Sir John hunted, and "the other two he went to the bench and the board of guardians, and very good justice he did." The imbalance between the amount of time he devotes to each pursuit throws into question the sincerity of the narrator's praise. To the extent that Sir John constrains the low-level abuser Grimes, we may infer that he wields a more legitimate authority over his county and over Tom himself. "Sir John," Kingsley tells us, "was a grand old man, whom even Mr. Grimes respected," in part because he could "send Mr. Grimes to prison when he deserved it, as he did once or twice a week."[126] Yet this sort of authority, as represented by the positive laws Sir John enforces, is suspect in its own right. The fact that he "own[ed] all the land about for miles" coupled with his enormous physical presence ("he weighed full fifteen stone") suggests an over-consumption of the land itself, as does the fact that he spends twice as much time hunting as he does doing "very good justice." Kingsley confirms this when he notes that Sir John "would do what he thought right by his neighbours, as well as get what he thought right for himself."[127]

Sir John's "Englishness" partially legitimates him as a legal authority. During Tom's rush to clean himself in the river, for example, he worries that the church doors will be closed to him if he does not get there in time, but Kingsley notes that "the good old English law would punish that man, as he deserved, for ordering any peaceable person out of God's house, which belongs to all alike."[128] Positive "English law" may yet be subservient to the higher, holy law represented by the universally accessible church, but at its best, then, this nationalized positive law may act as servant and protector of the greater law. (The connection between Sir John as English law-giver and church law is further emphasized by his hound who, at the start of the search for Tom, had "a throat like a church-bell" and "lifted up his mighty voice, and told them all he knew.")[129]

Yet even Sir John, as a representative of English law, is inadequate as an ultimate authority in a state of nature. He is unable to pursue Tom down Lewthwaite Crag—"Oh that I were twenty years younger, and I would go down myself!"—and must send "a little groom-boy" instead.[130] They arrive too late to dispense earthly justice to the wronged Tom, and Sir John lacks the understanding of physical or moral natural law necessary to make sense of Tom's fate. "[T]he keeper, and the groom, and Sir John made a great mistake, and were very unhappy (Sir John at least) without any reason," when they discover what they think is Tom's corpse.[131] The absence of "reason" suggests Sir John's failure to discern the governing principles of moral natural law at work. Furthermore, Kingsley emphasizes Sir John's failure to understand the scientific principles of nature that have occasioned Tom's metamorphosis: "Sir John did not understand all this, not being a fellow of the Linnaean Society; and he took it into his head that Tom was drowned."[132] On the one hand, Sir John's assumption is only common sense, as opposed to scientific guild knowledge at which Kingsley appears to poke fun. And yet Sir John proves incorrect in his assumption. Therefore, while positive law can, when used properly (i.e., "Englishly"), work in service of a natural moral order, Sir John's imperfections and ultimate impotence demonstrate that it alone is insufficient; it seems there are greater systems of law with claims to Tom's obedience.

Linguistic and narrative markers in the text suggest that the processes of the natural world do indeed point to higher, moral "natural law," and that obedience to Nature herself ought to be one of Tom's most important lessons. The natural authority responsible for Tom's moral education resides in the three great matriarchal figures of the tale, Mrs. Doasyouwouldbedoneby, Mrs. Bedonebyasyoudid, and Mother Carey, though Kingsley presents disembodied nature as an extension of matriarchy as well (describing salt water, for example, as "the mother of all living things"[133] and extracting Longfellow's description of "Nature, the old Nurse").[134] The pair of elaborately named sisters represent natural forces as a familiar duality: the loving mother and punitive teacher. Mrs. Bedonebyasyoudid describes her intended punishment for a particular moral failing: "when folks are in that humour, I cannot teach them, save by the good old birch-rod."[135] Despite Mrs. Beonebyasyoudid's nature goddess connotations, her birch rod is an important signifier of state-sponsored punishment: under the Whipping Act 1862, a criminal under the age of fourteen could, in lieu of being sent to prison, be whipped up to twelve strokes with a birch rod.[136] Its appearance at this stage in the story foreshadows the inevitability of positive law as necessary to mete out justice by the end.

It is in the character of Mother Carey that we can most clearly see the possible relationship between physical and moral systems of natural law: "[S]he was very old—in fact, as old as anything which you are likely to come across, except the difference between right and wrong."[137] Again, crucial to the fairy tale of child development is the essential dichotomy of "right and wrong." According to Kingsley here, the natural law of moral right and wrong pre-dates even the physical manifestations of nature, though nature herself has priority over everything else, including the positive laws and established Church that act as competing filters for this law of right and wrong. Her role, she tells Tom, is not to make things but to "sit here and make them make themselves."[138] This explanation tracks not only with Kingsley's view of evolution as an inevitable earthly process flowing independently from the initial creative act of Divine Providence, but with the potential and mandate for human beings to discern absolute "right and wrong" on their own, through the mediating presence of nature.

Despite the centrality of the maternal figure of nature as a dispenser of moral justice, however, the text is rife with a competing, Hobbesian view of nature as lawless and brutal, wholly divorced from any system of divine or human law. Indeed, the very fragmentation of the idea of maternal nature into a myriad of deeply contradictory figures suggests the impossibility of treating physical natural law as a straightforward mediator of moral natural law. When Tom encounters a family of otters—initially described as the "merriest, lithest, gracefullest creatures you ever saw"—the mother otter attacks Tom, exclaiming "Quick, children, here is something to eat, indeed!" and shows "such a wicked pair of eyes, and such a set of sharp teeth in a grinning mouth, that Tom, who had thought her very handsome, said to himself, *Handsome is that handsome does.*"[139] This representative of nature— even nature in the guise of yet another mother, engaged in the very natural act of providing for her young—is described as a "wicked old otter," perhaps due to the fact that her potential victim was the humanoid Tom.[140] The laws of physical nature are not benign when they conflict with the safety of a human being as made in God's image. Later on in the story, Kingsley seems to condone almost identical natural lawlessness during Tom's journey to the shiny wall, when a group of puffins "stayed behind, and killed the young rabbits, and laid their eggs in the rabbit-burrows."[141] Of this slaughter Kingsley only observes that it was "rough practice, certainly; but a man must see to his own family."[142] The language of morality used to condemn the mother otter's behavior contrasts sharply with the amoral view of the rabbits' death as part of the benign process of care-taking. While this pair of scenes may be a gesture toward the possibility of evolution and theology coming together through the maternal care of children, Kingsley lacks a coherent principle whereby natural physical laws of competition and survival can truly be reconciled with the system of "right and wrong" he believes to be paramount.

Kingsley's solution to this confusion over substantive justice is to fall back on the virtues of procedural justice. In light of what has gone before— the effort Kingsley has taken to deliver Tom from the hands of Mr. Grimes and the police to the isle of a nature goddess—the choice seems curious: the automatic dispensing of justice, without reference to personal pity or mercy, is an old ideal for the role of the common law judge, but hardly for an all-seeing, eternal God figure, particularly any version of the Christian god of mercy. Eighteenth-century legal commentator Giles Jacob summarizes this function of English common law judges: "*Judges* have not the Power to *judge* according to that which they think fit; but that which by Law they know to be right."[143] In his book on judicial duty, legal historian Philip Hamburger emphasizes the importance placed on judging in accordance with the laws of England:

already at an early date in the history of the common law the king's commissions to his judges specified their duty with the clause "*facturi quod*

ad iustitiam pertinet secundum legem, & consuetudinem Angliae." In other
words, they were to do that which pertains to judging according to the law
and custom of England.[144]

Even more to the point, in his nineteenth-century war against the idea
that children are incapable of forming criminal *mens rea*, Jerlinger Symons
emphasizes its un-Englishness: "[t]he assumption that all children under six-
teen offend without discernment appears to have been arbitrarily established
in France."[145]

Indeed Kingsley's primary dispenser of natural justice, Mrs.
Bedonebyasyoudid, wields a state-mandated birch rod. In other words, she
cannot operate solely within the confines of physical natural laws, as she did
with respect to the Doasyoulikes or to the trout, and she falls back on the
presumed righteousness of the English law. When Tom flees from Grimes
and the mob of Sir John's servants, we perceive him to have escaped a corrupting system of illegitimate human authority and punishment. Yet the
successive punishments he receives at the hands of Mother Nature herself
are suspiciously similar to the very systems of human punishment Kingsley
critiques in the early pages of the novel. Upon Tom's initial plunge into the
forest:

> [t]he boughs laid hold of his legs and arms, and poked him in his face
> and his stomach, made him shut his eyes tight . . . and when he got the
> rhododendrons, the hassock-grass and sedges tumbled him over, and cut
> his poor little fingers most spitefully; the birches birched him as soundly as
> if he had been a nobleman at Eton, and over the face too (which is not fair
> swishing, as all brave boys will agree); and the lawyers tripped him up, and
> tore his shins as if they had sharks' teeth—which lawyers are likely enough
> to have.[146]

That the forest not only hurts Tom but "birches" him makes explicit the
connection to Mrs. Bedonebyasyoudid, "the fairy with the birch rod"—and,
by extension, the institution of state-sponsored corporal punishment through
the Juvenile Offenders Act. But here she does not appear to exact any sort of
lawful punishment; Tom has done nothing wrong, and this birching—like
the earlier beating by Mr. Grimes—is comparable to an "unfair" form of corporal punishment within human institutions. Furthermore, the pun on the
word "lawyer"—referring to spiky lawyer vines, but with the overt reference
to "shark-like" attorneys—makes explicit that this encounter with nature is
an entanglement with a system of law possessed, like the court of Rosamund's
father in "The Lost Princess," of many of the same defects as the positive law
of earthly magistrates.

These parallels continue when we come to know Mrs. Bedonebyasyoudid in the flesh. She is first introduced as a reader of the *Waterproof Gazette*, which is printed "on the finest watered paper, for the use of the great fairy, Mrs. Bedonebyasyoudid, who reads the news very carefully every morning, and especially the police cases."[147] It appears paradoxical for a "great fairy" to rely on third-hand accounts of events printed in a commercial publication (presumably liable to the same sensationalistic errors as its land-based counterparts) in determining when and where she must dispense justice. Further, the reference to "police cases" confirms that the underwater realm is bound by systems of legal control identical to the earthly ones and that, indeed, Mrs. Bedonebyasyoudid's potency as a law-giver depends upon them for success. This reliance is self-conscious: when Tom first arrives at the sacred isle of the water babies, he sees that "instead of watchmen and policemen to keep out nasty things at night, there were thousands and thousands of water-snakes, and most wonderful creatures they were."[148] This contrast to the world of earthly criminal discipline suggests that the natural authorities here are superior. Yet at the very seat of Mrs. Bedonebyasyoudid's power—the prison in which Tom finds Mr. Grimes at the end of the story—order is maintained by disembodied police truncheons and blunderbusses, the synecdoche reminding us that only the essence of man-made authority is sufficient for punishing the greatest sinners like Grimes.[149] Thus, even the magical isle inhabited by justice personified devolves into the bureaucratized discipline suggested by Foucault.

In Mrs. Bedonebyasyoudid's cross-examination of Tom for having put a pebble into a sea anemone's mouth, she functions more as a common law court of justice than as an all-seeing divine being. First, she applies a familiar principle of criminal law which we have already seen MacDonald mock in "The Lost Princess," that ignorance of the law is no excuse: "if you do not know that things are wrong that is no reason why you should not be punished for them."[150] Mrs. Bedonebyasyoudid appears to operate as a human tribunal and not as a manifestation of the higher power. She reinforces this conclusion by describing her role as a law-giver in the dispassionate language endorsed by Giles Jacob in the eighteenth century: "I work by machinery, just like an engine; and am full of wheels and springs inside; and am wound up very carefully so that I cannot help going."[151]

We see yet another example of the obedience/autonomy opposition also familiar from MacDonald when, after this talk with Tom, she proceeds to punish legions of offenders who have harmed children through ignorance— foolish mothers, careless nursery maids, and "cruel schoolmasters," the last of whom she "birched . . . soundly with her great birch-rod."[152] Comporting with the "eye-for-an-eye" reading of Biblical vengeance, this episode demonstrates the need to discipline representatives of authority who abuse their power to discipline. Yet Mother Earth's earlier birching of Tom remains un-redeemed, a fact that sits uncomfortably with Mrs. Bedonebyasyoudid's use of the punishment on those who had used it inappropriately. Again we are faced with the paradox that, while highly aestheticized child punishment forms the very narrative logic of the text, it provides examples of penal authorities being punished themselves.

Kingsley attempts to resolve this instability with the third major episode in which the fairy appears in the role of law-giver and punisher: the occasion of Tom consuming all of the sweets in her cupboard. Here, Kingsley emphasizes her eschewing physical discipline, because if she had used corporal punishment, "she knew quite well Tom would have fought and kicked, and bit, and said bad words, and turned again that moment into a naughty little heathen chimney-sweep."[153] Yet Kingsley highlights this abstinence not as a rejection of physical punishment but of employing these techniques as an interrogation before Tom had actually confessed to the crime. He says,

> She leaves that for anxious parents and teachers . . . who, instead of giving children a fair trial, such as they would expect and demand for themselves, force them by fright to confess their own faults—which is so cruel and unfair that no judge on the bench dare do it to the wickedest thief or murderer, for the good British law forbids it.[154]

Even if she did not already know the truth, we are told, she would "not surely behave worse than a British judge and jury."[155] As with the episode of the sea anemone, this "great fairy," the embodiment of the forces of natural law, is defined almost entirely by her procedural function, which is that of an earthly, a particularly British, common law court.

Yet by separating the faces of benign, disciplinary, and even malevolent "Mother Nature"—and by linking her punitive authority to the conventions of the English common law—Kingsley undoes her legitimacy as a divine mediator. She emerges, in the end, like Sir John at the beginning: an alloy of the right and wrong in physical nature, interrelated with the right and wrong in positive law. The figure of Tom as a child criminal is crucial to the resolution of this ambivalence in a narratively coherent fashion—not only within this text but in the general cultural narrative by which earthly mediators must dispense justice to wrongdoers. Although Tom is, in many ways, an innocent initially unfairly subjected to earthly punishment, he is nonetheless —by virtue of his identity as an uneducated young chimney sweep—in need of punishment for the purposes of evolution into humanity.

For Kingsley, the project of determining who knows the difference between right and wrong is crucial, regardless of whether it is undertaken by Sir John, Mrs. Bedonebyasyoudid, or any English common law judge. Yet childhood allows a space for this inquiry to yield temporarily null results —Tom can commit murder, in the anthropomorphized natural world of a fairy tale, and be pardoned for it so long as he endures the subsequent process of punishment.[156] Furthermore, the relationship between Tom and his potential adult reader is a bit less fraught than in MacDonald's tales. Tom—an emblem of the category of corrupted-yet-reformable urban youth that had been created for the first time in the Victorian age—is malleable due to his age but not particularly interesting as a point of access to Salvation. Indeed at the end of the text, he returns to land to begin a life as a proper English gentleman. If Kingsley's "shadow text" makes Tom important to the reader's self-identification it is through the resolution of the traumatic crisis of legitimacy left open by MacDonald: the English law that imposes punishment through orderly procedural channels is the best system in the non-magical world for ensuring moral and cultural evolution for all of us. The difficulty, of course, is that no magical pardons are available for adults. I will, therefore, conclude with a final example of the fairy tale mode mediating the relationship between child and adult criminality and its attendant nineteenth-century anxieties, in the bildungsromans of Charles Dickens.

Dickens and the Inescapable Child Criminal

We have seen William York's punishment and banishment, reappear as a plot device in Victorian literary fairy tales. Indeed, the narrative structure of the pardon as an escape valve for tensions about possible systemic judicial imprecision link child and adult criminality. In Edward Said's familiar formulation, the Western construction of "the Orient" flows in part from the desire to define the West itself through its differences from the Eastern "other."[157] We can discern a similar process present—and formalized—in the institution of criminal punishment, a primary function of which is to express societal affirmation of shared moral principles by distinguishing and condemning those who violate them. The link between these two "otherings" is particularly apparent in the punishment of banishment, which links criminality with exclusion from physical space—a practice which the expansion of the British empire made increasingly well-utilized as an alternative to the death penalty throughout the eighteenth and nineteenth centuries. The discursive link between the child criminal and the Oriental "other" is particularly apparent in the use, by Victorian penologists such as Matthew Davenport Hill, of the term "City Arabs" to describe street urchins.[158]

As legal scholar Peter Goodrich puts it, a community's capacity to exclude strengthens the bonds between the remaining members:

The establishment of an identity, the constitution of a community, and the capture of subjectivity, are first a matter of establishing a collective . . . identity whose virtue will be matched only by the *evil* of those who do not belong to it.[159]

The work of Charles Dickens who, perhaps more than any other nineteenth-century writer, solidified the child criminal as a lasting part of the collective memory of criminality, requires mention for its illustration of these relationships. *Great Expectations* (1861) confronts the anxiety that, precisely due to the fluid nature of childhood identity—a third, temporary state of "otherness"—criminality may not be altogether excludable. The discipline asserted over Pip by his sister and the other adults at the start of the text establishes an immediate link between childhood and criminality, animated by submission to the potentially illegitimate exercise of authority.[160] Further, Pip's aid to Magwitch in his childhood becomes constitutive of his developing adult self: first materially so, because of his financial "expectations," but eventually even morally so, as evidenced by his sudden and almost irrational fixation on saving the man's life toward the end of the novel. Criminality still ends up excluded—the convict gets hanged and Pip must make his income and eventually win Estella (in Dickens's revised conclusion to the novel) without benefit of his inheritance—but as a bildungsroman, the text makes it clear that Pip's adult identity would not have evolved as it did in the absence of his child-like engagement with the criminal. The text also suggests that a healthy process of maturation entails the eventual fusion of adult and child selves, as well as a unification of the space of home with the space of empire.[161]

At the start of the text, Pip—like David Copperfield—is an object for the arbitrary penal action of his entire community, in particular through the bringing up "by hand" by his sister and the officious coercion of his Uncle Pumblechook, who "pushes him over" on his way to being bound apprentice to Joe "exactly as if [he] had at that moment picked a pocket."[162] Indeed, on the latter occasion the whole town mistakenly performs the process of exclusion reserved for criminals, asking "What's he done?" and "He's a young 'un, too, but looks bad, don't he?" with one person giving him "a tract ornamented with a woodcut of a malevolent young man fitted up with . . . fetters, and entitled TO BE READ IN MY CELL."[163] When he steals food for Magwitch, Pip begins to construct himself as a criminal as well, "fully expect[ing] to find a constable in the kitchen" waiting "to take [him] up"[164] and later on even being irrationally "disposed to believe that [he] must have had some hand" in Orlick's attack on his sister, as "a more legitimate object of suspicion than anyone else."[165] The community's construction of Pip as criminal by identity rather than by deed demonstrates the earlier-mentioned criminalization of childhood itself identified by Susan Margery.

The image of the child's body as a kind of lightning rod for the organized punitive instincts of a society is also strikingly clear in the early chapters of *David Copperfield*, in which the young David is subject to increasingly formalized systems of penal control. This is not, however, simply an aspect of childhood, or even impoverished childhood, that David transcends as he achieves adulthood. Through Mr. Dick's parallels to the child David and association with pre-"carceral" systems of social control Dickens maintains his proto-Foucauldian critique of penal discourse even into David's adulthood, and beyond the realm of juvenile discipline. Mr. Creakle's regime at Salem House so well illustrates Foucault's claims about nineteenth-century shifts in thinking about punishment it barely warrants much discussion.[166] But, briefly, the shift from Mr. Murdstone to Mr. Creakle as the figure of disciplinary oppression tracks with the shift Foucault identifies between the earlier practice of inflicting pain on a criminal's body in recompense for the highly individualized harm to a sovereign body posed by an act of crime, to the later practice of shutting criminals off in prisons. At the ruthless hands of Mr. Murdstone (who, like a sovereign, initially seeks dominance over his household through the demonstration of his uncontrolled right to punish), David's body becomes a site of sympathy for his mother (a stand-in for the polity to be controlled). David's lessons—though presided over by the vindictive Murdstones and inevitably culminating in physical abuse—are nonetheless a point of sympathetic contact between David and his mother, and a space for resistance on Clara's part: "the greatest effect in these miserable lessons is when my mother . . . tries to give me the cue by the motion of her lips."[167] The moment of David's own greatest act of resistance, in biting Mr. Murdstone to prevent further beatings and in the process physically marking the "sovereign's" hand (which was therefore subsequently "bound up in a large linen wrapper")[168] is the moment at which Murdstone's more personalized system of physical abuse appears insufficient and gives way to the carceral system at Salem House.

Salem House relies on the power of institutionalized processes to assert its authority over its inmates—like Mettray, blending the discourses of education and religious instruction into its bureaucratic program of control. Mr. Creakle's physical abuses—unlike the personalized tortures of Mr. Murdstone —are notable for their impersonality. He beats the boys routinely, as a matter of course and without any stated cause derived from actual threat to his sovereignty: in the bureaucratic style of the military, "like a trooper" he "laid about him, right and left, every day of his life."[169] And, of course, David's greatest suffering in this new system comes from its discursive authority to construct him as an anomaly in his community by means of the placard Mr. Murdstone directs be affixed to his back:

> What I suffered from that placard, nobody can imagine. Whether it was possible for people to see me or not, I always fancied that somebody was reading it. It was no relief to turn round and find nobody; for wherever my back was, there I imagined somebody always to be.[170]

David's terror of the literal legibility of his "criminality" within a community demonstrates the horrors of the discursive authority made possible by the same modern system of surveillance that had been lauded by reformer Robert Hall in his lectures on Mettray. David, of course, eventually escapes from the discursive violence of his childhood (which shifts, after his mother's death, into his self-identification as "the common drudge" Mr. Murdstone forces him to become by making him work in his bottling facility).[171]

Much more so than *Great Expectations,* however, *David Copperfield* entrenches the role of the fairy tale as an escape zone for the excesses of adult control over the child. Critics such as Alan Barr have noted the preponderance of fairy tale images throughout the text, connecting the young David's imaginative imposition of these tropes onto both his innocent adventures and his sufferings with the adult David's imagination of his financial challenges as a merely a "forest of difficulty" separating him from Dora in her "fairy bower."[172] Consistent with the chain of psychoanalytic thought from Freud to Bettelheim—which suggests that the traditional folk fairy tale structure, with its lack of ambiguity, vivid imagery, and use of magic, models the child's ego development—Dickens uses the fairy tale motif to extend David's childhood ego development into his adult world.[173] The idealized childhood Dickens constructs upon the ruins of earlier unhappiness serves to sustain an important adult fantasy in which childhood serves as a kind of origins story of innocence.

David's physical journey to Dover and rebirth as a talented schoolboy and eventual gentleman does not, however, extinguish the text's concerns about penal authority. Instead, Dickens displaces the trauma of punishment onto the character of Mr. Dick. From the outset, Mr. Dick represents an obvious double to David. Apart from the shared letter "D," (and the obvious phonetic connection between "Dick" and "Dickens," David's authorial alter ego), both Mr. Dick and David exist in a state of discursive flux due to the mutability of their names. David moves back and forth between David, Daisy, Davy, and—at the time he meets Mr. Dick—Trotwood and eventually "Trot," whereas Mr. Dick is in reality "Mr. Richard Babley," a name he "cannot bear."[174] Both characters are, therefore, uniquely susceptible to discursive construction by society at large. Furthermore, Mr. Dick's confused and oft-thwarted progress on his "Memorial" is a parallel to David's own more successful growth as a writer, and in particular to the specific biographical project purportedly represented by the text itself. Given the seeming doubling of the two characters, it is no wonder that they become "best of friends"[175] and David's long-deferred, transitional last moments of childhood (flying the kite and playing games with his schoolmates) take place with Mr. Dick, who even visits David at school in Canterbury for these activities, until David himself outgrows them.

Mr. Dick serves, however, not merely as a repository for David's frequently repressed child-like qualities, but as another potentially incarcerated body, thereby sustaining the concerns over institutionalized punishment developed in the earlier chapters of the book. From the moment we meet Mr. Dick, Aunt Betsey links him to a counterfactual in which he is an inmate of an asylum. "His own brother," she says, "would have shut him up for life" and "sent him away to some private asylum place,"[176] and this threat of incarceration continues throughout the text, with Aunt Betsey repeatedly concerned that asylum people have come to lock him up. In discussing Dick's supposed insanity she asserts the extent to which it—like the young David's "criminality"—is discursively constructed: he is "a little eccentric . . . though . . . not half so eccentric as a good many people" and "a great deal more sane than [his brother is] or ever will be, it is to be hoped."[177] She implies that Mr. Dick's "mind" possesses unique qualities of common sense and vision inaccessible to the rest of the world, thereby reinforcing the subjectivity of discursive claims to truth.

As a potential object of punishment, however, Mr. Dick serves a specifically historicized function within the text. His "memorial" is perpetually thwarted by the undesired reappearance of the head of King Charles I—"if [his execution] was so long ago, how could the people about him," Mr. Dick asks, "have made that mistake of putting some of the trouble out of *his* head, after it was taken off, into *mine*?"[178] Aunt Betsey echoes the suggested link between the symptoms of insanity and this moment of social upheaval: "He connects his illness with great disturbance and agitation, naturally, and that's the figure . . . which he chooses to use."[179] The regicide was, naturally, the most disruptive crisis in the English legal imagination and still felt in the eighteenth and nineteenth centuries. The notion that what had hitherto been conceived of as a divine right of rule could be subverted by earthly judicial authorities was a profoundly traumatic cultural event: with earthly judicial and political systems previously conceived of as mere instruments of a divine "natural" law, their use to do violence to the purported embodiment of that law raised basic questions about the sources of political authority generally and the nature of citizenship in a polity.

Against this backdrop, it is not surprising that Mr. Dick points to the anonymous and vaguely threatening "people about" the King as responsible for "putting" the trouble into his head. His description indicates the danger in the often arbitrary systems of discursive and bureaucratic control that may develop as an alternative to the simple, if tyrannical, framework of divine right embodied by a unitary monarch like Charles I. Mr. Dick suggests that his own supposed insanity has somehow resulted from the operations of these long-ago "people." It is not a leap to suggest here that the power released through the execution of the king and displaced into the more diffuse authority of "people" includes the power to construct such irregularities as "insane" behavior and to police them through the "carceral" mechanisms, subsequently identified by Foucault, which haunt Dickens's text. In any case, it is unsurprising that in the inherently individualistic project of a biography Dickens would situate the ego-development of his child protagonist against the backdrop of a social world often dangerous to individual identity and, even after David's triumph over the threat of homogenization, retain this threat as a source of uncertainty throughout the remainder of the text.

This summary treatment of the relationship between child criminality and adult identity in Dickens's two bildungsromans demonstrates that the stakes of the general debate over child criminality involved more than simply the question of juvenile *mens rea*. The nineteenth-century fairy tale genre explored that issue in ways that reveal a longstanding cultural discomfort with child punishment—a discomfort ostensibly manifested in the new statutory developments of the Victorian age. But, too, a reading of children's fairy stories against "adult" works like Dickens's demonstrates how the debate over child criminality reflected broader ongoing trauma over the potential illegitimacy of earthly punishment generally. Victorian children's writers used the motif of pardon—or its magical equivalent—to shore up these concerns in fairy land, emphasizing the widespread ambivalence over whether the common law itself recognized the pre-lapsarian nature of childish intent. On the one hand, writers such as MacDonald and Kingsley imply the necessity of penal structures supplied by the common law and its new statutory auxiliaries. Yet they also illustrate the possibility that hardwired into this system—to the extent that the pardon power may be necessary to protect the common law requirement of criminal *mens rea*—is the idea of its own insufficiency.

Notes

1. Foucault, "Discipline and Punish," p. 1636.
2. Ibid. pp. 1637–8.
3. Ibid. p. 1639.
4. In a laudatory lecture on his visit to Mettray, MP Robert Hall emphasizes the

role of collective surveillance in enforcing good behavior. He notes that the boys were divided into residential units known as "families," which self-policed their own members: "This certainly is a most powerful engine: the eyes of the whole society awake to prevent the offence from coming; the cares of the whole family applied to wean the wayward from his willfulness." Hall, "Extract from a Lecture on Mettray," p. 44.

5. Brewer, *By Birth or Consent*, p. 93.

6. Ibid. p. 193.

7. Ibid. p. 184.

8. Hale, *History of the Pleas of the Crown*, p. 13.

9. Ibid. p. 22. Athelstan may have, in the words of Hale's editor Solum Ellym, "[thought] it a pitiable case that a youth but twelve years old should be put to death" and increased the minimum age to fifteen. Nonetheless, executions of youths younger than fifteen continued. Ibid. p. 22.

10. Ibid. p. 22.

11. Dalton's *The Country Justice: Containing the Practice, Duty, and Power of the Justices of the Peace Out of Their Sessions* (1618) was a manual used by English justices which, after twenty editions, eventually became an important reference tool on English common law in the American colonies.

12. Brewer, *By Birth or Consent*, p. 207.

13. Hale, *History of the Pleas of the Crown*, p. 24.

14. Ibid. p. 24 (emphasis added).

15. Ibid. p. 24.

16. Ibid. p. 25.

17. Ibid. p. 26.

18. Ibid. p. 24. It should be noted that the legal significance of the ability to distinguish between right and wrong is not unique to the adjudication of child criminality. The so-called "M'Naghten" rules were passed by Parliament as a reaction to the 1843 acquittal of Daniel M'Maghten for the murder of Edmund Drummond (who he had mistaken for Prime Minister Sir Robert Peel). The rules stated, among other things, that in order for a defendant to benefit from the defense of insanity

> it must be clearly proved that, at the time of the committing of the act, the party accused was labouring under such a defect of reason, from disease of the mind, as not to know the nature and quality of the act he was doing.

This version of the insanity defense remains on the books in most former commonwealth jurisdiction, including all but four of the U.S. states.

19. The resolution of challenging legal questions through executive pardon was, likewise, common well beyond the context of juvenile offenders. In one of the most famous common law cases of all time, *R* v. *Dudley and Stephens* (1884),

a lifeboat full of shipwrecked men were found guilty of murder for killing and cannibalizing the weakest of their number. While it was acknowledged by the court that, had they not done this, the entire group would have perished, "necessity" was rejected as a defense to murder. The court was highly conscious of the risk of sanctioning utilitarianism and thereby giving the formal sanction to general lawlessness: "it is not suggested that in this particular case the deeds were 'devilish,' but it is quite plain that such a principle once admitted might be made the legal cloak for unbridled passion and atrocious crime." While the court therefore formally sentenced the defendants to death, public opinion was so strongly in their favor that it was a foregone conclusion that they would be pardoned by the Crown.

20. Brewer, *By Birth or Consent*, p. 210.
21. Ayelet Ben-Yishai provides an interesting account of a similar phenomenon in nineteenth-century law reports. She argues that in their vagueness and lack of detail these reports were "anti-narrative" in style as a reaction to challenges to the authority of the common law. Ben-Yishai, "Victorian Precedents," p. 383. Through their lack of case-specificity, such reports negotiated the tension between the individual case and the general rule, thus facilitating the authority of precedent-based reasoning. Ibid. p. 401.
22. *R* v. *Yorke* (1748), Fost. 70.
23. Ibid. p. 71.
24. Nodelman, *The Hidden Adult*, p. 224.
25. Ibid. p. 225.
26. Foster 70, 71.
27. Ibid.
28. Ibid. p. 72. In *Oliver Twist* (1837–39), the Artful Dodger was similarly expelled from the text via transportation. This chapter will discuss the relationship between childhood and the punishment of transportation in greater detail in the section on Charles Dickens below.
29. Brewer, *By Birth or Consent*, p. 183.
30. Ibid. p. 182.
31. Laurence, *History of Capital Punishment*, p. 18.
32. Knell, "Capital Punishment," pp. 204–5.
33. Devereaux, "Imposing the Royal Pardon," p. 126.
34. Knell, "Capital Punishment," p. 199.
35. Ibid. p. 199.
36. Carpenter, "Letter to the *Bristol Gazette*," p. 139.
37. Hendrick, "Constructions and Reconstructions," p. 40.
38. Knapp & Baldwin, *Newgate Calendar*, vol. 2, p. 18.
39. Shore, "Re-inventing the Juvenile Delinquent," p. 1. For a lengthier treatment of these arguments see Shore, *Artful Dodgers*.

40. Prior to Peel's creation, in 1828, of the Metropolitan Police Force with its "bobbies," the Bow Street Runners (founded by Henry Fielding, as discussed in the next chapters) had been paid by the central government to work for the magistrates' office, primarily to execute arrest warrants.
41. Saunders & Saunders, *Criminal Offences of Children*, p. 1.
42. Hall, *Law Relating to Children*, p. 2.
43. Platt, *The Child-Savers*, pp. 3–4.
44. Margery, "The Invention of Juvenile Delinquency," p. 117.
45. Ibid. p. 117.
46. Ibid.
47. Hill, "Practical Suggestions," p. 2.
48. Ibid. p. 4.
49. Banerjee, "The Child in Victorian Fiction," p. 488.
50. Ibid. p. 488.
51. Brown, "The Influence of Queen Victoria," p. 31. Brown notes how Disraeli referred to Victoria by Spenser's famous title for Elizabeth, and shows how little fairy tale tradition existed in England between the reigns of the two queens Ibid. pp. 34–6.
52. MacDonald, "The Child in the Midst," p. 106.
53.
> If any man desire to be first, the same shall be last of all, and servant of all. And he took a child, and set him in the midst of them: and when he had taken him in his arms, he said unto them, Whosoever shall receive one of such children in my name, receiveth me; and whosoever shall receive me, receiveth not me, but him that sent me.

Mark 9: 35.
54. MacDonald, "The Child in the Midst," p. 8.
55. Ibid. p. 3.
56. MacDonald, *Lilith*, p. 174.
57. MacDonald, "Letters," p. 364.
58. McGillis, "George MacDonald and William Wordsworth," p. 152.
59. Makman, "Child's Work is Child's Play," p. 127. This theme of death and resurrection through love reverberates through many of his children's tales, particularly "The Golden Key" (1867), "The Shadows" (1864), "The Lost Princess" (1874), and *At the Back of the North Wind* (1871).
60. MacDonald, "The Child in the Midst," p. 3.
61. Ibid. p. 4.
62. Ibid. p. 4.
63. Ibid. p. 5.
64. MacDonald, "Hands of the Father," p. 186.
65. See Sheley, "From Eden to Eternity," pp. 329–44.

66. MacDonald, *Complete Fairy Tales*, p. 104.

67. Ibid. p. 104.

68. Ibid. p. 103.

69. Ibid. p. 103.

70. Ibid. p. 106.

71. MacDonald's selection of his heroine's name is hardly coincidental. The pub-
    lication of his friend Charles Dodgson's *Alice in Wonderland* (1865) opened
    the door for his own foray into the world of the children's fairy tale. As Ulrich
    Knoepflmacher puts it, the two writers were linked by "a fascination with
    death, and, therefore, also with silence; a mixture of humor and morbidity
    . . . Carroll and MacDonald tapped energies that originated from an anti-
    linguistic otherworld that each identified with the early phases of childhood."
    Knoepflmacher, *Ventures into Childland*, p. 153.

72. MacDonald, *Complete Fairy Tales*, p. 104.

73. Ibid. p. 106.

74. Ibid. p. 110.

75. Ibid. p. 113.

76. Ibid. p. 119.

77. Ibid. pp. 116–17.

78. Ibid. p. 119.

79. Nodelman, *Hidden Adult*, p. 80.

80. Ibid. p. 80.

81. Ibid. p. 227.

82. Ibid. p. 232.

83. Ibid. p. 234.

84. Ibid. p. 238.

85. Ibid. p. 246.

86. Ibid. p. 243.

87. Ibid. p. 242.

88. Ibid. p. 281.

89. Ibid. p. 294.

90. Ibid. p. 232.

91. Ibid. p. 236.

92. Ibid. p. 238.

93. Ibid. p. 256.

94. Ibid. p. 273.

95. Ibid. p. 285.

96. Ibid. p. 285.

97. Ibid. p. 291.

98. Ibid. p. 264.

99. Ibid. p. 277.

100. Ibid. p. 277.
101. Ibid. p. 295.
102. Ibid. p. 298.
103. Ibid. p. 298. The king's proclamation serves the same function as the common law principle that "ignorance of the law is no excuse" for committing a crime (or *ignorantia legis neminem excusat*).
104. Ibid. p. 299.
105. The real-world implications of nonsensical fairy tale logic resulting in unjust punishment has been more broadly discussed in the context of *Alice in Wonderland*. Many scholars agree that the character of the Queen of Hearts should be read as Queen Victoria. Jussawalla, *The Red King's Dream*, *Alice Companion*, and *New Horizons* (book review), p. 160 (citing Jones & Gladstone and Stoffel). Parker B. Potter has even traced the frequent judicial references to her famous declaration "Sentence first—verdict afterwards!" (generally by appellate courts identifying procedural injustice in the courts below). Florence Becker Lennon acerbically observed that

> the immaturity of the three queens in the *Alice* books in no way slandered England's Queen. Even in her old age, she never progressed in ethics or statesmanship beyond the notion of personal virtue her governess had taught her in childhood.

Lennon, *Life of Lewis Carroll*, p. 11. While a more thorough treatment of the law of *Alice in Wonderland* is beyond the scope of this chapter, the intertextualities between Carroll's and MacDonald's work are so clear that it is impossible to avoid the echoes of the Queen of Hearts in this scene. Interestingly, the Queen's overly punitive application of law in that text—against the Knave of Hearts, her courtiers, and the child Alice herself—was likewise mitigated by the royal pardon of the King of Hearts.
106. MacDonald, *Complete Fairy Tales*, p. 299.
107. Ibid. p. 300.
108. Ibid. p. 262.
109. Kingsley, "Natural Theology," p. 320.
110. Ibid. p. 320.
111. As Darwin described Kingsley's impression,

> A celebrated author and divine has written to me that "he has gradually learnt to see that it is just as noble a conception of the Deity to believe that He created a few original forms capable of self-development into other and needful forms, as to believe that He required a fresh act of creation to supply the voids caused by the action of His laws."

Darwin, *Origin of Species*, p. 481.

112. Gillian Beer has discussed Kingsley's use of Darwinian theories in the novel, particularly Darwin's challenge to Malthus's theories on the deleterious effects of overpopulation. Like Darwin, Beer argues, Kingsley presents biological profusion as a positive phenomenon, and she notes that Kingsley "grasped much of what was fresh in Darwin's ideas while at the same time retaining a creationist view of experience." Beer, *Darwin's Plots*, p. 138. John Hawley has explored Kingsley's attempts to reconcile the claims of Christianity with those of science, arguing that Kingsley, "in choosing the commitment of faith of strict empiricism . . . became for many, in an age of increasing dichotomy between the realms of science and religion, a model of a Christian who hoped that the truths of both would ultimately coalesce." Hawley, "Kingsley and the Book of Nature," p. 479. Earlier, Arthur Johnston also explored the role of science in *The Water-Babies*. Johnston, "Kingsley's Debt to Darwin," pp. 215–19.

113. Immel, Knoepflmacher & Briggs, "Fantasy's Alternative Geography," p. 231.

114. Petch, "Law, Equity, and Conscience," p. 131.

115. Symons, "On Juvenile Crime," p. 85.

116. Ibid. p. 85.

117. Ibid. pp. 86–7.

118. Ibid. p. 87.

119. Ibid.

120. Foucault, "Discipline and Punish," p. 1638.

121. The name "Grimes" may be a reference to the servant of the thuggish Tyrell in William Godwin's *Caleb Williams* (1794). In this text Godwin's protagonist repeatedly scorns the Burkean conception of the rule of law and the rights of Englishmen in the face of actual criminal procedures which reflect only the distribution of political power, not legal reasoning.

122. Kingsley, *Water-Babies*, p. 2.

123. Foucault, "Discipline and Punish," p. 1643.

124. Kingsley, *Water-Babies*, p. 2.

125. Ibid. pp. 2–3.

126. Ibid. p. 2.

127. Ibid. p. 3.

128. Ibid. p. 25.

129. Ibid. p. 30.

130. Ibid. p. 30.

131. Ibid. p. 35.

132. Ibid. p. 35.

133. Ibid. p. 61.

134. Ibid. p. 113. From *The Fiftieth Birthday of Aggasiz* (1857).

135. Kingsley, *Water-Babies*, p. 109.

136. 25 & 26 Vict. c. 18, s. 2.

137. Kingsley, *Water-Babies*, p. 128.
138. Ibid. p. 130.
139. Ibid. p. 47.
140. For all of his belief in natural selection as a manifestation of God's will, Kingsley's conception of absolute moral "right and wrong" did not stop at the edge of the woods; even animals acting according to physical natural law, he argued, were capable of violating moral law by committing acts that would be criminal for human beings, despite their asymmetrical exclusion from Salvation and inability to make godly laws of their own or be bound by human positive law. In response to a letter from a man who had watched his friend be consumed by a tiger, Kingsley said of the killing:

> a wrong and a crime I believe it to be, and one which God knows how to avenge and to correct when man cannot. Somehow—for He has ways of which we poor mortals do not dream—at the hand of every beast will He require the blood of man.

Kingsley, "Capital Punishment" pp. 54–5. *The Water-Babies* contains episodes, such as this one with the otter, in which animals are judged by this moral natural law of right and wrong, yet Kingsley never reconciles these moments with the numerous other instances in which he seems to endorse the view of "nature red in tooth and claw" as a necessary feature of God's system of selection.
141. Kingsley, *Water-Babies*, p. 122.
142. Ibid. p. 122.
143. Jacob, *Every Man His Own Lawyer*, p. 549.
144. Hamburger, *Law and Judicial Duty*, p. 105.
145. Symons, "On Juvenile Crime," p. 86.
146. Kingsley, *Water-Babies*, p. 14.
147. Ibid. p. 80.
148. Ibid. p. 87. Possibly an allusion to Coleridge's *The Rime of the Ancient Mariner*, suggesting magical retribution:

> Beyond the shadow of the ship,
> I watched the water-snakes:
> They moved in tracks of shining white,
> And when they reared, the elfish light
> Fell off in hoary flakes.

149. Kingsley, *Water-Babies*, pp. 148–9.
150. Ibid. p. 92. This doctrine, *ignorantia juris non excusat*, is of ancient application in both common and civil law countries in the criminal context.
151. Ibid. p. 92.
152. Ibid. p. 94.

153. Ibid. p. 100.

154. Ibid. p. 100. The use of fright to force confession suggests the procedures of the Inquisition which, coupled with the elements of anti-Catholicism throughout the rest of the text, serves here as a latent counterpoint against which "good British law" can be defined.

155. Ibid. p. 100.

156. This observation raises a new question: does romanticizing, through fairy tale, the cycle of child crime, punishment, and pardon run the risk of encouraging error by suggesting that magical reversal is always available? Such questions —raised by critics of fantasy such as Maria Edgeworth—reflect the serious concern raised by the judge in York's case: the dangers of children being able to commit serious crimes "with impunity."

157. Said defines "Orientalism" as "a way of coming to terms with the Orient that is based on the Orient's special place in European Western experience" and argues that "the Orient has helped to define Europe (or the West) as its contrasting idea, image, personality, experience." Said, *Orientalism*, pp. 3–4.

158. Hill, "Practical Suggestions," p. 2.

159. Goodrich, "Antirrhesis," p. 83.

160. Muriel Whitaker has discussed Dickens's account of Pip's upbringing as an allusion to the Puritan tradition, diametrically opposed to the Romantic notion of childhood, which held that the child was stained with sin and capable of being damned to hell even prior to the age of reason, Whitaker, "The Proper Bringing Up," p. 152.

161. By contrast, Jack P. Rawlins has argued that *Great Expectations* should be read as a failed attempt by Dickens to "dream a healthy relationship with the child within him," noting that the text begins with Pip "methodically wronged by the adult world around him" but ending with him "as the single unforgiven source of it." Rawlins, "Great Expiations," p. 668.

162. Dickens, *Great Expectations*, p. 105.

163. Ibid. p. 105.

164. Ibid. p. 21.

165. Ibid. p. 120.

166. The phrase "brought up by hand" appears literally to indicate that a child has been brought up on the bottle rather than breast-fed; C. J. P. Beatty has sourced the expression as coming from an eighteenth-century medical text called *A Treatise on the Diseases of Children, with Directions for the Management of Infants from the Birth; especially such as are brought up by Hand* (J. Mathews, London, 1784). Beatty, "Probable Source," p. 315.

167. Dickens, *Great Expectations*, p. 65.

168. Ibid. p. 70.

169. Ibid. p. 97.

170. Ibid. p. 90. Brontë's Jane Eyre, discussed at length in the next chapter, under-goes a nearly identical—and identically traumatic—punishment during her school days at Lowood.
171. Ibid. p. 184.
172. Barr, "Mourning Becomes David," p. 65.
173. For the most comprehensive work on Dickens's use of the fairy tale see Stone, *Dickens and the Invisible World*.
174. Dickens, *David Copperfield*, p. 212.
175. Ibid. p. 226.
176. Ibid. p. 214.
177. Ibid. p. 214.
178. Ibid. p. 212.
179. Ibid. p. 215.

Part III

The Rape Victim as Evidence

4

The Rape Novel and Reputation Evidence

Rape is the paradigmatic individual trauma. It is a total bodily violation that, unlike murder, is typically survived, leaving the victim with long-term psychological disruption. But, unlike more publicly accessible events like an assault with its visible wounds, rape fades into the realm of the private due both to the inarticulate nature of the wounds it leaves and the evidentiary and definitional challenges to proving it happened at all. One thread of cultural trauma theory shows how individual trauma may never become cultural trauma unless it is discursively acknowledged as such.[1] While even our twenty-first-century society struggles to fully recognize rape trauma, eighteenth-century society was particularly unlikely to acknowledge it unless the "prosecutrix" fit a particular formal common-law definition of a truth-telling victim. If we search for the eighteenth-century rape victim in the common law memory, we find her[2] primarily in the rules of evidence that gave her formal existence. This chapter will consider how those rules themselves, challenged by new literary conceptions of character, gradually became a form of chronic trauma in the common law imagination.

According to the common law rule, as understood in the eighteenth century, an alleged victim's "positive Oath of a Rape, without concurring circumstances, is seldom credited."[3] As Blackstone somewhat more decorously put it, "the party ravished may give evidence upon oath . . . but the credibility of her testimony, and how far forth she is to be believed, must be left to the jury upon the circumstances of fact that concur in that testimony."[4] Specifically:

> [I]f the witness be of good fame; if she presently discovered the offense and made search for the offender . . . these and the like are concurring circumstances, which give greater probability to her evidence. But, on the other side, if she be of evil fame . . . if she concealed the injury for any considerable time after she had the opportunity to complain . . . these and the like circumstances carry a strong, but not conclusive, presumption that her testimony is false or feigned.[5]

In other words, a victim's account of a rape was insufficient in and of itself to meet the Crown's evidentiary burden of proof. But her good or evil "fame"— the subjective narratives created about her in public discourse—could either elevate her account to the realm of legal truth or relegate it to that of falsehood. It is therefore unsurprising that eighteenth-century rape prosecutions, even more so than today's, took the form of dual trials: of both the defendant and the victim. Yet this evidentiary emphasis on a rape victim's public "fame" seems incompatible with the purported goal of legal adjudication: the search for external fact with deliberate blindness to the role of perception in creating it.

Through its unique capacity to depict subjectivity, fiction dramatizes these epistemological problems of perception. Jan-Melissa Schramm argues that "an analysis of the relationship between evidence and the generation of assent in courts of law and in acts of reading must examine the role of eye-witnesses in the reporting of an 'event.'"[6] For Schramm, the key question in comparing these two genres is whether an eyewitness's act of perception creates meaning or whether meaning "resides in fact external to the witness."[7] Schramm demonstrates how, in eighteenth- and nineteenth-century fiction, this contingent aspect of testimony serves most frequently as proof of a defendant's innocence. The novel form has similar exonerative possibilities for victim testimony, through its ability to discredit public perception as an objective proxy for factual information about a victim's character. It deploys narrative against the objective evidentiary presumptions that would define away a rapist's crimes against certain victims.

The eighteenth century saw a general explosion in interest in individual character as an aesthetic topic, one that has been assumed to relate to the rise of the sentimental novel and the so-called "inward turn" of the British reader.[8] In the standard account, over the course of the eighteenth century, the personal became an increasingly more valued subject for literary exploration, as opposed to the formerly popular externalized narratives about great events and public life.[9] Yet historians such as William Robertson and Edward Gibbon likewise deployed character as a lens for explaining historical events: an acknowledged role of the late-eighteenth-century British historian was "to unmask and penetrate the natural temper of an individual and infer motives from the individual's public and private actions."[10] The concept of individual character was thus culturally important not only to novelists depicting personal consciousness, but as "a source of evidence to which the historian could appeal in his interpretation of motivating forces such as zeal, interest, resentment, intrepidity, and impetuosity."[11] The historiographic role of character, therefore, parallels its evidentiary relationship to external fact in the legal context. Under certain circumstances, the common law rules of evidence treat natural character as relevant proof of a party's motive for acting. Yet in law as in history—as Neil Hargraves notes of Gibbon's treatment of human character released from the bounds of feudalism—character promises to "harmonize the internal and the public . . . constantly undergoing redefinition and adjustment."[12] In the eighteenth century, then, at the same time the aesthetic depiction of individual character was enjoying a century-long cultural ferment as evidence of particularity, it remained a vehicle for narratizing public and communal events.

This chapter will discuss the specific interaction between literary and legal narratives about rape victim character during the eighteenth and early nineteenth centuries. I begin with a short survey of the development of rape jurisprudence and the evidentiary relevance of victim reputation to proof of rape under the common law through the mid-1700s. I then move on to demonstrate the centrality of victim reputation evidence to Samuel Richardson's seminal rape novel *Clarissa* (1748) and its critical responses. I argue that Richardson challenged the prevailing legal understanding by depicting both the discursive contingency of his heroine's character and the frequent contradictions between evidence of particular facts about Clarissa and her "general" reputation. The decades of eighteenth-century discourse about Clarissa's character contributed to a long cultural memory of uncertainty about what constitutes an "innocent" victim who can be said to be legally susceptible to being raped. Yet I also suggest that the somewhat polarized public response to the text and its protagonist demonstrate the power of the monolithic legal conception of character and anxieties over its disruption. Finally, I show how early nineteenth-century jurisprudence on the relevance and proof of victim character in rape trials reveals ongoing common law anxiety over the relative importance of public perception and specific facts in legally recognizing the factual trauma of rape.

A History of English Rape

In medieval England, rape was taken seriously, yet a woman's sexuality was conceived as the property of her male guardian, who could lose it if he failed to defend it adequately.[13] In *Lancelot, the Knight of the Cart* (1175–1181), Chrètien de Troyes depicts knightly codes of chivalry as forbidding sexual assault on a woman traveling alone, yet allowing a knight who defeats a woman's traveling companion to have his way with her.[14] While Malory takes a more progressive view, adding to the oath of the Round Table the vow to "strengthen [women] in their rights and never to enforce them, upon pain of death," he was jailed twice for rape.[15] Chaucer also depicts rape as a significant offense in "The Wife of Bath's Tale," where Guinevere and her ladies sit in judgment of a knight who casually rapes a maiden, imposing the death sentence should he fail, within a year, to answer the question of what women want. Caroline Dunn notes that the medieval religious tradition casts woman into Eve's role of sexual temptress: "women could hope to change their behavior and follow the model of the converted prostitute Mary Magdalene, but their fundamental nature, according to many male theorists, remained unchanged and susceptible to sex."[16] It was during the medieval period that medical writers developed the fallacy that forcible sex could not result in pregnancy, a belief that would haunt rape jurisprudence for centuries.[17]

In the early medieval period, the rapists of virgins were most frequently prosecuted, both because the crimes were somewhat easier to prove medically and because the theft of a woman's "treasure" was considered the most serious form of the offense.[18] In that era, one could say that the victim's prior character for chastity was functionally an element of the offense. By the fourteenth and fifteenth centuries, however, the number of reported victims who were wives or widows came to outnumber the cases of deflowering.[19] The Crown did not prosecute rape until the thirteenth century; before that, the only recourse was for the victim to prosecute by private appeal with the county court, as was common for a wide range of crimes. This era solidified the evidentiary requirement that the victim raise an alarm immediately after the event and document it by showing her physical injuries or torn clothing to the bailiff or county coroner.[20] Rape appeals, like all others, required pleadings using highly specific language. As Dunn notes, "Rape narratives, like other legal texts, are highly formulaic . . . and the Latin record is probably far removed from the words uttered by the rape victim when she first reported the assault."[21] Due to the use of scribes as intermediaries, medieval rape narratives "hardly provide modern scholars with an accurate rendering of the medieval female voice."[22] Even once the possibility of indictment by the Crown became available, however, the use of appeals by rape victims remained steady across the fourteenth and fifteenth centuries.

Punishments for rape consequent to these private appeals were severe, usually death or castration. Thirteenth-century jurist Henry de Bracton cited mutilation as the appropriate punishment, urging that:

> There must be member for member, for when a virgin is defiled she loses her member and therefore let her defiler be punished in the parts in which he offended. Let him thus lose his eyes which gave him sight of the maiden's beauty for which he coveted her. And let him lose as well the testicles which excited his hot lust.[23]

In 1275 Edward I's Statute of Westminster created the possibility of prosecution by the Crown and specified two years' imprisonment plus fines as punishment in such cases. However, the statute also explicitly preserved the victim's "common right" to prosecute her appeal and indeed extended the period during which she could bring it to forty days, thus codifying and facilitating the traditional punishment of death or mutilation. (This double system of enforcement makes particular sense when taking into account the lack of any formal prison system during this period; the Crown's prescribed means of punishment could not be used widely.) The Statute also took care to specify that it applied not only to virgin victims, mandating that "none do ravish, nor take away for Force, any Maiden within Age . . . nor any Wife or Maiden of full Age, nor any other Woman against her Will."[24]

This rape statute came to occupy an interesting and conflicted place in the legal imagination all the way into the nineteenth century. While Matthew Hale correctly summarized in his 1736 *History* how the public and private remedies worked together[25]—a view echoed in the Victorian age by Pollock and Maitland[26]—sixteenth-century commentator Sir William Straundforde appears to have introduced a competing, and incorrect, understanding into the history of the common law in his *Les Plees del Coron* (1557). Straundforde, believing the two-year sentence to be the sole remedy remaining after the legislation, says

> Edward I . . . seems through the law made at Westminster I to have relaxed this penalty. And then, in view of the outrages which followed the said law, at his next Parliament held at Westminster . . . the offence of rape ceased to be a felony.[27]

William Hawkins absorbed this history into his *Pleas of the Crown* (1716), adding that "the smallness of the punishment prov[ed] a great encouragement to the offence."[28] Blackstone and early eighteenth-century treatise-writer Edward Hyde East adopted this interpretation too, and by the nineteenth century William Oldnall Russell was concluding that "this lenity . . . is said to have been productive of terrible consequences."[29] As Bruce MacFarlane notes, however, none of these authors explained what these consequences were or cited any authorities for the proposition.[30] The commentators' amorphous general dismay over under-prosecution contrasts sharply with the skeptical attitudes toward individual victim accounts evinced by the actual common law rules with which this chapter opened. This contradictory discursive framework allowed rape to be, at once, constructed in the cultural memory as an unenforceable crime of horrible violence and yet vanish into impossibility when claimed by a non-ideal, corporeal female body.

The confusion over this issue could relate to the fact that, perhaps due in part to the severity of the punishments, conviction rates were extremely low; while the scarcity of records makes it difficult to know for certain, most studies during the time period have found 0 to 20% of cases in their samples ending in conviction.[31] Importantly, however, even in cases without official judicial sanction, the defendant might suffer other community sanctions such as being outlawed or forced to marry his victim. Dunn notes that "a woman who won her claim received no recompense other than personal satisfaction that justice was served, as the convicted offender's chattels were forfeited to the Crown, not her," and that therefore both parties may have had an incentive to settle the matter out of court.[32]

In any case, between the Statute of Westminster and the late seventeenth century, very little evolution in legal thinking about rape specifically or criminal law generally took place, in part due to the idea that Edward I's legislative innovations had become fixed and permanent.[33] In the eighteenth and nineteenth centuries, however, the common law of rape and its proofs developed substantially. Two elements of proof interact most significantly with the introduction of literary subjectivity in the eighteenth century and warrant particular attention. The first is the requirement that a rape be accomplished "by force," an element upon which most of the great treatise writers, save Hale, were unanimous.[34] The second is the primary topic of this chapter: the relevance of the sexual character of the victim to both the issue of consent and her general testimonial veracity. Because the two are somewhat interrelated, we will briefly consider the legal basis for each element.

Force

With respect to the question of force, some courts required a showing of the victim's active resistance before they would deem a rape to have been committed. Gregory Durston has noted that—in part due to the increased prevalence of extra-marital intercourse in the eighteenth century (in contrast to prior centuries prior and the subsequent Victorian era)—courts were chary of imposing a capital sentence for what was, in reality, a "seduction." Yet of course the definition of seduction was itself highly malleable. One witness in another man's rape trial, Henry Williams, testifies that he would never force a woman to have sexual relations "otherwise than by talking her over, and making her drink, as a Man must always do in such Cases; for you know a Woman must be coax'd a little, though she's never so willing."[35] From a legal standpoint, it became the woman's responsibility to repel all such attempts at "coaxing."

On the basis of lack of evidence of force, courts overturned or declined to hand over for prosecution cases with facts that would shock a contemporary audience: for example, the case of a woman who explained that she failed to resist because she was paralyzed with fear,[36] and a case in which a twelve-year-old workhouse inmate raped by her father said she had not objected because "he said if I did he would never come and see me anymore."[37] As one nineteenth-century court put it,

The resistance must be up to the point of being overpowered by actual force, or of inability, from loss of strength, longer to resist, or, from the number of persons attacking, resistance must be dangerous or absolutely useless, or there must be dread or fear of death.[38]

At the heart of this legal premise lay a gross medical misunderstanding, that rape was not physically possible without consent. In *The Elements of Medical Jurisprudence* (1787) physician Samuel Farr (ostensibly adapting the 1767 treatise of a Swiss professor, as "nothing of the kind had ever been published in this country") says that while attempted rape might be possible:

> [T]he consummation of a rape, by which is meant a compleat, full, and entire coition, which is made without any consent or permission of the woman, seems to be impossible, unless some very extraordinary circumstance occur: for a woman always possesses sufficient power, by drawing back her limbs, and by the force of her hands, to prevent the insertion of the penis into her body, whilst she can keep her resolution entire.[39]

Almost a hundred years later, celebrated nineteenth-century gynecologist Dr. Lawson Tait remained "perfectly satisfied that no man can effect a felonious purpose on a woman in possession of her senses without her consent" because, after all, "you cannot thread a moving needle."[40] Another related medical myth likewise helped shape the definition and proof of rape: the idea that conception is only possible when sexual intercourse is accompanied by desire.[41] As Farr writes, "without the enjoyment of pleasure in the venereal act no conception can probably take place."[42] Due in part to the precedent-based nature of common law jurisprudence (combined with judges' lack of scientific training), this bit of folklore can be traced from its medieval beginnings through this nineteenth-century incarnation, and even into the political rhetoric of today.[43]

The evidentiary importance of force to the possibility of a rape can be traced not only in the treatises and case law, but through the narrative accounts eighteenth-century victims gave on the stand, which seem to share an emphasis not only on resistance but on resistance to the point where it became physically impossible to continue. In *Lidwell's Trial*, discussed at length later on, the prosecutor took care to ask the victim Sarah Sutton if she had "given him any resistance," to which she replied, "as long as my strength would enable me."[44] Complainant Ann Cooper, also discussed further below, goes into more explicit detail about her struggles, testifying that:

> [S]he was down upon the ground striving, and crying out till she was almost dead; that she still resisting and crying out, he hit her several blows on the face, stopped her mouth, held her by the throat; and she at last recovering

herself upon her knees, though quite spent with striving and crying out, he flung her across a low table and did lie with her there, [the rapist's accomplice] all the while holding the door on the outside.[45]

And, casting doubt on the character of the alleged victim, the editor of the account of Captain Hugh Leeson's rape trial notes, "[I]t is very natural for her Sex to exert themselves in their own Defence when Violence is done contrary to their Inclinations, and to leave some Marks of their Displeasure upon the Persons that Attack them."[46] From these examples, we see that the story of a "compleat" rape was entirely one-dimensional; as a definitional matter rape slips away into consent the moment the woman stops struggling to her utmost.

Character

A victim's character became important to a rape prosecution for two different reasons. Her character for truthfulness was relevant in the same way it was (and is) for all witnesses generally and was, therefore, an issue simply because she was testifying.[47] The separate question of her character for chastity was also relevant to the specific factual question of consent.[48] As a nineteenth-century American opinion so memorably asked, "will you not more readily infer assent in the practiced Messalina, in loose attire, than in the reserved and virtuous Lucretia?"[49] The basic assumption was that a woman who had consented to one man was more likely to have consented to any other man. The court here uses classical imagery to construct the well-worn Madonna/whore dichotomy: under the common laws of evidence, a woman who is neither a paragon of virtue nor of sin is narratively impossible. Some cases took it still further, with courts allowing—in rape cases and beyond—character evidence about a woman's sexual "looseness" to impeach her character for truthfulness as a witness, where they would not allow it for a man. Another American court sums this up:

> It is a matter of common knowledge that the bad character of a man for chastity does not even in the remotest degree affect his character for truth, when based upon that alone, while it does that of a woman.[50]

(The idea that a man's "bad character for chastity" was a subject for amusement, as opposed to the condemnation required by a woman's, will be explored below.)

The means by which the common law allows character evidence to be given in general sits in awkward tension with the hearsay bar preventing a witness from testifying to facts outside of his or her direct knowledge. Witnesses —character witnesses or otherwise—are generally barred from speaking to facts another person has told them.[51] Yet under the English common law, character witnesses may only testify to the party's reputation for the relevant aspect of character (whether it be truthfulness or, in the case of a rape victim, chastity). They may not give evidence as to specific facts demonstrating a party's character. The paradox of this evidentiary practice should be obvious: while ostensibly barring testimony about facts the witness has heard from others, the evidentiary rules invite testimony on a generalized communal narrative about the individual whose character is in question. In other words, a witness need have no personal experience with the party's character, only membership in a community that has exposed him or her to a collective view of the party's reputation for that character. This practice invites a kind of collective hearsay premised on the idea that, while testifying to the information given by a third-party individual may be unreliable, testifying to information derived from a communal narrative, expressed clearly enough that the witness has become aware of it, is likely to be probative.

In the case of alleged rape victims in the eighteenth century, the archive demonstrates both how an individual's testimony could channel communal narratives about a victim's sexuality inside the courtroom during a specific trial and the way published accounts of these trials actively attempted to contribute to the legally significant communal reputation of an alleged victim outside the courtroom. The relationship between commercially consumable texts and legal reputation mirrors, in this way, the role of the adultery compendiums which Chapter 1 described as serving self-consciously punitive functions. Here, because the published accounts of rape trials and the character of victims presented therein necessarily contributed to a rape victim's reputation for either chastity or promiscuity, they took on a legal function in and of themselves.

As an example of the first function, the rape trial of Jacob Wykes and John Johnson, summarized in a collection of criminal trials called *The Bloody Register* (1764), is representative. Ann Porter accuses Wykes, the inn-keeper of the Glebe Tavern on Drury Lane, of raping her with the assistance of Johnson while she was waiting for his porter to dispatch a letter she had brought for a resident who was not in at the time. In addition to Porter's account, several witnesses testify on her behalf. Her landlord testifies that

> when she came home her gown was torn, all the sleeve off, her apron and
> her smock torn, her arm black and blue; that she told him she had been
> used by the prisoner as before declared, and that he threatened if she made
> a noise he would murder her.[52]

In his defense, Wykes himself says that Porter had consumed two half-pints of wine while waiting for the response to her letter and then left quietly; he testifies that his wife was present during the entire time the rape allegedly occurred, but he does not produce her as a witness. The account of the trial given by the *Bloody Register* suggests that the remaining substance is devoted to Porter's character. Her landlord gives opinion evidence about her chastity, based on his personal experience of her five-month stay with him:

> [S]he had lodged with him five months, had always behaved herself very modestly, and he never knew anything to the contrary; that had she been otherwise she should never have come into his house; that she always kept very good hours, had no company resorted to her, worked very industriously at her needle, and as he had been informed, had a husband at sea, who sent her sometimes ten pounds, sometimes thirty pounds at a time.[53]

In contrast to the specificity of the landlord's opinion evidence, Wykes produces a group of character witnesses to give reputation evidence against Porter. (Daniel Singleton, a bailiff, also provides one piece of first-hand evidence, upon which he bases his opinion of her immorality, that once, when she had employed him and his partner to arrest someone for impregnating her, she had "took his hand and put the middle finger of his right hand to her body, and directed him, &c.")[54]

Beyond that statement from Singleton, however, this group of witnesses serves primarily to refract narratives generated by an assumed community beyond the courtroom. Singleton adds that "by relation she had ruined half a hundred families."[55] A Mr. Jennings testifies that

> she made it her business (as they call it) to trap people by pretending to be with child by them, be ravished, &c, that he thought there was not so notorious a woman upon the face of the whole earth.[56]

Jennings only names one such person, "Mr. Butler, a gentleman in the Fleet," but adds that Mr. Butler himself "had produced no less than thirty-seven evidences against her."[57] Finally, an unnamed officer of the court testifies that Porter is "the oldest bite, and oldest whore in town, that she had ruined several that he knew."[58] Regardless of whether there is any underlying truth to these claims—it is impossible to be certain from our vantage point—they are significant in the extent to which they intentionally admit hyperbole into the realm of legal truth. While it is unlikely that her notoriety exceeded that of anyone else on earth, or even that she had been involved in scandals with fifty different married men, it is nonetheless legally relevant that such was her reputation: by this process, fiction becomes formally reified into legally relevant fact. We don't know who these half-hundred families are, or the nature of the thirty-seven other pieces of evidence. But the three witnesses in the courtroom stand in for a whole universe of facticity that slips away from direct scrutiny. After this evidence, Porter herself testifies "she was as innocent of all as an Angel in Heaven," thereby responding to hyperbolized narrative with one of her own (and also, of course, shifting the question of guilt or innocence from the actual defendant to herself).[59] In the end, the jury acquits Wykes and Johnson.

The zero-sum relationship between the defendant's and victim's morality implicit in these competing hyperboles is driven by the dichotomous Madonna/whore cultural narrative of feminine sexuality described earlier: it is not enough for the victim to be telling the truth about the specific incident; she must be either an "Angel in Heaven" or the most "notorious woman in the world." But it should also be at least noted in passing that, in the judicial context, the popularity of this dichotomy can be explained by the psychological literature on how juries receive evidence. In seminal research conducted in the 1980s and 1990s, Janet Pennington and Reid Hastie found that juries do not simply evaluate whether individual pieces of evidence, when taken together, meet the requisite burden of proof. Rather, they look to the two competing stories offered by each side and determine which is the most internally, narratively coherent.[60] If one understands this fact at an empirical level, the increased importance of the Madonna/whore dichotomy becomes clear. In the absence—so common in rape cases even in our modern era—of physical evidence, the work done by background cultural narratives to fill in the dots becomes disproportionately important. It is simply a more coherent narrative for the victim to be Lucretia or Melassina, rather than any shade of grey in between.

It should also, of course, be observed that much of the hyperbole recounted in the published compendium could be the poetic license of the transcriber or editor. Yet this potential for paraphrasing brings us exactly to the secondary legal function noted above: the role of cultural texts about rape victims and rapists in constructing a person's all-important, legally-recognized reputation. In other words, the relationship between reputation evidence given on the stand, its translation into the culture through texts such as the *Bloody Register*, and its reconstitution back into legal fact, is cyclical.

Consider, for example, the 1715 trial at the Old Bailey of Captain Hugh Leeson for the rape of Mrs. Mary May. It appears that Leeson and Mary's husband were imprisoned in the same debtor's prison, where Leeson continued to reside after his debts were already discharged. On the day in question, May alleged that Leeson raped her in an upstairs room.[61] In his defense, Leeson accused May of seeking his death in retribution for his rejecting her sexual advances. Leeson was convicted and sentenced to death but subsequently pardoned by the Crown due, it seems, to a combination of his connections at Court[62] and the general reluctance, mentioned earlier as a possible explanation for jury acquittals, to impose capital punishment in these cases, in the absence of milder alternatives.

After these events, Leeson had published—ostensibly through the assistance of an anonymous "friend" who mediated with the publisher—an account of the proceedings, intended to refashion his reputation. The text, *Captain Leeson's Case: Being an Account of his Tryal* (1715), opens similarly to the adultery compendiums, with dual punitive purposes: "As to the Jury, he leaves them to Publick Censure, and submits himself to the Judgment of all Gentlemen and others, from whom he promiseth himself a more favorable Sentence."[63] These two purposes—restaging his own trial in the public sphere and condemning the jury itself for un-law-like behavior—wind through the entire account and both turn on his theory of the misapplication of reputation evidence both for himself and against May.

With respect to the jury's alleged misconduct, his sole piece of direct evidence comes from a conversation his friend purportedly had with a juror who told him he "did not think it worthwhile" to differ with the rest of the jury who voted guilty "because he knew the Gentlemen had such an Interest in Court, that he would not die for it."[64] Leeson uses this fact to situate his self-rehabilitating narrative in the context of a general tradition of English legal exceptionalism: by lamenting his jury's departure from "the Honour and Regard to Truth, which is generally professed by English Juries."[65] The text rests its assumption that the jury's verdict was not only wrong but grossly irresponsible almost entirely on character evidence, seen as a zero-sum dichotomy between the Captain's impeccable morality and May's. The account concedes that May had a number of character witnesses in her favor but points out that "there were other Witnesses, who said she was a Woman of a Scandalous Life, and one Swore he heard her Husband tax her with Clapping him,"[66] testimony later recharacterized as "undeniable Proofs brought in against [May] by undeniable Witnesses of a continued pursuit of Evil Courses in a Libidinous way of Life."[67] By contrast, Leeson's witnesses swore to "his Conduct . . . almost from his Cradle to that very time, to be Honourable and Praiseworthy."[68] In line with the false logical dichotomy implicit in these hyperboles, the text likewise portrays the verdict as a categorical refutation of all of the defense's witnesses who, "notwithstanding they had good Characters given of them likewise, were of no manner of use to [the jury], and might as well have stay'd away as appear'd in Court, as this Verdict implies."[69] The assumption that belief in any aspect of Leeson's character witnesses' testimony must result in an acquittal, such that a conviction compels the conclusion that they were of no use to the Jury at all, rests on the conception that the communal narrative embodied in reputation evidence about chastity is more probative of the truth of the matter than testimony about the specific incident in question. This weight of reputational history on the construction of legal truth will be seen in the literary texts explored later in this chapter.

As promised in the introductory language, the Leeson text invites the public to perform a jury function, by collecting the evidence the actual jury had not found sufficient to overcome the evidence against him. The account given is not presented in pure narrative form but in the conventional structure of legal logic known as "arguing in the alternative." After presenting the primary argument that Leeson's reputational narrative should trump May's, he moves on to present two additional theories of the case, each sufficient to exonerate but inconsistent with one another. The first is that had Leeson, in fact, been "prone to it" Mary May would have been

> last in his thoughts as being old and disagreeable and no way capable of exciting anything like desire of enjoyment in a Man, who he might, without Vanity say, had in his Power to make Application, and not without Success, to those of her Sex that were more amiable and engaging.[70]

In other words, the virtuous Captain, upstanding since the cradle, seems confident of his ability to seduce high enough quality women to render it unnecessary to rape an unattractive one. The third option the text presents is that "if she was known Carnally, which the Person condemn'd altogether denies, that knowledge must have been obtain'd by her own consent."[71] The argument here is that Mary May's behavior was so flirtatious that Leeson could have had relations with her by consent. With its three alternate lines of argument, the text replicates the same slippage between legal and factual truth that occurs whenever adjudication produces a verdict through formal evidentiary channels. The disparity between each of these independently coherent narratives reveals the spaces in which ambiguities and subjectivities reside; always a problem in legal fact-finding generally, but heightened in the context of rape, with its particular evidentiary challenges.[72]

In any case, the legal function of the Leeson account extends beyond merely his second judgment in the public sphere. It is part of a series of similar published accounts of rape trials in which the victim—as implied about both Porter and May—has allegedly set up the defendant for hanging, usually in an attempt to extort money or in retribution for being scorned by him. *The Boarding-School Rape* (1704) summarizes the trial of the mother and uncle of a pre-adolescent girl who testifies that they forced her to accuse the plaintiff of rape, in the hopes of being bought off. *The Case of Lord Drummond in Relation to a Rape* (1715) attempts the same character-clearing function as the Leeson account, although in this case after a dismissal as opposed to a conviction. This account, subtitled to clarify that the alleged victim, Elizabeth

Galloway, was "a common prostitute," opens with an expression of outrage that rapes must be prosecuted and judged in the first place, when the comparative moral reputations of the parties are so clear:

> The Nature of Rape is so very perplex'd, and the perpetration of it on Adult Persons so very difficult, that it requires something of an implicit Belief to be credited; however, since our Laws enjoin those that sit in Judgment in such Cases to make their Determinations suitable to the Oaths given in before them, and the Verdict of the Jury, and we have frequent Instances of Persons lying under Sentence of Death for these Crimes, it may not be improper to submit an Account of as Black a Contrivance, as ever was set on Foot, against the Life of a Gentleman sprung from as good Blood as any in Scotland, to Readers Perusal, under Pretence of His endeavoring singly by Force to violate the Chastity of a Woman, whose Inclinations to Acts of Lewdness for some Years before, had made her incapable of any Struggles in Defence of her good Name or Reputation.[73]

This introduction encapsulates a number of the eighteenth-century cultural mythologies about rape—most notably the fact that its perpetration is physically "difficult," the idea that earlier "Acts of Lewdness" precluded a woman from being a victim, and the ever-present idea that a victim's "Defence" of her Reputation should be the central question in a rape adjudication. This account dramatizes its subject as part of a kind of epidemic of false rape accusations, the fear of which constituted a potential collective trauma in its own right. Here the author suggests that the plaintiff, a prostitute who had successfully brought a paternity suit against Lord Drummond but turned out subsequently not to have been pregnant, had been emboldened by "having heard of the Success which an Infamous Woman called Mary May had against Captain Leeson."[74] The end of the account features a postscript mentioning that, the same week as the Leeson case, a "well-practis'd Lady of the same Religious Hundreds of DRURY, likewise endeavor'd to do the same Thing by another Man of Quality."[75] (The Drummond account is also particularly interesting insofar as its political/historical context. Because Lord Drummond's father was, at the time, in France, supporting the cause of James II, the author accuses the justice of the peace of being particularly eager to arrest Lord Drummond "out of his Zeal for the Cause to grant one against the Son of a Lord who was avowedly in the Interest of the Pope, and the Pretender.")[76] These texts work together, then, to create a cultural narrative about false rape accusations which—by cross-referencing one another—likewise contribute to the reputation of the specific parties involved, not merely socially but potentially as a formal evidentiary matter in the event that the "infamous" Mary May ever testifies again in court.

Performing Rape in the Eighteenth Century

While the cases discussed in the previous section involve ostensibly factual accounts of real trials, they bleed into a general eighteenth-century discourse about rape, which playwrights theatricalized satirically. Scholars of seventeenth-century Restoration drama have explored the connection between fictional and actual rape during that era. Jean Marsden observes that the fascination with rape as a subject for theatrical spectacle coincided with the introduction of female performers in the seventeenth century, which allowed the male gaze to be deployed, in reality, across the third wall whenever a theatergoer observed a scene of ravishment.[77] Derek Hughes points out that the early years of the Restoration saw relatively few theatrical rapes despite the presence of female performers and argues, instead, that the eventual popularity of the subject came from the "unprecedently complex exploration of sexual behavior which was developing at this very time."[78]

Either way, by the eighteenth century, rape had become a common enough literary subject that Henry Fielding could use it frequently—for example, as both a plot device and metaphor for political corruption in the love comedy *Rape Upon Rape* (1730), in which the trial of a wrongly accused rape defendant provides occasion for Fielding to send up the corrupt judiciary. Susan Staves describes Fielding's use of attempted rape in his novels as "a natural topos of comedy" noting that his comedic novels such as *Joseph Andrews* (1742) and *Tom Jones* (1749) are rife with scenes of attempted sexual violence against women that never succeed.[79] Staves argues that this recurring theme reflects the underlying anxiety that—precisely due to the assiduous attempts of men in pursuit of female beauty—there would soon be no chaste women at all. She asks:

> What better way to ally masculine fears that no pure women remained than to repeat stories of solicitations of chastity proceeding all the way to violence, to show chastity tested not only by persuasion but also by more extreme assaults, and then to allay masculine anxiety by triumphant comic conclusions in which female chastity is preserved?[80]

Staves' observation provides an explanation for the tension between concerns about rape as a generalized threat to virtue and skepticism about the actual virtue of individual victims. Further, if she is correct, this suggests that even the figure of the genuine, honest rape victim could be co-opted to serve masculine needs.[81] The rape victim can thus be conceived as doubly violated—first bodily, by the rapist, and then rhetorically, by the rape discourse, which erases the trauma of the act and uses the victim for other purposes.

One of the most famous rape trials of the eighteenth century provides a perfect example of this double-objectification. Notorious rake Colonel Francis Charteris—nick-named "the Rape-Master General of England"—was convicted of the rape of his maid Ann Bond (and subsequently pardoned, though he died shortly thereafter, likely from a disease contracted while in prison). Unlike many of the defendants discussed in the previous section, Charteris could not present a defense premised on his own reputation for chastity as it was universally reviled—indeed, Bond testified that when she had been offered employment with him he had given an assumed name; once she discovered who her employer was she resolved to leave his service. His defense consisted of a colorful condemnation of her character, and particularly her sexual reputation in rural Lancashire, from whence she had come to London.

After his conviction, the Charteris trial inspired a wellspring of published accounts, satires, and poetry.[82] Most represented Charteris as a scoundrel and prime object for satire; William Hogarth, for example, included him in the series *The Harlot's Progress* (1732), depicting him in the background, masturbating, as the protagonist Moll is seduced into a life of prostitution by a procuress.[83] Hogarth himself made much of the fact that *The Harlot's Progress* and his other comic paintings were explicitly intended as "characters" as opposed to "caricatures": critics have observed that he wanted the same sort of recognition for depicting character as that received by authors such as DeFoe for their literary characters such as Moll Flanders.[84] Hogarth even created two engravings, *Characters and Caricatures* (1743) and *The Bench* (1758), to demonstrate the distinction between these modes of representation. That *The Bench* depicts, among its array of faces, a panel of bewigged judges suggests Hogarth's awareness of the legal valence to his chosen aesthetic mode.

In any case, despite the condemnation implicit in these literary depictions of the rapist's criminal character, they nonetheless—by centering the rapist himself as the subject for humor or contempt—transform the victim's character into a caricature. A popular print depicts Charteris in profile, standing at the bar with his thumbs tied together, accompanied by a poem:

> Blood!--must a colonel, with a lord's estate,
> Be thus obnoxious to a scoundrel's fate?
> Brought to the bar, and sentenc'd from the bench,
> Only for ravishing a country wench?
> Shall gentlemen receive no more respect?
> Shall their Diversions thus by Laws be check'd?
> Shall they b'accountable to Saucy Juries,
> For this or t'other pleasure? ---H__'ll & Furies!
> What man thro' Villainy would run a Course,

And ruin Families without remorse
To heap up Riches—if when all is done
An ignominious Death he cannot Shun?[85]

While the poem mocks the entitlement to sexual lawlessness associated not only with Charteris but with upper-class rapists generally, it nonetheless reduces Ann Bond herself to the character of "country wench"—satirically trivialized to convey Charteris' outrageous sense of entitlement, yet nonetheless invisible in the poem alongside concerns over Charteris as a figure of social destruction. Indeed an anonymous satirical epitaph to Charteris takes this point even farther. While mock-lauding the deceased because he, "with an inflexible constancy and inimitable uniformity of life, persisted in spite of age and infirmity, in the practice of every human vice," the author goes on to describe Charteris as

> the only person in his time who would cheat without the mask of honesty; who could retain his primeval meanness after being possessed of ten thousand pounds a year, and who having done every day of his life, something worthy of a gibbet, was once condemned to one for what he had not done.[86]

The author is preoccupied with Charteris' pecuniary vices—the victims of which were no doubt primarily his male trading partners—while actively disavowing his rape of Bond. As in Hogarth's print, in this epitaph, Charteris' sexual aggression renders him a figure for contempt and mockery, but in both cases, he has no victim. Moll, of course, was becoming a prostitute, whose consent was all but assumed as a legal matter.[87] And in proclaiming Charteris' innocence, the epitaph imputes—due, perhaps, to the persistent saint/sinner conception of feminine morality—a similar character to Bond. In any case, all of these texts elide Ann's point of view as a victim, rendering her an object —whether innocent or complicit—in the broader "Rape-Master" narrative.

This satirist's elision of Ann's bodily trauma from his comical depiction of Charteris' crime dramatizes a communicative problem with trials generally, one that is not unique to the eighteenth century. Elaine Scarry's work on the inexpressibility of physical pain is helpful to our understanding the limitations of the trial as a means of access to the truth of a rape victim's suffering, even today. As Scarry puts it, "when one hears about another person's physical pain, the events happening within the interior of that person's body may seem to have the remote character of some deep subterranean fact, belonging to an invisible geography that . . . has no reality."[88] I have argued elsewhere that a victim's testimony has the potential to invert—through speech—the "absence of world" (to use Scarry's term) she experiences at the hands of her assailant while in the throes of physical pain.[89] Yet the potential for this world recreation through communication is limited to the extent that it is channeled through the formal procedural engines of a trial. A prosecutor controls the presentation of the case against the defendant and determines the location and function of a victim's testimony with the effect of enhancing the articulation problem Scarry identifies.[90] (This diminishing of the rape victim's voice somewhat parallels the general absence, lamented by Caroline Norton, of the alleged adulteress's testimony from the crim-con prosecution of her lover by her husband.) The preceding pages show a similar problem at work in both the formal evidentiary procedures and social discourses—such as the saint/sinner dichotomy—through which rape accounts became legible in the early eighteenth century. Like one part of a spectacle on a stage, observable only from the removed vantage of the audience and driven by a higher, singular narrative purpose, the rape victim's voice is difficult to extricate from its context or treat as a proxy for the unobservable truth that is the trauma of sexual violation and violence. Specifically, old common-law evidentiary presumptions about victim character allowed socially-created victim reputation to alter the legally cognizable truth concerning the contested acts—an epistemological process that inflicts traumas of its own. In the next section, I will discuss how Samuel Richardson implicitly used the narrative subjectivity of the novel form to challenge the architecture of these evidentiary proofs.

Narrative Coherence and Clarissa's Reputation

In the first major English novel about rape, *Clarissa* (1748), Samuel Richardson uses an epistolary format and repeated emphasis on legalism to present his readers with what is, essentially, a question of legal fact-finding: based upon the various subjective pleadings in the form of letters by various characters, who is culpable for Clarissa's violation and death? Much excellent scholarship has focused on the power of the new novel form to probe one of the core eighteenth-century evidentiary principles mentioned above: the presumption of consent in the absence of force. Frances Ferguson has famously argued that Richardson illuminates the inherent problems with evidentiary law that would establish proof of consent by mistakenly equating epistemology with psychology.[91] In self-justifying his conduct, Lovelace "needs the formulae of consent . . . that would belie Clarissa's resistance and establish [despite her unconsciousness] that she was there" by continually framing "the rape that she did not consent to with the events that she did participate in—the elopement, residence in the same house."[92] Fundamentally the novel form allows the reader to follow Clarissa's subjective account of her protracted efforts to avoid the crisis of the rape, which culminates in her violation while unconscious. This chronology implodes the old common-law notion that consent is co-extensive with a lack of physical resistance—even when the victim has affirmatively consented to interactions shy of rape.

Several scholars have also read *Clarissa* in the historical context of eighteenth-century discourse about consent theory. As Gillian Brown observes, the plot in which a daughter must be compelled by her parents to marry against her will "evokes the republican rhetoric of violated filial rights that figured so urgently and effectively in American revolutionary politics."[93] Yet a legal and moral focus on consent posed problems for women in a world where their actual choices were circumscribed by law and culture. (Brown reads Hannah Foster's best-selling novel *The Coquette* (1797) as a depiction of "the perimeter within which female consent in eighteenth-century America operated" and a warning to women against engaging in "voluntary" coquetry due to its tendency to sustain those self-limitations.)[94] Sandra MacPherson discusses *Clarissa* as a contribution to the political debate surrounding the Marriage Act of 1753, which sought to prevent the abuses of clandestine marriages the validity of which, under canon law, turned primarily on the parties' easily-feigned consent, as opposed to formal, state-mandated processes such as licenses and the publishing of banns.[95] She argues that Richardson dramatizes the abuses of the old legal commitment to intentionalism and shows how Lovelace may believe himself protected in his dealings with Clarissa by the common law doctrine that "to one who is willing, no wrong is done."[96] The weight of this scholarship supports the significance of this new literary genre to challenging an objective assumption of the common law around a question of sexual violation.[97]

I argue that *Clarissa* likewise troubles the second evidentiary principle discussed above: the relevance of the victim's character to proof of rape. The multiple subjectivities of the epistolary format challenge the common law treatment of a rape victim's character as objectively knowable and absolute. The text also exposes the circularity of the particular common law rule admitting hearsay-like "general" reputation evidence while excluding testimony about specific facts. Specifically, Richardson shows the gap between immediate, individual points of view and public "fame," which we get only third-hand through reports from letter writers on conversations they had had with characters the reader never directly accesses. Clarissa's struggle to protect both her physical bodily integrity and her socially-constructed reputation demonstrates the epistemological incoherence of generalized reputation evidence serving as legal proof against rape. Ultimately, by dramatizing the separate and only partially overlapping realities of reputation and particular fact, Richardson calls into question the heightened legal relevance of the former in rape cases.

The novel is organized as a series of overlapping adjudications of the heroine's unfairly implied criminality; her orientation toward nearly every character in the novel is that of a defendant before a judge.[98] Both the Harlowe family and Lovelace characterize their own criminal intentions toward Clarissa—which amount to only slightly differing forms of rape—as "trials" in the explicitly judicial sense of the term. During the lengthy period during which her family members make increasingly barbaric attempts to force Mr. Solmes upon her, Clarissa imagines her rebuttals as legal documents, noting she is "tired with making declarations and pleadings on the subject."[99] Furthermore, Clarissa describes her family's "strict search" of her room for her "papers" in the same language associated with the general warrants that allowed, until restricted by the courts in the 1760s, both Star Chamber and Parliament free rein to search for books and other publications in order to restrict speech.[100] The literary depiction of Clarissa as a criminal defendant mimics the centrality of reputation evidence to the basic structure of the evidentiary proof of rape as summarized by Blackstone at the start of this chapter: where the victim is "of evil fame" the law presumes she is lying. Thus, the would-be rapists in the text can, as a legal matter, define away their offenses by changing the external narrative of Clarissa's respectability. In convicting her for "bad fame" they exonerate themselves.

Indeed, Lovelace imagines his enduring efforts to seduce Clarissa as "trials . . . mortifying to her niceness" with the specific purpose of undermining her public reputation for good character. Invoking the archaic common law term for character evidence, he asks, "[i]s virtue to be established by common bruit only? Has her virtue ever been *proved?*"[101] In planning her "trial" Lovelace taps into the general anxiety Susan Staves identifies over the potential impossibility of genuine feminine virtue: "If I have not found a virtue that cannot be corrupted, I will say there is not one such in the whole sex."[102] (Later, during his many attempts to rationalize his schemes, he uses the importance of reputational damage as a red herring to obscure the harm of the physical violation he contemplates, complaining

> [s]he cannot bear to be thought a woman, I warrant!—and if, in the last attempt, I find her *not* one, what will she be the worse for the trial?—No one is to blame for suffering an evil he cannot shun or avoid.)[103]

He thereby justifies his conduct by eliding the trauma of bodily violation itself through the circular logic that Clarissa will not be publicly condemned for it—a logical fallacy symmetrical to the actual rule that such trauma should be presumed not to exist where public condemnation has been established via reputation evidence.

Clarissa's only real opportunities to preserve her character arise in her testimony to an imagined third tribunal—that of her best friend Anna Howe.

In the text's very first letter Anna suggests the potential exculpatory function of letter writing, urging Clarissa to make a testimonial record in writing:

> I know how much it must hurt you to become the subject of the public talk; and yet upon an occasion so generally known it is impossible but that whatever relates to a young lady, whose distinguished merits have made her the public care, should engage everybody's attention. I long to have the particulars from yourself, and of the usage I am told you receive upon an accident you could not help and, in which, as far as I can learn, the sufferer was the aggressor.[104]

Anna's suggestion emphasizes the gap between the accepted character evidence generally embodied in public report and the actual truth accessible through the "particulars" of a subjective account—precisely the sort of evidence that would typically be inadmissible to rebut evidence of a general reputation for bad character. Furthermore, Anna suggests that the public may have a legitimate claim to Clarissa's good behavior, flowing from her earlier position as a moral role model for young ladies. She urges, therefore, that "If anything unhappy should fall out from the violence of such spirits as you have to deal with, your account of all things previous to it will be your justification."[105] The default position here is that, once again, the burden is upon Clarissa to "justify" conduct that the reader comes to understand as involuntary, and—like a criminal defendant—in doing so she is responsible to the community as a whole for the public harms her behavior may have caused. Clarissa thus exemplifies the double trauma I described earlier: her body is to be used for either the financial or sexual gratification of others and, beyond that, she must be utilized in the public sphere as either a cautionary paragon of corruption or a wrongfully-accused figure of pity. Anna's assumption that such public objectification "hurts" Clarissa makes the equivalence between these two forms of trauma explicit.

At the heart of all of these layers of imagined criminal adjudication lies Clarissa's prosecution of herself, which surfaces from time to time as an even more important—though possibly more challenging—case in her mind than any of the others. At the outset, Clarissa asks Anna to pray for her, "that I may not be pushed upon such indiscreet measures as will render me inexcusable to myself: for that is the test, after all; the world's opinion ought to be but a secondary consideration."[106] In prioritizing her own opinion over the that of the rest of the world she indicates that it is a closer approximation of the actual moral truth of her situation; yet later she finds it almost too complicated to ascertain: "I am, in my own opinion, a poor lost creature: and yet cannot charge myself with one criminal or faulty inclination."[107] Where even Lovelace acknowledges that every step of the way Clarissa has done everything in her power to preserve her virtue, her uncertainty about her criminal status seems to be based on a theory of attenuated causation flowing from her initial exchange of letters with him against the command of her father. She describes his first attempted rape as "[t]his last evil . . . the remote, yet sure consequence of my first—my prohibited correspondence!"[108] The logical confusion on these points may flow from the fact that the common law allows reputation evidence only in the form of a general narrative of public "fame," and not through specific facts. She cannot point to a particular instance of "criminality" on her part, but that is less legally relevant than her generalized impression of her guiltiness.

With respect to Lovelace's character, reputation evidence manages to capture reality partially, while eventually slipping away from it in dangerous ways. At the start of the novel, Clarissa's brother "justified his avowed inveteracy [toward Lovelace] by common fame," which at first seems untrustworthy given the spiteful and self-interested behavior of James Harlowe, Jr. himself.[109] Anna attempts to piece together a true "character" for Lovelace by causing inquiries to be made amongst his uncle's servants and his tenants and comes up with a mixed review. Lord M's steward "believed he kept no particular mistress, for he had heard *newelty*, that was the man's word, was everything [to] him."[110] Of Lovelace's alleged seduction of his innkeeper's daughter, "Rosebud," Anna declares, "I really believe the man is innocent. Of this *one* accusation, I think, he must be acquitted."[111] She also reports that "Mr. Lovelace had a very good paternal estate, and that, by the evidence of an enemy, all clear."[112] Anna's conclusion—again reflecting the judicial role she has taken upon herself, and the significance of the various piece of evidence she has collected—is that "he is guilty of an inexcusable fault in being so careless as he is of his reputation."[113] This "verdict" suggests the possibility of reputation being distinct from reality, while somehow erasing the evidence of particular instances of poor conduct that indicated the physical presence of other violated feminine bodies.

By the time Mr. Solmes is about to present Clarissa with specific evidence of Lovelace's criminal misconduct—the alleged rape of Miss Betterton, who dies in childbirth—her refusal to hear the evidence against "the poor criminal" seems somehow reasonable in light of the partial discrediting of reputation evidence the text has demonstrated.[114] (Even when we find out the particulars of the Betterton affair, their precise significance remains blurry, as Miss Betterton herself refused to prosecute him for rape.) As Clarissa puts it,

> I believe Mr. Lovelace is far from being so good as he ought to be: but if every man's private life were searched into by prejudiced people, set on for that purpose, I know not whose reputation would be safe.[115]

Nonetheless, though the text remains slippery about giving Clarissa (and the reader), concrete proof that Lovelace's reputation is an accurate proxy for character, by the end it becomes clear that his nature may be even worse than his reputation suggests.

On the other side of the coin, however, Richardson presents the probative value of reputation as less reliable and deeply destructive when brought to bear upon Clarissa—perhaps in part due to her comparative powerlessness to control it due to her gender. From the start it is clear that—as the rape laws suggest—her reputation is one of the most important aspects of her intrinsic worth. She begs her mother to be "the guardian of [her] reputation" which she feels would be tarnished if she entered into an illegitimate marriage with someone she despises.[116] Her mother subsequently remarks, in response to Clarissa's defense of her responsible conduct as a housekeeper, "[y]ou have been richly repaid in the reputation your skill and management have given you."[117] Her sadistic brother James demands "if you have a real value for your reputation, show it as you ought. It is yet in your own power to establish or impair it."[118] The assertion of Clarissa's "power" is obviously both cruel and preposterous, as the scenario in which she has been locked away to prevent her from marrying Lovelace was entirely conceived by her family to force her into a non-choice between reputations of dutiful child and "giddy" harlot, designed to make her do their bidding. Lovelace, too, uses reputation to control Clarissa against her will. She tells Anna he claims that "all the world gave me to him," suggesting that it would be going against the public will for her to reject him (and, further, that she was a commodity for the public to do with as it chose for largely narrative purposes).[119]

Throughout her confinement in London, Clarissa's understanding of her reputation controls her, even when she barely has contact with the world outside of Mrs. Sinclair's house of ill-repute. In alluding to the changing views of "the public," which obviously has no direct contact with Clarissa at this point in the narrative, Richardson discredits the probative value of reputation evidence as proof of Clarissa's veracity as a testifying victim. When she first arrives there Lovelace tells her "[t]he public voice is in [her] favour."[120] Later, however, she asks, "could the giddiest and most inconsiderate girl in England have done worse than I shall appear to have done in the eye of the world? Since my crime will be known without the provocations."[121] This moment establishes the crucial importance, to truth formation, of Clarissa's subjective experience of her abduction and the events leading up to it.

But Lovelace gives the text's darkest account of the function of reputation evidence and the reasons for its potential unreliability when he observes:

She has already incurred the censure of the world. She must therefore choose to be mine for the sake of soldering up her reputation in the eye of that impudent world. For who that knows me and knows that she has been in my power, though but for twenty-four hours, will think her spotless as to fact, let her inclination be what it will?—And then human nature is such a well-known rogue, that every man and woman judges by what each knows of themselves.[122]

Lovelace's description moves beyond the suggestion that reputation evidence may be incomplete due to a lack of subjective fact but that it might also be distorted by the subjective interpretations of the men and women who produce it. The text suggests that this concern may be heightened in cases where a feminine character for virtue must be constructed, as we see the enhanced pleasure taken by Mrs. Sinclair and her ladies of ill-repute in reducing Clarissa to what they consider to be their level.

Richardson seems to blame the social and legal conditions of their world for the stifling of a rape victim's subjectivity. Lovelace brags that

[a] rape, . . . to us rakes is far from being an undesirable thing. Nothing but our law stands in our way, upon that account; and the opinion of what a modest woman will suffer, rather than become a *viva voce* accuser, lessens much an honest fellow's apprehensions.[123]

In other words, the law, which promises significant retribution, in theory, poses no real threat to the rapist because a woman's socially policed reputation will suffer if she raises her voice in a courtroom. Richardson captures, here, the paradoxical manner in which being a rape victim was itself a mark against testimonial capacity.

The novel seems to understand the relationship between legal and social rules, and the need for testimonial strategies to articulate truth despite them. Periodically, however, Richardson links this imperative to an overall project of law-making and statecraft. Anna, for example, questions the arbitrary control of Clarissa's parents as potentially illegitimate in the language of Lockean liberalism: "AUTHORITY! What a full word is that in the mouth of a narrow-minded person, who happened to be born thirty years before one!— . . . should not parents have *reason* for what they do?"[124] Later on Anna compares the loss of power by a wife after marriage to "the feeble struggles of a sinking state for its dying liberty."[125] (As I will discuss in the next chapter, Charles Brockden Brown situates his rape narrative against similar concerns about political legitimacy in *Ormond*.)

On the other side of the discourse, Lovelace describes his own illegitimate exercise of brute authority:

[m]any and many a pretty rogue had I spared, whom I did not spare, had my power been acknowledged and my mercy been in time implored. But the *debellare superbos* should be my motto, were I to have a new one.[126]

The reference comes from the *Aeneid* and translates into "tame the proud" —an expression of public duty.[127] With that choice of expression, Lovelace imagines himself not only as a conqueror but "a lawgiver"—an identity he explicitly adopts much later on when devising imaginary legislation that would allow spouses to change partners once a year.[128] Musing on his scheme shortly after having raped Clarissa, he asserts that it would result in "absolutely annihilating four or five atrocious or capital sins—rapes, vulgarly so called; adultery and fornication."[129] Richardson's association of his villain with the process of lawmaking seems to indict actual English lawmakers for the state of affairs that have facilitated Clarissa's victimization, an identification reiterated later when Clarissa "held up to Heaven, in a speechless agony, the innocent [marriage] licence . . . as the poor distressed Catalans held up their English treaty."[130] Though here the reference is to treaty law, Clarissa's voicelessness in the face of English authority suggests an imperative for formal legal change.

Clarissa created a significant stir in the public imagination. As the editor of a recent compendium of eighteenth-century written responses to the text notes,

the range and intensity of response to this one work provides an exceptionally multi-faceted mirror by which to read the culture of the second half of the eighteenth century [as] some of the most famous and influential intellectuals of Europe . . . used Richardson and his greatest work to debate esthetics and literary form, human psychology, public morality, the education of young people, the private relations of men and women.[131]

Due to its innovative format and provocative subject matter, *Clarissa* prompted a decades-long discourse, much of which centered specifically around the character of its heroine.

English divine and classics scholar Henry Gally produced the first serious essay on the question of literary character in "A Critical Essay on Characteristic-Writing" (1725), the introduction to his translation of *The Moral Characters of Theophrastus*. In it he developed the concept of "Characteristic-Justice" to measure the skill with which an author adheres to "nature in creating characters:

Since every Feature must be drawn exactly to the Life, great Care must be taken, that the Strokes be not too faint, nor yet too strong: For Characteristic-Justice is to be observ'd as strictly by the Writers of this

Kind, as Poetic-Justice is to be by Poets. That Medium must be copied, which Nature it self has mark'd out; whatever falls short of it is poor and insipid, whatever is above it is Rant and Extravagance.[132]

The critical discussion of character in *Clarissa* reflects a similar concern with accuracy and hyperbole. Richardson's proponents lauded his skill at rendering distinct characters through the epistolary form; for example, the author of the introduction to the French translation noted that "[t]he style of every letter is excellently adapted to the character of the writer."[133] Beyond literary aesthetics, however, the late eighteenth-century cultural commentary about *Clarissa* reveals an epistemological clash between proponents of the *moral* value of a consistently drawn, monolithic character and critics who noted the disruptive potential of concrete exceptions. While the individual trauma of rape can hardly be said to manifest in these conversations, the discourse reflects an incipient cultural trauma around the processes of identifying a particular woman as either raped or culpably "fallen." The recurring anxiety over the respective moral virtues of general and specific literary character evidence anticipates a judicial debate over this same problem with respect to reputation evidence in the early-nineteenth century common law.

In a 1748 letter to the editor of *The Jacobite's Journal*, printed while the novel was still being published in serial, Henry Fielding lamented the various conflicting criticisms of Clarissa's character:

> She is too cold; she is too fond. She uses her father, mother, uncles, brother, sister, lover, friend, too ill, too well. In short, there is scarce a contradiction in character which I have not heard assigned from different reasons to this poor girl, who is as much the object of compassion as she can be, and as good as she should be described.[134]

Fielding suggests that negative views of Clarissa—though wholly contradictory among themselves—all tended to hyperbole, just as his positive characterization paints her as the epitome of wronged goodness.[135] Mary Whortley Montagu, by contrast, laments over what she sees as hyperbolic positive accounts of Clarissa's character, telling her daughter that

> [e]ven that model of perfection, Clarissa, is so faulty in her behavior as to deserve little compassion. Any girl that runs away with a young fellow without intending to marry him should be carried to Bridewell or to Bedlam the next day. Yet the circumstances are so laid as to inspire tenderness . . .[136]

Montagu suggests that Clarissa's general reputation for "perfection" is less probative of moral respectability than the specific circumstances of her flight with Lovelace, which render her criminal. While differing in their ultimate conclusions, both Fielding and Montagu object to the totalizing quality of public accounts of Clarissa's character.

In stark contrast, other commentators praised Richardson precisely for the hyperbolic consistency of Clarissa's character, on the grounds that uniformity suggested truth-to-nature. For example, in 1778, the Scottish poet Anne MacVicar Grant declared, "[n]ever, sure, were characters so well drawn, discriminated and supported . . . [Clarissa's] in particular. Never was anything so uniformly consistent, so raised above common characters, and yet so judiciously kept within the bounds of nature and probability."[137] Abigail Adams gave similar praise in 1785, stating

> in his amiable portraits Richardson was master of the human heart; he studied and copied nature; he has shown the odiousness of vice, and the fatal consequences which result from the practice of it; he has painted virtue in all her amiable attitudes.[138]

Adams's treatment of the concept of idealized, personified virtue as an element of nature is structurally similar to the evidentiary principle that generalized reputation best captures the factual truth of a rape victim's testimonial veracity: both rely on a constructed yet coherent narrative to transmit facticity.

The writings of other commentators, however, reveal discomfort with precisely this epistemological proposition. In his 1766 "Sermon to Young Women," well-known minister and ethicist James Fordyce describes Richardson to his female audience as

> an author to whom your sex are under singular obligations for his uncommon attention to their best interests. But particularly for presenting, in a character sustained throughout with inexpressible pathos and delicacy, the most exalted standard of female excellence that was ever held up to their imitation.[139]

Yet he goes on to offer a qualification:

> I would be understood to except that part of Clarissa's conduct, which the author meant to exhibit as exceptional. Setting this aside, we find in her character a beauty, a sweetness, and artlessness—what shall I say more?—a sanctity of sentiment and manner, which, I own for my part, I have never seen equaled in any book of that sort; yet such, at the same time, as appears no way impracticable for any woman who is ambitious of excelling.[140]

Like Grant and Adams, Fordyce presents caricature as the best proxy for natural reality: Clarissa is, at once, the paragon of feminine virtue and yet an attainable, practical role-model. Unlike those writers, however, Fordyce stumbles a bit over the specific evidence of Clarissa's indiscretions. Similarly to a judge excluding specific fact evidence, he sets these instances aside as "exceptional." This discomfort with the contradiction between the general and the specific appears even more explicit in later commentary. American clergyman Enos Hitchcock conceded in 1790 that "[Richardson's] Clarissa has been considered by good judges as the most finished model of female excellence which has ever been offered for their imitation" but argues that

> even this great master in the science of human nature has laid open scenes, which it would have been safer to have kept concealed; and has excited sentiments, which it would have been more advantageous to early virtue not to have admitted.[141]

Like so many other writers, Hitchcock aligns idealized general feminine morality with the idea of the natural, in opposition to the specific scenes of sexual desire which he implies are unnatural because they are dangerous. Similarly, Whig historian Catharine Sawbridge MacAulay Graham worries that Richardson

> is not sufficiently correct in his ideas to set forth in his heroine an exact pattern of moral loveliness, nor to draw such a character of his rake, as should render him disgustful to the giddy part of the female sex.[142]

In her view, it seems, Clarissa's character should have been unalloyed by desire, while Lovelace's should have been monolithically vulgar.

Tom Keymer has demonstrated how Richardson's use of "forensic realism" contributed to what he identifies as the "legal paradigm" at the end of the novel.[143] Keymer notes that Richardson had written critically of the criminal justice system's failures to protect rape victims due to their delicacy, penury, and tender-hearted fear of taking their ravishers' lives.[144] To fill the space of the prosecution Clarissa herself refused to mount, Keymer argues, Richardson's book "will gather, arrange and present all the evidence relevant to the case, accumulating the testimonies of the parties concerned and submitting them to the reader for judgment . . . the literary equivalent of a trial."[145] Some of Richardson's contemporaries may have seen the text's applicability to real-world rape prosecutions. For example, William Shenstone lamented of the vast degree of detail that "[n]othing, but fact could authorize so much particularity, and indeed not that; but in a court of justice—."[146] Scholars have already noted Richardson's legal significance as a contribution to the debate over the 1753 Marriage Act. The remainder of this chapter will explore how the debate Clarissa sparked over literary proofs of character similarly echo in the criminal jurisprudence on rape victim character evidence.

Reputation and Specific Fact Evidence in Nineteenth-century Rape Trials

The rape case-law of the early nineteenth century reveals a conflict between the common law rules that prohibit proof of character through anything other than general reputation evidence and the legible fear that truth lies in specificity. Relatedly, the centrality of a victim's character to rape cases occasionally put pressure on the general common law rule barring proof of a witness's good character unless first impeached by the other party. During this period, jurists often spoke of these rules as though they were concrete and immutable yet, on other occasions, ignored them or acknowledged the epistemological gaps they created.

For example, the detailed published reports of a pair of Irish trials show how sentimentalized narratives about victim identity transcended evidentiary restrictions in contrasting ways. On April 22, 1800, Thomas Lidwell was arraigned in Dublin for the alleged rape of Mrs. Sarah Sutton, the wife of his good friend Jacob. According to Mr. Plunket, the prosecutor, Lidwell is, like Jacob Sutton, "a gentleman of considerable property and of a family highly respectable."[147] Throughout the proceedings, the presiding judge, the prosecutor, and the defendant himself comment repeatedly on how unfortunate it is that a gentleman of such good breeding and an otherwise spotless record should have fallen into such debased circumstances. This evidence is consistent with the rule allowing the defendant, alone, to bring affirmative evidence of his good character to demonstrate a lack of propensity to commit a crime.[148] Indeed, even when Lidwell's jury returns a verdict of guilty, it is with a recommendation for mercy based upon his "previous uniform good character."[149] Nonetheless Mrs. Sutton testifies that while she was visiting the Lidwell family in Osberstown, County Kildare, Lidwell had repeatedly attempted to separate her from his wife and daughter, behaved increasingly rudely—on one occasion jokingly tripping her to make her fall into the grass —and finally, on the day she decided to leave early to get away from him, made a last-minute excuse to prevent his daughter from joining them on a carriage drive to run an errand. During this trip, he drove off the road into a sandpit, dragged Mrs. Sutton out of the carriage, threw her "violently upon the ground" and did with her "as he pleased."[150] After the rape, Lidwell drove Mrs. Sutton back to his estate, where she took refreshment and departed on her journey home. It was several weeks before she told her husband what happened and they took legal action.

Lidwell's prosecutor uses subjective evidence of victim character to subvert the common law rules that tend to presume away certain victim trauma. In his opening statement, he observes that a woman of a strong and determined disposition would have probably given immediate vent to her just resentment; she would have burst into a passionate declaration of her injuries to the first stranger whom she saw on the road, or to the family as soon as she returned.[151]

He thereby anticipates one of the chief objections of defense counsel, embodied in the extract from Blackstone with which this chapter opened: the great evidentiary importance of a rape victim immediately raising an outcry. Lidwell's prosecutor addresses these objections by constructing an affirmative portrait of Mrs. Sutton's character. He notes that while "other dispositions would be differently affected," she was "a woman gentle, timid, retiring, a mind the reverse of a strong or firm one, in a strange country, without friend or acquaintance; she did not proclaim upon the public road the history of her own shame and sorrow."[152] He goes on to paint a sentimental scene of the victim's anguish upon returning from her trip: "the moment she was alone with her mother, the very morning after her return, she burst into an agony of grief, and disclosed the whole transaction."[153] She initially defers to her mother's urging that she conceal the attack from her husband lest he "abandon her and her children" or else "lose his life by seeking vengeance."[154] Yet Sarah Sutton "pined under the consciousness of what had passed; her husband used to find her pillow wet with her tears."[155] After weeks of this untenable state of affairs, she finally confides in her husband, who reacts lovingly and insists that they prosecute his supposed friend.

In reading the published account of this trial it is, as always, difficult to discern to what precise extent the sentimental language and refined storytelling was the oratory of the prosecutor and how much was the embellishment of the volume's editor. Either way, however, it is clear that the legal and cultural biases—strong even now and nearly insurmountable in the early eighteenth-century—against rape victims who delay before bringing charges were at least partially mitigated in this turn-of-the-nineteenth-century case by an understanding of the subjective components of the victim's character. Sarah Sutton is presented—perhaps even fetishized—as a tormented protagonist facing a range of romantic, familial, and emotional pressures specific to her situation and personality, which override the legal presumption about her delayed outcry. Indeed, the sole illustrated plate in the published account places Sarah, elevated on the witness stand at the center of the picture, with the prisoner shrouded in darkness and nearly out of the frame to the left. The caption, "that is he," refers to the moment in the transcript at which the prosecutor asks her to identify the prisoner and "much embarrassed, and after some time, raising her hand, and for the first time during her examination, looked towards the dock, and pointing to the prisoner, said '*that is he.*'"[156]

This aesthetic mode of valorizing rape testimony, which made Sarah's testimony legally compelling and commercially narratable in 1800, in contrast to some of the earlier eighteenth-century depictions, shows the influence of the rise of the novel form and its contributions to the understanding of subjectivity in the real-world criminal courtroom. Like Richardson, the prosecutor has successfully disrupted a stock evidentiary presumption—that genuine rape victims report the crime immediately—by integrating exceptional competing facts into an overall narrative of his protagonist's idealized moral character.

The 1824 case of *R* v. *Madders &. Kelly* involved a similarly appealing complainant, at least in the account that appeared in Richard Rowe's case reports. The facts of the case are fairly horrifying: Ms. Ivy is searching for her nurse's home in Waterford after dark. Due to revolutionary activity in County Wexford, the city is heavily patrolled by soldiers, a number of who gang-rape her. According to the victim, she first encounters Madders and Chambers, who each rape her with the help of the other. She then seeks help from a passing serjeant, Kelly, who offers her protection in the guardhouse where he, too, rapes her. The prosecution attempts to lead the testimony of the victim's aunt, Mrs. Shaw, who testifies that "Miss Ivy had an extremely virtuous education, and always conducted herself with the strictest propriety."[157] While crown counsel notes that "similar evidence was admitted at Lidwell's trial,"[158] the court deems it irrelevant as "there has not been the smallest attempt to impeach the correctness of Miss Ivy's conduct."[159] The court thereby correctly applies the rule against evidence bolstering the character of a witness whose veracity has not been impeached; nonetheless, in referring to the Lidwell case the prosecutor suggests the rule was or should have been in flux as applied to testifying rape victims.

The case report itself, however, fills in the gaps to construct the victim's character for the audience outside the courtroom. A footnote on the first page of the case describes her as "a young lady, elegant in her person and manners, the daughter of the late Mr. Ivy, an eminent Attorney in Waterford, who amassed an immense fortune by his profession."[160] Furthermore, the case editor enters the realm of literary description when he notes that, at the sight of one of the defendants, "the idea of what she had suffered, worked so forcibly on her mind, as to throw her into convulsions; her lamentable cries pierced every heart."[161] This description translates objectively observable facts—i.e., a witness's demeanor in the courtroom—into a plurality of subjective truths: not only the "idea" causing trauma within the victim's mind but the residual traumatic effect on the hearts of the courtroom audience. At this moment, Rowe is telling us, the reader, about the process of telling. He implicitly recognizes the doubled individual trauma of a rape victim objectified by the process of becoming public evidence. Like Richardson, he presents this particular form of individual trauma to the public for potential incorporation into the collective memory of rape.

Furthermore, despite the formal exclusion of the victim's good character from this trial, it creeps back in as relevant to what appears to have been an attempt at a defense based on the mistaken belief in consent. When Kelly's counsel cross-examines Ms. Ivy he elicits the fact that, when Kelly encountered Madders with the victim after the first assault and asked who she was, Madders said she was a servant maid who lived on the quay, who had been walking with him upon meeting him on the quay. Ivy testifies that

> I told the serjeant that I was niece to Mrs. Shaw. Upon his dragging me into the entry, I cannot say or form any belief as to whether the serjeant thought me a very different person from what I really was.[162]

In other words, counsel for the defense appears to be suggesting that his client's failure to apprehend her genteel status, and his potentially mistaken belief that she had been "walking" on the street like a prostitute, suggests he believed her to be consenting to sex.[163] In Ms. Ivy's next words, she appears, herself, to blur the concepts of identity and character, noting that she "could not conceive whether the serjeant mistook her character."[164] The efforts of the defense prove unsuccessful: the court finds both defendants guilty and sentences them to hang. While formally excluded from the trial, then, the victim's respectable character remains relevant not only in the rape narrative being sold to and consumed by the public, but in the subtext of the adjudicatory process itself. And like in *Lidwell's* case, and unlike in the comic seventeenth- and early-eighteenth-century accounts, the public character of the rape victim has become one of tragic, accidental violation.

While rape victims with notably "good" characters made for good sentimental prose by early nineteenth-century legal reporters, the allowance and nature of evidence of "bad" victim character produced more case law. The 1812 case of *R* v. *Hodgson*[165] provided the first clear nineteenth-century statement of the rule that a victim could refuse to answer questions about whether she had had sexual relations with a man other than the defendant, and that the defense could not proffer collateral evidence to show that she had. The court noted that "the witness was not bound to answer these questions as they tended to criminate and disgrace herself"[166] and that collateral evidence was inadmissible because the Crown "could not come prepared to answer them."[167] *Hodgson* would echo throughout the rape jurisprudence of the nineteenth century, construed as a statement of judicial concern that the complainant not acquire a criminal character through the reputation-forming process of the trial itself.[168] In 1821 Baron Wood echoed this view in *R* v. *Hall*, holding that an alleged rape victim was not compellable to answer the question of whether she had had sexual connection with a third party (her employer) and asking "[i]f persons put up into that box, are to be hunted, and terrified as to the whole history of their lives, who would become a witness?"[169] The court also notes that even if the victim had slept with the third party "that has nothing to do with the Prisoner at the bar; she has no right to be ill-treated on that account."[170] This judicial concern for the reputation-destroying potential of the trial proved somewhat evanescent: many decades later, defense counsel in the 1871 rape case of *R* v. *Holmes & Furness* would refer to the early nineteenth-century as "a period where a more extensive protection was allowed to witnesses than now."[171]

Furthermore, whatever the *Hodgson* rule accomplished in the way of victim protection, it seems to have been limited to barring impeachment through specific evidence. Just five years after *Hodgson*, *R* v. *Clarke* (1817)[172] affirmed the rule that, while the defense could not attack an alleged victim's character through particular acts, general "[e]vidence that the woman had a bad character previous to the supposed commission of the offence is admissible."[173] In this case, the prosecution, arguing against both specific and general evidence of bad character, notes the logical paradox of the rule on reputation evidence. Crown counsel urges that it is unfair that the victim's "character might be taken away by general evidence . . . without subjecting the witnesses, who gave such general evidence, to a prosecution for perjury, since they could not be indicted on such general evidence."[174] While the Crown's argument on reputation evidence did not prevail, the fact that it was made at all represents, like the court's discussion in *Hodgson,* an awareness of the perverse cycle of reputation evidence to potentially generate its own irrefutable legal truth.

In any case, despite the strongly-stated rule in *Hodgson*, even specific facts about the victim's sexual history managed to make their way into evidence in the nineteenth century. In *R* v. *Robins* (1843),[175] Lord Coleridge held that it was "not immaterial to the question whether the prosecutrix had had this connection against her consent to show that she had permitted other men to have connection with her, which, on her cross examination, she had denied." In *R* v. *Barker* (1829),[176] while Justice Park officially expressed doubt whether, after *R* v. *Hodgson*, the defense could proffer particular acts of intercourse by the victim,[177] the court eventually allowed the questions: "[w]ere you not, on Friday last, walking the High Street of Oxford to look out for men?" and, "[w]ere you not, on Friday last, walking in the High Street with a woman reputed to be a common prostitute?"[178] While the court appears to treat these questions as evidence of general looseness (courts regularly treated the general fact of being a prostitute as within this category[179]) they nonetheless appear to violate the *Hodgson* rule insofar as they were intended, as Judge Curwood noted, "to try the credit of the woman" with evidence of a highly specific instance (the events of the preceding Friday night).

The uncertainty sparked by the *Hodgson* case persisted in *R* v. *Martin* (1834),[180] where the court claimed to follow it by allowing evidence to be given of the previous intercourse between prosecutrix and defendant but not with other men. Nonetheless, Justice Williams cast doubt on *Hodgson* through a highly personal lens, stating, "I was one of the counsel in the case of *Rex.* v. *Hodgson*" and using that participation as a basis for declaring

> the doctrine, that you may go into general evidence of bad character in the prosecutrix, and yet not cross-examine as to specific facts, I confess does appear to me to be not quite in strict accordance with the general rules of evidence.[181]

Here the personal memory of a participant in the trial that created a legal rule becomes enfolded into precedent casting doubt on the rule itself.

The rule allowing only general bad reputation evidence endured as a legal matter throughout the nineteenth century, though the cases nonetheless reflect its discursive instability. In *R* v. *Cockcroft* (1870), the court allowed the cross-examination of the complainant (rather than forbidding the question, as the *Hodgson* court had done) but forbad the defendant to introduce collateral evidence once she refused to answer.[182] Nonetheless, only a year later in *R* v. *Holmes and Furness* (1871), the question of whether a third party could give testimony that a rape victim had had sex with him arose again and the trial court, while refusing to allow the testimony, nonetheless reserved the issue for the Court of Crown Cases Reserved.[183] Despite the defense counsel's argument that *Hodgson* was dead letter and that, because "the prosecutrix stands in a peculiar position in relation to the charge," therefore "great latitude is allowed as to evidence affecting her general character," the Court concluded the rule was clear that the defense may not lead contradictory evidence once the victim states she has not had connection with another man.[184] The Court reaffirmed, however, that general looseness of character would be admissible and relevant because "such evidence has a direct bearing on the issue of consent or non-consent on the part of the prosecutrix."[185]

At around the same time, another case revealed persistent ambivalence over general reputation in a slightly different sexual context: the character of the defendant in an indecent assault trial. In *R* v. *Rowton* (1865), the court adhered to the rule that the prosecution could lead reputation evidence to impeach the defendant's character only to rebut his affirmative good character evidence. The Crown witness had proposed to testify,

> I know nothing of the neighbourhood's opinion, because I was only a boy at school when I knew him, but my opinion, and the opinion of my broth-

ers, who were also pupils of his, is that his character is that of a man capable of the grossest indecency and the most flagrant immorality.[186]

While Lord Cockburn reaffirmed the rule that "general character alone . . . can afford any test of general conduct . . . and, therefore, proof of particular transactions, in which the prisoner may have been concerned, are not admissible,"[187] he expressed doubt about the epistemological coherence of such a rule and implies that it is sometimes ignored in practice:

> As the law stands, no one could contend that evidence of specific facts is admissible, although one fact would weigh more with the jury than any evidence of general reputation. The fact is, that this part of our law is an anomaly . . . In practice, it is true, the rule is somewhat relaxed. The evidence of witnesses gains weight by being introduced with a statement of the opportunity they have had for forming a correct judgment . . . Facts, though they would be much stronger evidence, are excluded . . .[188]

In other words, witnesses, while prevented from testifying directly to specific transactions involving the defendant, may obliquely testify to more than general reputation through their responses to questions about their bases for knowing him or her. In dissent, Chief Justice Erle went even further and stated that witnesses should be able to testify directly to their personal opinions of the defendant. He stated that this was, in fact, already the rule, that "[d]isposition may be ascertained either from the personal experience of the witness or the general opinion of others" and noted that he had "never heard a witness examined to character without his being questioned as to his personal experience."[189] He also concluded that this rule makes the most sense normatively because "[p]ersonal experience gives a cogency to the evidence such as mere report can never import. General rumour is the general inference from a number of specific statements; and those statements are derived from personal experience."[190]

Thus by the mid-nineteenth century, we see judges discussing the use of character evidence in rape and sexual assault cases as though the rules are discursively unstable. Jurisprudential ambiguity as to the comparative probative value of reputation and "specific fact" evidence of character is particularly significant due to the way in which the common law renders the characters of the defendant and victim constitutive of the offense of rape itself. Richardson suggests the epistemological problems attendant to reputation evidence in *Clarissa*, which itself set off a public debate about how evidence of specific exceptions to a party's general character made it more or less "natural." Echoes of these literary debates manifest in the novelistic features of nineteenth-century rape jurisprudence whenever it raises the possibility of its narrative artificiality on the question of reputation evidence. Ultimately, of course, somewhere behind the concentric layers of social and legal discourse about victim reputation lies the trauma of the sexual violation itself. And in the spaces where literary subjectivity unsettles traditional evidentiary discourse about reputation, the secondary trauma of rape—the discursive construction of a victim's character—enters the collective memory.

Notes

1. Alexander, "Toward a Theory of Cultural Trauma," p. 10.
2. I use female pronouns to discuss rape victims in this chapter because the law of the time period I consider conceived of rape as a male-on-female crime.
3. Jacob, *Every Man His Own Lawyer*, p. 461. This curt formulation comes from the instructional volume *Every Man His Own Lawyer, or A Summary of the Laws of England, in a New and Instructive Method* (1768) by "self-help" legal author Giles Jacob.
4. Blackstone, *Commentaries*, vol. 4, p. 141.
5. Ibid. p. 141.
6. Schramm, *Testimony and Advocacy*, p. 2.
7. Ibid. p. 3.
8. For a classic account of this evolution see Ian Watt's *The Rise of the Novel* (1957).
9. Deirdre Lynch has broken the public reception of literary character into two distinct phases defined by their relationship to consumer culture. In the early eighteenth century, she argues, character helped consumers navigate "the systems of semiotic and fiduciary exchange . . . that made a commercial society go" Lynch, *Economy of Character*, pp. 5–6. By contrast during the sentimental phase of the late eighteenth century,

   > [p]eople's transactions with books came to be connected in new ways, first, to their endeavors to find themselves as 'individuals' and to escape from their social context, and, second, to their endeavors to position themselves within an economy of prestige in which cultural capital was distributed asymmetrically and in which not all who read were accredited to 'really read' literature

   Ibid. p. 6.
10. Hargraves, "Revelation of Character," p. 24.
11. Ibid. p. 29.
12. Ibid. p. 35.
13. Dunn, *Stolen Women*, p. 52.
14. de Troyes, "Lancelot," p. 202.
15. Malory, *Works*, vol. 1, p. 120.
16. Dunn, *Stolen Women*, p. 53.

17. The late thirteenth-century legal text *Britton* (long falsely attributed to John le Breton, Bishop of Hereford) states, for example, "no woman can conceive if she does not consent." *Britton*, p. 154.

18. Dunn, *Stolen Women*, p. 59.

19. Ibid. p. 62.

20. Ibid. p. 68.

21. Ibid. pp. 68–9.

22. Ibid. p. 69.

23. Bracton, *De Legibus*, vol. 2, pp. 414–15.

24. *Statutes of the Realm*, 3 Edw. 1 c. 13.

25. Hale, *History of the Pleas*, vol. 1, p. 627.

26. Pollock, *History of English Law*, vol. 2, pp. 514–15.

27. MacFarlane, "Historical Development of the Offense of Rape", p. 12 n35.

28. Hawkins, *Pleas of the Crown*, vol. 1, p. 109.

29. Russell, *A Treatise on Crimes*, vol. 1, p. 556.

30. MacFarlane, "Historical Development of the Offense of Rape", p. 12.

31. Roger D. Groot found no convictions between 1189–1216. Groot, "The Crime of Rape *temp.* Richard I and John," p. 329. John Marshall Carter found 21 percent of 145 thirteenth-century cases ending in conviction. Carter, "Rape in Medieval England," p. 108. Also looking at a thirteenth-century sample, Barbara Hanawalt found convictions in nine percent of 60 prosecutions. Hanawalt, *Crime and Conflict*, pp. 272–3. In Yorkshire at the turn of the fifteenth century Karen Ellis found an 18% conviction rate. Ellis, "Gaol Delivery in Yorkshire, 1399–1407" p. 38. Yet Edward Powell found no convictions on 280 indictments in the midland counties between 1400–1429. Powell, "Jury Trial at Gaol Delivery," p. 101. Nor did Philippa Maddern in a study of 216 accusations from the King's Bench rolls from 1422–1442. Maddern, *Violence and Social Order*, pp. 102–3.

32. Dunn, *Stolen Women*, p. 76.

33. As stated by Victorian treatise-writer Fitzjames Stephen, "From the days of Bracton to those of Coke (1644), an interval of at least 350 years, there was an extraordinary Dearth of writers on English law." Stephen, *Criminal Law of England*, vol. 2., p. 202.

34. See, for example: East ("Rape is the unlawful carnal knowledge of a woman *by force* and against her will," East, *Pleas of the Crown*, vol. 1, pp. 43–4); Coke ("Rape is when a man hath carnal knowledge of a woman *by force* and against her will," Coke, *Laws of England*, vol. 2, 180); and Blackstone (Rape is "the carnal knowledge of a woman *forcibly* and against her will" Blackstone, *Commentaries*, vol. 4, 139) (italics all mine). By contrast, Hale defines rape as "the carnal knowledge of any woman above the age of ten years 'against her will,' and of a woman child under the age of ten years with or against her will." Hale, *History of the Pleas*, vol. 1, p. 628.

35. Proceedings of the Old Bailey, 8 December 1731, Trial of John Ellis (quoted in Durston, "Rape in the Eighteenth-Century Metropolis," p. 23).

36. *R v. Adkins*, Old Bailey Proceedings, sessions ending 18 September 1751.

37. *R v. Sherwin*, Old Bailey Proceedings, sessions beginning 31 January 1779.

38. *R v. Rudland* (1865), 4 F. 495.

39. Farr, *Elements*, p. 42.

40. Quoted in Edwards, *Female Sexuality*, pp. 122–6.

41. Ibid. p. 121.

42. Farr, *Elements*, p. 43.

43. In 2012 United States Rep. Todd Akin famously explained that "If it's a legitimate rape, the female body has ways to try to shut that whole thing down."

44. *Lidwell's Trial*, p. 28.

45. *Bloody Register*, vol. 2, p. 187.

46. Roberts, *Leeson's Case*, p. 14.

47. 4 *Wigmore* § 1104. See also *Phipson on Evidence* (1898) (stating that the bad general character of a prosecutrix is material, "not only to her credit but to the issue, and is therefore admissible whether she be, or not be, cross-examined." *Phipson*, p. 175 (citing *R v. Gibbons*, 31 L.J.M.C. 98, 99–100).

48. *R v. Ryan* (1846), 2 Cox C.C. 115.

49. *People v. Abbot* (NY 1838), 19 Wend. 192.

50. *State v. Sibley*, 131 Mo. 519 (Mo. 1895). As John Henry Wigmore, author of the most influential treatise on the common law of evidence, puts it, the rules must "be interpreted to permit *the woman's character as to chastity* to be considered, inasmuch as this trait may be *inextricably connected with a tendency to unveracity in charges of sex offences*." 1 *Wigmore* §§ 62 & 200 (3d ed. 1940).

51. The hearsay rule only began to solidify in English common law during the course of the eighteenth century. It is generally considered to have been articulated in most complete detail in *Wright v. Tatham*, 7 Adolph. & E. 313, 386 (Exch. Ch. 1837), a case involving proof of a testator's competence via letters written to him. Apart from becoming the leading hearsay case, it was also the inspiration for Dickens's *Bleak House*.

52. *Bloody Register*, vol. 2, p. 187. By way of clarification, although these witnesses were testifying about facts related to them by the defendant, their statements would not be considered hearsay if they were not offered for the truth of the matter asserted, but for the purpose of showing the victim's prior state of mind in order to bolster her statements on the stand. In other words, they could be offered to show that she is not lying on the stand as her story is consistent with what she said at the time. They might also fall into a particular exception to the hearsay rule, admitting excited utterances on the theory that when someone is in a state of high emotional dudgeon they are less likely to be intentionally prevaricating.

53. Ibid. p. 189.

54. Ibid. p. 190.

55. Ibid. p. 190.

56. Ibid. p. 190.

57. Ibid. p. 190.

58. Ibid. p. 190.

59. Ibid. p. 191.

60. Pennington & Hastie, "Juror Decision Making," p. 501.

61. Available at <www.oldbaileyonline.org> (last accessed 2 March 2019) (27 April 1715, trial of Hugh Leeson and Sarah Blandford (t17150427-43)).

62. Durston, *Whores and Highwaymen*, p. 361.

63. Roberts, *Leeson's Case*, p. ii.

64. Ibid. p. 4. This use of the pardon to bifurcate the formal legal narrative of guilt and its physical consequences has been discussed in Chapter 3.

65. Ibid. p. 24.

66. Ibid. p. 8.

67. Ibid. p. 16.

68. Ibid. p. 16.

69. Ibid. p. 9.

70. Ibid. p. 17.

71. Ibid. p. 13.

72. As noted barrister William Garrow said in an opening statement at the Old Bailey in 1789, the "nature of the offence . . . is almost always attended with a secrecy which makes it necessary for Courts and Juries to find their way as they can, and to judge from the probability and improbability of the story told by the person who complains of the injury" (quoted in Durston, *Whores and Highwaymen*, p. 1).

73. Roberts, *Lord John Drummond*, p. 4.

74. Ibid. p. 9.

75. Ibid. p. 11.

76. Ibid. p. 9.

77. Discussing Otway's *The Orphan* (1680), she argues "the rape becomes the physical manifestation of the desire perpetrated by the rapist but implicit in the audience's gaze. Thus the audience, like the rapist, 'enjoys' the actress, deriving its pleasure from the physical presence of the female body." Marsden, "Rape, Voyeurism," p. 186.

78. Hughes, "Rape on the Restoration Stage," p. 228. For example, in female playwright Aphra Behn's *The Rover* (1677) the rake Willmore's attempted rape of Florinda (in a case of mistaken identity) is treated comically, but the genuine threat to virtuous women is clear. Another significant—and unusual—entry during this period was Nicholas Rowe's *Tamerlane* (1701), which is the first

English drama to treat rape within a marriage as tragic (in this case by the Turkish emperor Bajazet on his unwilling wife Arpasia). Anne Greenfield has shown how the "unprecedented" text subtly reminds viewers that "a wife did and should have sexual autonomy, even when that autonomy conflicted with her husband's desires." Greenfield, "Marital Rape in *Tamerlane*," p. 58.

79. Staves, "Comedy of Attempted Rape," p. 86.

80. Ibid. p. 90.

81. Fielding's is hardly the only work to betray this preoccupation. For example, the introduction to a popular English edition of Kleist's work containing two prominent stories involving rape, "The Marquise of O . . ." (1801) and "Amphitryon" (1807), characterizes the tales as "revolv[ing] entirely around the seeming misconduct of a virtuous young woman." Jean Wilson has argued that, counter to this characterization, Kleist's works actually subvert the comic structure to which they ostensibly conform and "arouse the reader's resistance to . . . romanticized narratives of sexual violation." Wilson, "Heinrich von Kleist's *Amphitryon*," p. 116.

82. Including, very loosely, Fielding's *Rape Upon Rape*. Rivero, *Plays of Henry Fielding*, pp. 77–9.

83. *Prints and Drawings in the British Museum*, p. 710.

84. Lynch, *Economy of Character*, p. 63.

85. *Prints and Drawings in the British Museum*, p. 710.

86. Ibid. pp. 710–11.

87. Under the civil law of the Continent a prostitute was legally incapable of being a rape victim. On this point Blackstone distinguishes the English common law, which recognizes the rape of a prostitute as such, "because the woman may have forsaken that unlawful course of life." Blackstone, *Commentaries*, vol. 2, p. 141. Blackstone hereby implies that a prostitute who has not reformed would not be capable of being raped—his concern is simply that it might be too difficult to tell and thus her profession should not be held against her.

88. Scarry, *Body in Pain*, p. 3.

89. Sheley, "Reverberations of the 'Victim's Voice,'" p. 1261.

90. Particularly in cases where the victim is not given the opportunity to make a narrative statement about her experience of an event.

91. Ferguson, "Rape and the Rise of the Novel," p. 108.

92. Ibid. p. 104–5.

93. Brown, "Consent, Coquetry, and Consequences," p. 625.

94. Ibid. p. 628.

95. MacPherson, "Lovelace, Ltd." p. 101.

96. Ibid. p. 116.

97. As Jan-Melissa Schramm puts it, "if legal strategies of proof and persuasion are imitated throughout the novel, it is an explicit rejection of the publicity of the

law and its patriarchal biases which generate the very production of *Clarissa* in its epistolary form." Schramm, *Testimony and Advocacy*, p. 88.

98. Thomas Beebe, noting how legal language was devoured by an eighteenth-century public interested in the relationship between law and power, speculates that Richardson read Alexander Pope's will, which was published during the time he was writing *Clarissa*. Beebe, "Doing Clarissa's Will," p. 160. Richardson's inclusion of entire legal documents such as Clarissa's will and the marriage license obtained by Lovelace certainly suggests an intentional effort to capture the details of the legal frameworks in which his characters operate.

99. Richardson, *Clarissa*, p. 344.

100. Ibid. p. 320.

101. Richardson, *Clarissa*, p. 427.

102. Ibid. p. 429.

103. Ibid. p. 868.

104. Ibid. p. 39.

105. Ibid. p. 40.

106. Ibid. p. 182.

107. Ibid. p. 565.

108. Ibid. p. 381.

109. Ibid. p. 48.

110. Ibid. p. 50.

111. Ibid. p. 286.

112. Ibid. p. 78.

113. Ibid. p. 75.

114. Ibid. p. 315.

115. Ibid. p. 316.

116. Ibid. p. 91.

117. Ibid. p. 94.

118. Ibid. p. 119.

119. Ibid. p. 168.

120. Ibid. p. 326.

121. Ibid. p. 382.

122. Ibid. p. 575.

123. Ibid. p. 897.

124. Richardson, *Clarissa*, p. 85. Judy Cornett has read Clarissa herself as a "naïve juror" in a Lockean system in which jurors were expected to rely on a combination of natural reason and their experience to judge the creditworthiness of the evidence before them. For Cornett, "Clarissa's story exposes . . . the inadequacy of the Lockean model of cognitive self-sufficiency for knowers who are innocent and powerless." Cornett, "The Treachery of Perception," pp. 191–2.

125. Richardson, *Clarissa*, p. 277.

126. Ibid. p. 162.
127. "Remember, Roman, these will be your arts: to teach the ways of peace to those you conquer, to spare defeated peoples, to tame the proud."
128. Richardson, *Clarissa*, p. 872.
129. Ibid. p. 872.
130. Ibid. p. 887.
131. Bueler, "Introduction," p. xi.
132. Gally, "A Critical Essay," p. 38.
133. von Haller, *A Critical Account of* Clarissa, p. 22. The Abbé Joseph de la Porte noted that in his letters Lovelace, in particular, "displays all the distinctiveness of his character." "The Rest of the Letters of Clarissa," p. 72.
134. Fielding, "Letter to *The Jacobite's Journal*," p. 8.
135. Samuel Johnson shared Fielding's moral admiration for the text, declaring that Richardson "taught the passions to move at the command of virtue."
136. Montagu, "Letter to Lady Bute," p. 57.
137. Grant, "Letter to Miss Ewing," p. 277.
138. Adams, "Letter to Lucy Cranch," p. 279.
139. Fordyce, "Sermon to Young Women," p. 341.
140. Ibid. p. 341.
141. Hitchcock, *Memoirs of the Bloomsgrove Family*, p. 352.
142. Graham, *Letters on Education*, p. 354.
143. Keymer, *Richardson's* Clarissa, pp. 218–19.
144. Ibid. p. 219.
145. Ibid. p. 221.
146. Shenstone, "Letter to Lady Luxborough," p. 245.
147. *Lidwell's Trial*, p. 3.
148. Phipson, *Law of Evidence*, p. 173.
149. *Lidwell's Trial*, p. 90.
150. Ibid. p. 17.
151. Ibid. p. 5.
152. Ibid. pp. 5–6. The Suttons resided in Queen's County.
153. Ibid. p. 6.
154. Ibid. p. 6.
155. Ibid. p. 6.
156. Ibid. p. 23 (italics in original).
157. Rowe, *Reports of Interesting Cases*, p. 353.
158. Ibid. p. 354.
159. Ibid. p. 353.
160. Ibid. p. 343.
161. Ibid. p. 344.
162. Ibid. p. 352.

163. The relevance of evidence of "street walking" to an alleged rape victim's character for chastity is more directly considered in the *Barker* case, discussed below.

164. Rowe, *Reports of Interesting Cases*, p. 353.

165. Russ. & Ry. 211.

166. Ibid. p. 211.

167. Ibid. p. 212.

168. As Justice Parke noted to a jury around this time, however, the discursive
mutability of the victim's character was also a motivation for false accusations:
"[i]n transactions of this kind, the injured party is not always altogether innocent. She has perhaps made some advances, and, it sometimes happens, that a
person, who with more or less reluctance has given her consent, will afterwards,
for the purposes of protecting her character, be ready to deny it, and support it
at any expense." *Anonymous* (1830), York Sp. Assizes, 1 Lewin 293.

169. Rowe, *Reports of Interesting Cases*, pp. 353–4.

170. Ibid. p. 353.

171. 25 LT. 669, 670–671.

172. 2 Stark. Rep. 241.

173. Ibid. p. 244. See also *R* v. *Tissington,* 1 Cox C.C. 48 (1843).

174. 2 Stark. Rep. 243.

175. 1 Cox C.C. 55.

176. 3 C. & P. 588.

177. Ibid. p. 588.

178. Ibid. p. 590.

179. See, for example, *R* v. *Clay* (5 Cox C.C. 146).

180. 6 C. & P. 562.

181. Ibid. p. 562.

182. 11 Cox C.C. 410.

183. 25 LT. 669.

184. Ibid. p. 671.

185. Ibid. p. 671.

186. 169 ER. 1497, 1499.

187. Ibid. p. 430.

188. Ibid. p. 430.

189. Ibid. p. 430.

190. Ibid. pp. 430–1.

5

Literary Rape Trials and the Trauma of National Identity

Despite Richardson's occasional references to the broader project of law-making, his primary legal contribution to rape discourse in *Clarissa* was to show the importance of subjectivity in generating truths about the legally significant "facts." This focus on the interior and the specific contrasts with the historical, nationalistic trauma discourse characterizing, for example, the relationship between adultery literature and jurisprudence described in Part I. Yet rape discourse carries nationalistic implications as well. At the most basic level, it makes explicitly English judgments about sexual morality. For example, Blackstone describes the common law definition of rape as distinguishing England from the rest of Europe because, while civil law does not recognize the rape of a prostitute as a crime,

> the law of England does not judge so hardly of offenders, as to cut off all opportunity of retreat even from common strumpets . . . It therefore holds it to be a felony to force even a concubine or harlot; because the woman may have forsaken that unlawful course of life.[1]

English rape law thereby constructs prostitution as a potentially transitory state of being, in contrast to the discursively static harlots of the Continent.

More dramatically, eighteenth-century English writers used the motif of sexual violation to express cultural trauma over national identity and political stability in the face of the upheavals in France. British royalist Edmund Burke captured the horrors of the overthrow of French monarchy with reference to the sexualized physical violation of Marie Antoinette:

> A band of cruel ruffians and assassins . . . rushed into the chamber of the queen, and pierced with an hundred strokes of bayonets and poniards the bed, from whence this persecuted woman had but just time to fly almost naked . . . The king . . . and his queen, and their infant children (who once would have been the pride and hope of a great and generous people) were then forced to abandon the sanctuary of the most splendid palace in the world, which they left swimming in blood . . .[2]

This chapter considers how nineteenth-century literary adjudications of rape complicated the ongoing jurisprudential project of defining English law as distinct from the civil law generally and the traumatic French legal order specifically. On the one hand, nineteenth-century texts contribute to this reassuring dichotomy by dramatizing continental violence as leading to rape. Yet these texts also seem to share a fear that the historically cumulative common law structure has the potential to function similarly to the literary Gothic, in which history facilitates sexual violence in the present.

Rape and Revolution

We can find an example of the common law of evidence overtly mediating the particular, the historical, and the national in the rape context at the turn of the nineteenth century, across the Atlantic. The adoption of English common law in the American colonies was not, as legal scholar William Stoebuck explains, inevitable.[3] Stoebuck notes that colonists would raise a demand for the "common law of England" on occasions where they felt oppression from the English government, but in those cases they were referring to the aspects of constitutional law associated with political freedom, such as trial by jury.[4] The eventual reception of the common law by the colonies—which appears to have been completed by the time of the Revolution—was an apparently organic, American process, with little effort by the English home government to impose it from the top down.[5] Therefore, American Founding-era common law discourse throws particularly salient light on the values attributed to the system at a time when it had only recently been re-recognized amidst the tumult of revolution. In the wake of the Revolutionary War, American novelist Charles Brockden Brown would, in the novel *Ormond* (1803), expand the evidentiary problems in rape jurisprudence discussed in the prior chapter into anxieties about national identity.

Brown, one of the first and most prolific American novelists, relocated the horrors of the European Gothic tradition—which relegated evil to the peripheral spaces of mountain castles and monasteries—to the towns and civic spaces of early America.[6] His work frequently restages the classic Gothic psychological drama of the self "massively blocked off," as Eve Sedgwick puts it, "from something to which it would normally have access."[7] For Brown that something was, to use the phrase of his biographer Peter Kafer, the "revolutionary reverberations" of the 1770s and 1780s which saw, among other things, his father and twenty-five fellow Philadelphia Quakers arrested as suspected royalists, driven through the city in an open cart, and exiled in the Virginia wilderness for a year.[8] The traumas of the revolutionary period are legible in Brockden Brown's fiction, which is preoccupied with the threats posed by the criminal not only to the individual but to the deeply fragile communities of American nation and state. Brown's concern with the criminal is, perhaps, unsurprising; his family had intended for him to become a lawyer, and he spent six years at the Philadelphia law offices of Alexander Willcocks before abandoning his legal work, which he appears to have found morally dubious, in 1793.[9] His literary career began in New York, where he moved in intellectual circles deeply impacted by the radical democratic philosophies of such English authors as Mary Wollstonecraft and William Godwin. Brown's literary work would, in turn, influence a younger generation of British authors, including Mary Shelley, who reread his novels while working on *Frankenstein* (1818) and *The Last Man* (1826).[10] His work is therefore significant in the development of the English common law discourse discussed in this book, not only due to the contiguity (particularly at the beginnings of the Republic) of English and American common law but also due to literary cross-pollination.

Brown's most famous novel *Wieland* (1798) is subtitled "An American Tale," thus explicitly nationalizing the repressed evils he narrates. The text abounds with the theme of criminality hidden beneath homely exteriors —the invasion of the domestic by the evil and the supernatural. A visitor named Carwin comes to stay with the narrator and her brother Wieland; they soon begin hearing voices foretelling death and destruction. Though it turns out that Carwin is utilizing the powers of ventriloquism to torment them while concealed in Clara's bedchamber, his plot, combined with religious hysteria and dementia, drives Wieland himself to murder his family. Through Wieland's hysterical rampage Brockden Brown presents crime as an outgrowth of the idealized American domestic sphere. Early on Clara notes that "moral necessity, and calvinistic inspiration, were the props on which my brother thought proper to repose," in contrast to his friend Pleyel, who was "the champion of intellectual liberty, and rejected all guidance but that of reason."[11] These contrasting ideologies illustrate a philosophical tension of the American founding: the austere virtue of New England puritanical republicanism contrasted with the Enlightenment philosophy of reason espoused by the Anglican elite, including many of the Founders.[12] Clara describes Wieland's religious fervor as coupled with an enthusiasm for American nationhood and with a sort of voyeuristic pleasure of spectatorship similar to that discussed earlier in the context of Restoration drama: "revolutions and battles, however calamitous to those who occupied the scene, contributed in some sort to our happiness, by agitating our minds with curiosity and furnishing causes of patriotic exultation."[13] Here, Wieland's specifically American brand of Puritan religiosity evolves into the act of ultimate criminality: the murder of his wife and children out of the belief that he is executing God's will.

This picture of criminality as deeply other—relegated in Clara's mind to the realm of the diabolic—and yet in some ways both growing from and destructive of national identity, resonates with developments in penology in Philadelphia during the time Brown was writing.[14] Furthermore, at a more simplistic level, *Wieland* dramatizes the confrontation of criminality in a world without systematized police protection: Clara's investigations expose Carwin's ruse, and Carwin himself saves Clara from her brother's final murderous fit.[15] Wieland is punished through a traditional literary means—suicide—while Clara receives the traditional reward of marriage. The state is present in *Wieland* not as a regulative or coercive force, but as an aspect of the characters' American identities. Being "American"—much like being Christian—is but one element of Clara's innocence, yet the state and nation have no active agency in the novel. As in most of the European Gothic tradition, crime and innocence separate themselves through the self-help of the characters.

Unlike the archetypical Gothic heroines, however, Brockden Brown's female victims—while innocent—do not suffer from the surfeit of sentimentality that he found objectionable in the English novel. His renditions of sexual violence against women may be read against Richardson's, whose heroine Brockden Brown critiqued in an 1800 article in *The American Register*, saying "Clarissa's mind was not sufficiently imbued with the importance of conforming our actions and feelings to the will," a point which Paul Lewis interprets as a defense of Brockden Brown's own "more fully rational heroines" through the observation that "a stronger Clarissa would have been able to survive her accumulated woes."[16] Julia Stern goes so far as to cite *Clarissa* as a necessary pre-condition for *Ormond,* observing that "female homoeroticism in *Ormond* erupts from its interdicted position as a crucial subtext of the Richardsonian seduction plot."[17] Due to the resonance of the Clarissa/Anna friendship with the Constantia/Sophia friendship in the later text, Stern sees *Clarissa* as "the great textual precursor for *Ormond's* depiction of romantic friendship between women."[18]

In *Ormond,* as in *Wieland*, Brockden Brown emphasizes the self-help of the characters and the potential horrors lurking beneath the surface of American domestic and urban spaces. Yet he structures this text as not only an unveiling of the villain's criminal intentions—Ormond's plan to rape the heroine Constantia—but as a form of regulated testimony about the victim herself. It therefore operates, much more so than *Wieland*, against an implied backdrop of Anglo-American evidentiary jurisprudence. Julia Stern sees Brockden Brown's choice of a female narrative voice as an important feature of an overall project of resistance to the "abiding patriarchalism" of the American Founding.[19] Stern shows how *Ormond* reveals the author's hostility to the "regime of the fathers" inaugurated during the post-Revolutionary constitutional era when "masculine bands" became legitimized through the sheer authority of language, embodied in constitutional documents.[20] I will build upon this observation to suggest that the text's structural features reveal not only the anxieties Stern identifies surrounding the authority of foundational legal texts but also ambivalence over the judicial systems of truth-production which they re-established in the new American republic.

The novel opens as a second-person account by an unknown narrator to an unknown auditor, purporting to sketch Constantia's character. While we later learn that the former is Constantia's best friend Sophia Courtland and the latter a potential suitor Constantia has met in Europe after the events of the novel, the initial anonymity of the proffer suggests a formal, fact-gathering function. Indeed, the narrator immediately disclaims any entertaining or artistic purpose in giving the account, acknowledging that

> [y]ou are desirous of hearing an authentic and not a fictitious tale. It will therefore be my duty to relate events in no artificial or elaborate order, and without that harmonious congruity and luminous amplification, which might justly be displayed in a tale flowing merely from invention.[21]

With this opening, the text creates an immediate epistemological problem: where the "artificial order" of a "fictitious tale" obscures access to truth, what formalistic innovations facilitate it? As in *Clarissa,* the narrator appears to adopt the evidentiary procedures of legal adjudication.

First and foremost, Sophia is occupied with testifying to the rape victim's character—the centrality of which to credibility was the topic of the previous chapter. Although the novel—like a rape trial—appears to be "about" the titular villain Ormond, the narrator begins the tale with the character of the victim, noting that "Constantia . . . has numerous defects" and admitting her (Sophia's) own bias as a witness, conceding "[y]ou will readily perceive that her tale is told by her friend."[22] Yet she alludes explicitly to the accepted evidentiary proofs of bias in a character witness by urging "I hope you will not discover [in the narrator herself] many . . . glaring proofs of a disposition to extenuate her errors or falsify her character."[23] This language prioritizes—as do the common law rules of evidence—firsthand observations of relevant facts in determining whether a witness is qualified to testify, and the relevance of bias in evaluating the credibility of character testimony about another witness's truthfulness.[24] Much later in the text, when Sophia explains how she became reunited with Constantia after time abroad, she lauds the extraordinary effectiveness of deriving truth from observation. Upon randomly encountering Constantia's cousin after returning to the US, she says "I was powerfully struck by the resemblance of her features to those of my friend, which sufficiently denoted their connection with a common stock."[25] The cousin, for her part, "was deeply affected by the earnestness with which I expatiated on her cousin's merits, and by the proofs which my conduct had given of unlimited attachment."[26] In other words, the two accurately exchange both proof of ancestral identity and evidence of character in one first, face-to-face encounter.

With regard to her account of Ormond's character, too, the narrator Sophia emphasizes both the importance and limitations of her observations, claiming "I have shown him to you as he appeared on different occasions, and at successive periods to me. This is all that you will demand from a faithful biographer."[27] The alternate title of the novel is, in fact, "The Secret Witness," denoting Ormond's surveillance of Constantia through a wall of her apartment but also suggesting the centrality of witnesses to the text's process of truth-formation.[28] Indeed, at the end of the novel, Sophia constructs the suitor himself—acting as judge up to that point—as another potential witness with a testimonial capacity of his own, stating "[o]f [Constantia's] personal deportment and domestic habits you have been a witness. These, therefore, it would be needless for me to exhibit."[29] Beyond just reinforcing the importance of a witness's knowledge, this observation explicates other aspects of the legal mode in which the text operates. First, the narrator acknowledges her formal function as a legal advocate, characterizing her presentation of the novel's events as the equivalent to evidentiary "exhibits." Second, she underscores the official evidentiary relevance of "habit" in predicting an individual's future conduct.[30] The narrator concludes by telling the suitor that "[i]t is sufficient to have related events which the recentness of your intercourse with her hindered you from knowing but by means of some formal narrative like the present":[31] the problem of "knowing" lies at the heart of the novel, which has self-consciously adopted a legal method for truth-construction in the absence of knowledge.

Beyond the centrality, as in *Clarissa,* of common law evidentiary procedure within the text, the narrative framework reveals an additional preoccupation with external common law systems writ large. The text's constant implicit comparison of the American and French Revolutions politicizes the common law itself; Blackstone's assertion, in Book Four of the *Commentaries,* of the superiority of English criminal law to the civil law systems of the European countries would become even more significant in an age where English identity had become threatened by the trauma of French-style political upheaval. The connection to England Americans maintained by adopting the common law, with its emphasis on historical continuity, was just one way in which American identity remained in flux, against competing claims of kinship made by the French Republic. Where Brockden Brown is preoccupied, in

Wieland, with the specifically *American* incarnation of Gothic criminality, in *Ormond*, he explores how it is shaped by the American political and legal order. Sophia makes it clear to Constantia's suitor from the outset that these institutions were in some ways necessary pre-conditions for the events of the novel, claiming that:

> The modes of life, the influence of public events upon the character and happiness of individuals in America, are new to you. The distinctions of birth, and the artificial degrees of esteem or contempt which connect themselves with different professions and ranks in your native country, are but little known among us.[32]

Here she suggests that the all-important character of the actors in the crimes she describes have an inescapably public component, derived from the facts of the Revolution and the establishment of the American Republic. Sophia provides a bookend for this observation at the conclusion of the novel, in the passing explanation of her temporary disappearance from the events of Constantia's life due to a marriage and relocation abroad:

> I found that the difference between Europe and America lay chiefly in this:—that, in the former, all things tend to extremes, whereas in the latter, all things tended to the same level. Genius, and virtue, and happiness, on these shores, were distinguished by a sort of mediocrity. Conditions were less unequal, and men were strangers to the heights of enjoyment and the depths of misery to which the inhabitants of Europe are accustomed.[33]

Here she seems to anticipate Tocqueville's account in *Democracy in America* (1835),[34] and establishes continuity between her roles of, first, character witness for Constantia and, second, political historian. This narrative framing device, then, creates two threads of legal discourse which will continue through the eventual rape narrative itself: first, the epistemological function of evidentiary procedures and, second, the characteristics of the Anglo-American common law that become relevant to Constantia's victimization.

Yet despite the stated emphasis on legal truth-finding in the novel's framing device, the plot casts repeated doubt on the possibility of legally relevant firsthand witnessing as a means of access to truth. In the first place, throughout the text, Brockden Brown remains ambivalent about the efficacy of formal law. When Constantia's father gets bankrupted by a duplicitous apprentice and consequently forced to take work as a legal copywriter in a public office, Brockden Brown takes the opportunity to give a Dickensian polemic (from a similarly informed perspective) on the drudgery and, most importantly, irrelevance of formal legal practice to the vindication of truth:

The task assigned him was technical and formal. He was perpetually encumbered with the rubbish of law, and waded with laborious steps through its endless tautologies, . . . and hateful artifices. Nothing occurred to relieve or diversify the scene. It was one tedious round of scrawling and jargon; a tissue made up of the shreds and remnants of barbarous antiquity, polluted with the rust of ages, and patched by the stupidity of modern workmen into new deformity.[35]

While echoing Dickens on the sheer oppression of legal writing as a physical enterprise,[36] Brockden Brown also depicts the cumulative historical structure of the common law itself as grotesque. As in *Wieland,* the horror in *Ormond* derives from the tale's precise historical location at the crossroads between the medieval European gothic aesthetic and the new, potentially dangerous political ideals of the American republic. He identifies precisely this uncanny discord in the union of "barbarous antiquity" and modern "stupidity" in the common law; like the more traditionally gothic Frankenstein's monster (which perhaps this description influenced), it is a biological "tissue" manipulated into "deformity."

Similarly, when Constantia discovers that the treacherous apprentice, Craig, has turned up in Philadelphia, she immediately dismisses the possibility of legally vindicating her family's wrongs because "the law was formal and circuitous. Money itself was necessary to purchase its assistance. Besides, it could not act with unseen virtue and instantaneous celerity. The co-operation of advocates and officers was required."[37] Apart from the age-old problems of legal access and efficiency, which Constantia critiques, she also emphasizes the importance of "unseen virtue," suggesting that the very process of formal "seeing" intended to bring truth to light in court through witnesses was less virtuous than non-testimonial processes. Primarily, however, she concludes that "[j]ustice must be bought" and that although "[a]ll [Craig] had, according to the principles of social equity, was hers . . . The proper instrument of her restoration was law, but its arm was powerless, for she had not the means of bribing it into activity."[38] While this straightforward denouncement of legal epistemology seems to clash directly with Sophia's attention to legal testimonial process in the framing device, her subsequent narrative incursions into the action of the text throw it into further doubt. In introducing her listener to the titular villain she remarks:

I know no task more arduous than a just delineation of the character of Ormond. To scrutinize and ascertain our own principles is abundantly difficult. To exhibit these principles to the world with absolute sincerity can hardly be expected. We are prompted to conceal and to feign by a thousand motives; but truly to portray the motives and relate the actions of another, appears utterly impossible.[39]

She has tasked herself with speaking to the (eventual) villain's character and —particularly preoccupied with being "just" and speaking to "motives"— remains aware of the legally significant aspects of her tale. Yet in recognizing her limitations as a narrator, Sophia casts explicit doubt on the fundamental possibility of a character witness providing meaningful information to an adjudicator. Indeed Brockden Brown—like Richardson before him—by using Sophia's point of view rather than that of an omniscient narrator, suggests that the role of the novelist may be limited to the assembly of testimony rather than the production of stable truth.

Despite this, and in contrast to *Clarissa*, the text acknowledges the dangers of abandoning the protections and logic of the common law. First, the fateful apprenticeship Constantia's father had formed with Craig was notably founded on "[a] sort of provisional engagement . . . unattended . . . by any legal or formal act."[40] Furthermore, when the thuggish merchant Balfour becomes Constantia's first suitor, she analyzes the situation—accurately so far as we can tell from Sophia's account—through an intellectual framework adherent to both common law evidentiary commitments and higher-level Anglo-American political ideals. In this instance, at any rate, "[i]t was no difficult task to ascertain this man's character":[41] however else the text may problematize character judgments, here they prevent an unfortunate marriage. Furthermore, Constantia considers the potential union through the social contractarian language of John Locke, the frequently-cited theoretical foundation for not only the post-Enlightenment British legal order but for American constitutionalism. Unmarried and impoverished, "she was at least mistress of the product of her own labour," whereas if she married Balfour, she would be "bereft even of personal freedom."[42] Brockden Brown thus echoes—approvingly insofar as it drives a positive plot outcome—Mary Wollstonecraft's application of natural rights philosophy and social contractarianism to the case of women's rights.[43] In so doing, he elevates the language itself and the Anglo-American legal institutions it justifies. Furthermore, Constantia is motivated by a commitment to legal legitimacy; she is horrified at the idea of swearing matrimonial vows to Balfour because "to vow an affection that was not felt, and could not be compelled, and to promise obedience to one whose judgment was glaringly defective, were acts atrociously criminal."[44] In this manner she defines a potential individual and political (due to the implied sovereign role of the husband) contractual arrangement as illegitimate, not under some theory of natural law but the positive law of her state embodied by the word "criminal."[45]

Critics have divided over what to make of Brockden Brown's seemingly contradictory use of revolutionary feminist philosophy in this text. Some have read the text as an indictment of republicanism, in the United States as well as France.[46] Others, such as Lewis and Stern, take his Wollstonecraftianism at face value and emphasize the rationality and independence of characters like Martinette. Hana Layson has attempted to harmonize these positions, arguing that Brockden Brown

> explores the consequences of [the French] Revolution's failures for a feminism that shares its philosophical origins, a feminism that is itself deeply committed to reason as the means of liberation. Ultimately Brown's meditation of sexual injury becomes sharply critical of masculinity and rationality and of Wollstonecraft for so eagerly embracing them.[47]

I would go a step further and argue that Brockden Brown bifurcates the novel's concerns, between the shortcomings—evidentiary and otherwise—of the Anglo-American legal system and its opposition to the potentially violent continental systems, as represented by the rapist Ormond. The text does not contemplate republicanism as a monolithic phenomenon, but as one channeled by national identity. This choice necessarily elevates the importance of choice of legal system as both a regulative framework and symbol of national character.

When a disastrous plague strikes Philadelphia, Constantia experiences it as a crisis both epidemiological and political. She considers that

> [c]ontagious diseases . . . periodically visited and laid waste the Greek and Egyptian cities [and] constituted no small part of that mass of evil, political and physical, by which that portion of the world has been so long afflicted [yet] [t]hat a pest equally malignant had assailed the metropolis of her own country—a town famous for the salubrity of its air and the perfection of its police—had something in it so wild and uncouth that she could not reconcile herself to the possibility of such an event.[48]

For Constantia, health and legal legitimacy are continuous; that a biological plague has descended on American shores suggests the corruption of legal institutions typically associated with the depraved aristocratic European settings of the English Gothic novel.[49] Indeed the very house in which Ormond's sister Martinette shelters during the plague had been formerly inhabited by the quintessential proponent of democracy, William Penn. In *Clarissa,* Colonel Morden likewise explicates the link between continental disease and sexual depravity as threats to the wholesome Anglo order; having encountered Lovelace in Paris, he observes that "foreign fashions, foreign vices, and foreign diseases too, often complete the man."[50]

Martinette—who had taken up arms in the French Revolution before her arrival in America—eventually becomes a flashpoint for the text's ambiguity around the relative merits of the American state. Constantia is horrified by the fact that Martinette's pleasure at Robespierre's overthrow "was mentioned without any symptoms of disgust or horror" at "[t]he blood which it occasioned to flow."[51] Her reaction mirrors that of British conservatives, such as Edmund Burke, for whom the participation of women in the bloodshed of the French Revolution was a mark of its brutalizing effects. Yet her very American identity turns on a similar violent break from precisely the institutions Burke represents. As Martinette has been separated from her brother since adolescence and is therefore non-culpable for his depraved behavior it is unclear whether the reader should share Constantia's distress at Martinette's comfort with lawless violence or accept the latter's statement that she is "an adorer of liberty, and liberty without peril can never exist."[52] The question becomes further complicated when the contrast between the revolutions implicates the question of gender rights originally raised by Constantia in rejecting Balfour. When asked by Constantia how a woman's heart, in particular, can be inured to bloodshed, Martinette retorts —again deploying Wollstonecraftian rationality speech—"Have women, I beseech thee, no capacity to reason and infer? Are they less open than men to the influence of habit? My hand never faltered when liberty demanded the victim."[53] The exchanges between Constantia and Martinette leave us uncertain as to whether the perceived lawlessness of the French democracy renders it better or worse than its American equivalent. Yet, as embodied in the two allied yet very different women—even with Burkean, anti-feminist conservatism as the third principle implicitly aligned against them both—the two republican orders remain distinct discursive constructs.

Ormond himself—who, after unsuccessfully attempting to lure Constantia into a sexual union outside of marriage, resorts to attempting to rape her—appears to be a paradigmatic example of continental philosophy run rampant. As described by the self-admittedly unreliable narrator Sophia, Ormond lives his life according to a program of supposedly rational hedonism. Grotesquely parroting the philosophes, he "reasons" that, due to the pragmatic impossibility of doing good for others, the proper course of action is to live to do good for himself:

> It did not follow . . . that virtue and duty were terms without a meaning, but they require us to promote our own happiness and not the happiness of others. Not because the former end is intrinsically preferable, not because the happiness of others is unworthy of primary consideration, but because it is not to be attained . . . Principles, in the looser sense of that term, have little influence on practice.[54]

Like his sister, Ormond prefers liberty to legal order, but his take on the social contract differs from hers diametrically in its overt sexism. Marriage, for Ormond, is "absurd" due to "the general and incurable imperfection of the female character."[55] Before he meets Constantia, Ormond declares, echoing her own narrower rejection of marriage to Balfour specifically, that "[n]o woman can possess that worth which would induce me to enter into this contract, and bind myself, without power of revoking the decree, to her society." He conceives of his relationship with his first mistress Helena as "rational" in the Enlightenment sense, using Lockean language to describe it as "indebted for its value on the voluntariness with which it was formed, and the entire acquiescence of the judgment of both parties in its rectitude."[56] Yet he rejects the possibility of marriage, blending the rhetoric of social contractarianism with Thermidorian contempt for the oppressions of all traditional institutions:

> The terms of this contract were, in his eyes, iniquitous and absurd. He could not think with patience of a promise which no time could annul . . . To forego the liberty of choosing his companion, and bind himself to associate with one he despised; to raise to his own level whom nature had irretrievably degraded.[57]

That this French revolutionary philosophy eventually justifies Ormond's decision to provoke Craig to murder Constantia's father and, eventually, his attempt to rape Constantia suggests that the text settles on the American republic, with its faulty common-law system and predatory capitalist Balfours, as preferable to the utterly unbound depravity of Ormond.

Brockden Brown, however, complicates even this value judgment in his disposition of the legal questions in the text. After Constantia kills Ormond to try to escape rape, the narrator notes that "[h]er act was prompted by motives which every scheme of jurisprudence known in the world not only exculpates but applauds" and that "to state these motives before a tribunal hastily formed and exercising its functions on the spot was a task not to be avoided though infinitely painful."[58] Unlike Clarissa and Tess Durbeyfield (discussed below)—and despite the dim view taken of the law elsewhere in the text—Constantia is not doubly victimized by both her rapist and the justice system. Despite—or perhaps because of—the novel's structure as a defense of her character, no one ever more than perfunctorily questions her justification in taking Ormond's life. Assuming we believe the account of events related by Constantia to Sophia and by Sophia to her listener, the disposition of Ormond's death with as little additional pain to Constantia as possible exemplifies a legal system doing substantively good justice. Here, the gap between legal truth and "the real" seems minimal. Yet, in contrast to the uniquely American and French political and legal characters sketched by the narrator throughout the text, Brockden Brown takes care to specify (albeit inaccurately) that the justification for homicide available in cases of attempted rape is universally recognized. In suggesting that the common law, here, is doing no more than "every scheme of jurisprudence known in the world," he tacitly limits any positive conclusions that may be drawn about the Anglo-American system.

If the text's ultimate judgment on Anglo-American law remains ambiguous, so too, and more subtly so, remains its judgment on the function of evidentiary witnessing. In the last chapter, I surveyed the scholarship asserting that the increased understanding of perceptual subjectivity throughout the late eighteenth and nineteenth centuries laid the groundwork for a more capacious treatment of victim subjectivity in rape trials. Interestingly, in *Ormond*—despite the more just outcome for Constantia compared to her literary counterparts—Brockden Brown critiques her capacity to access objective truth through her subjective apprehension of her experiences. Repeatedly, Constantia—while canny in many other episodes of the text, particularly in her relationship with Balfour—falls prey to Ormond's trickery because of a lack of imaginative capacity to perceive motives beyond those physically before her eyes. Ormond first attempts to seduce her by "appear[ing] as devout as herself in his notions of the sanctity of marriage."[59] Sophia, as narrator, notes that Constantia is particularly susceptible to such a scheme because—despite her archetypically pious name—"[m]atrimonial as well as every other human duty was disconnected in her mind with any awful or divine sanction. She formed her estimate of good and evil on nothing but terrestrial and visible consequences."[60] In other words, Constantia's moral reality is entirely materialist. While, unlike Ormond, she behaves entirely virtuously despite this fact, Constantia's lack of interest in higher truth is a deeply problematic characteristic for a nineteenth-century heroine.

When Sophia arrives back in Philadelphia, meets Ormond, and learns of the suspicious death of Constantia's father, she sizes the situation up immediately in language quite condemnatory of her friend:

> Rightly to estimate the danger and encounter it with firmness are worthy of a rational being; but to place our security in thoughtlessness and blindness is only less ignoble than cowardice. I could not forget the proofs of violence which accompanied the death of Mr. Dudley.[61]

Through Sophia's gloss, the reader suspects that Constantia's gullibility—which, despite her intention to flee the country to escape Ormond, eventually leads her first to a deserted house to which she is inevitably pursued by her would-be ravisher—is culpable in its own right. We learn that Ormond—like Carwin in *Wieland* and Lovelace in *Clarissa*—has been privy to all her private conversations with Sophia through the characteristically gothic device of a hidden chamber between apartments. When he visits Constantia shortly before she plans to write him a letter bidding him farewell, he reveals this knowledge as though he is the text's sole omniscient knower: "Perhaps," he says sarcastically, "I know not the contents of the letter which you are preparing to write."[62] That Constantia—thus confronted with Ormond (as Clara was by Carwin in *Weiland*) as a repository of omniscience—nonetheless voluntarily isolates herself in a remote location implies a willful blindness that the text—much like its contemporary court opinions—comes close to associating with consent.[63]

In the rape scene itself, the obviousness of her particular danger becomes clear to Constantia immediately; when an unknown intruder begins to open the door of the room, she is sitting in "the first suggestion of her fears" is that "Ormond's was the hand that opened [it]."[64] When presented with this direct evidence, she concludes, again in legalistic language, that "[t]he motives of this unseasonable entrance could not be reconciled with her safety."[65] The conclusion seems so obvious, and so delayed that it tends to compromise Constantia's overall credibility as a witness to the events of the text. Once Ormond enters the room, he gives several disturbing speeches—straightforwardly declaring his intent to rape Constantia and understanding that her suicide will be the regrettable but necessary upshot of the event. Yet in so doing he makes a pair of speeches that condemn Constantia, first as a witness, and then as an agent of justice herself. First he asks:

> Must this meeting, which fate ordains to be the last, be so short? Must a time and place so suitable for what remains to be said and done be neglected or misused? No. You charge me with duplicity, and deem my conduct either ridiculous or criminal. I have stated my reasons for concealment, but these have failed to convince you. Well, here is now an end to doubt. All ambiguities are preparing to vanish.[66]

Beyond serving the function of "unblinding" her "senses," as Ormond later puts it, this speech highlights Constantia's persistence in misinterpreting ambiguities as a moral failing, (though it would seem to shore up, as a legal matter, Constantia's subsequent justification for taking Ormond's life in self-defense—the text is clear that "all" ambiguities have gone). Yet Ormond continues to condemn Constantia's culpable blindness, specifically relating to her failure to investigate her father's murder:

> [T]hy father is dead. Art thou not desirous of detecting the author of his fate? Will it afford thee no consolation to know that the deed is punished? Wilt thou suffer me to drag the murderer to thy feet? Thy justice will be gratified by this sacrifice. Somewhat will be due to him who avenged

thy wrong in the blood of the perpetrator . . . art thou equally devoid of curiosity and justice?[67]

This observation that Constantia's insistence on material evidence has caused her to be unjust complicates the account we receive of her eventual act of self-defense. At the moment in which she contemplates whether to kill herself (as Clarissa threatens) or attempt to kill Ormond, the chapter ends and the next begins with Sophia's point of view as her search for Constantia finally leads to the correct deserted house. When she first finds her friend she can only see her through the keyhole:

> A figure, with difficulty recognized to be that of my friend, now appeared in sight. Her hands were clasped on her breast, her eyes wildly fixed upon the ceiling and streaming with tears, and her hair unbound and falling confusedly over her bosom and neck.[68]

When Constantia recognizes that Sophia has arrived, she exclaims, "I am imprisoned!" and "Ah, why comest thou so late? Thy succour would have somewhat profited if sooner given; but now, the lost Constantia—."[69] At this moment, through the limited frame of view introduced by the device of the keyhole and Sophia as the belated firsthand witness, we cannot be certain either that Ormond is already dead, or indeed that Constantia has successfully prevented the rape. Constantia's use of the word "lost" to describe herself could refer to her violation as surely as to having committed homicide; it is only after Sophia arrives again with help to break down the door that Ormond's body comes into view.

Furthermore, when Sophia asks Constantia, "I hope . . . that nothing has happened to load you with guilt or with shame?" the latter's response is likewise ambiguous:

> I know not. My deed was scarcely the fruit of intention. It was suggested by a momentary frenzy. I saw no other means of escaping from vileness and pollution. I was menaced with an evil worse than death. I forebore till my strength was almost subdued: the lapse of another moment would have placed me beyond hope.[70]

In this passage, Constantia speaks simultaneously in both the legally precise language appropriate for the rape victim and for the criminal defendant. Forbearing "till [her] strength was almost subdued" fulfills the elusive element of force that would have been required to define Ormond's act as rape, had he been successful. But in noting that her deed was not "the fruit of intention," she seems to go out of her way to deny the level of *mens rea* necessary to support a charge of murder in the first degree—intention, or "malice aforethought." In light of these dual assumed identities, Constantia's response that she "knows not" whether she should feel guilt or shame could imply either uncertainty as to her justification in killing or her failure to successfully prevent the rape. Either way, this moment doubly demonstrates Schramm's point about nineteenth-century literary testimony acting as proof of innocence.

Sophia steps in to reinforce this effect as a narrative intermediary for Constantia's testimony, re-contextualizing both her friend's statements and her firsthand observations:

> These words sufficiently explained the scene that I had witnessed. The violence of Ormond had been repulsed by equal violence. His foul attempts had been prevented by his death. Not to deplore the necessity which had produced this act was impossible; but, since this necessity existed, it was surely not a deed to be thought upon with lasting horror, or to be allowed to generate remorse.[71]

Sophia's function here mimics that of defense counsel at trial, imposing narrative order on the defendant's account of events, synthesizing it with other evidence, and relating it to the jury. This testimonial intermediating role for defense counsel was already taking shape in the United States at the time Brockden Brown was writing, though, as the next section will discuss, it would not be introduced in England for over two decades. Here, Sophia's summary of events demonstrates how a novelist may use the narrative voice to resolve the ambiguities resulting from multiple points of view.

In summary: on one level Brockden Brown imports many of the same concerns over victim subjectivity that Richardson uses to complicate common law understandings of character and force in *Clarissa*. Yet by placing them in a historically specific, Founding-era American context, he also politicizes and problematizes the basic structure of common-law truth construction as a first principle, associated with the historical trauma of post-revolutionary choice of legal regimes. The novel's Gothic structure, with its implicit threat of sexual violation, invites us to examine the potential for the historically inevitable common law to support similar trauma in an Anglo-American setting. The dangers of hyper-historicism in constructing legal truths about rape would continue to be a literary concern as the nineteenth century progressed.

Ormond was not the last nineteenth-century novel to posit a relationship between rape trauma and revolutionary national identity. Dickens's treatment of this subject a bit longer after the historical fact in *A Tale of Two Cities* (1859) is more famous. The narrative link between the novel's eponymous cities is forsworn French aristocrat Charles Darnay's relocation to London, where he marries the daughter of Dr. Manette, a former prisoner of the

Bastille under the *ancien régime*. When Darnay returns to Paris mid-Reign-of-Terror he stands trial as an aristocrat and the Revolutionary Tribunal sentences him to the guillotine as vengeance for his father's and his uncle Marquis de Evrémonde's long-ago fatal rape of a peasant girl and murder of her family. The damning evidence of the sins of Darnay's forbears comes from a letter recovered from Dr. Manette's jail cell, where the Evrémondes had imprisoned him to ensure his silence after he tended to their victims. In it, he relates the events of the rape and his confinement, including a denouncement of the Evrémondes and their heirs, not foreseeing that one such heir would become his beloved son-in-law.

In Albert Hutter's psychoanalytic reading, the novel correlates family and nation, using the language of psychological conflict to portray social upheaval and the restoration of social order.[72] Hutter notes that the rape itself and the acts of vengeance it sparks are proxies for the broader national class conflict and that, "within the structure of the *Tale* [Manette's letter] acts like a traumatic memory, reliving the significant antecedent events of the entire plot at the climax of Darnay's second trial."[73] While the novel lacks the explic-itly legal forensic structure of *Clarissa* and *Ormond*, the climactic revelation of the trauma of the rape and its importance to the novel's characters through a testimonial document embedded in a formal criminal proceeding invites the reader to contemplate the relationship between sexual violence and the legal procedures of truth-gathering. Scholars have elsewhere well-explored Dickens's use of legal process as a proxy for the toxic aspects of British national identity, particularly in *Bleak House* (1852–1853).[74] They also have observed how his later depiction of the British nation as cordoned-off and insular shifted to a more cosmopolitan perspective with *Little Dorrit* (1856–1857).[75] In *A Tale of Two Cities,* however, Dickens dramatizes the evidentiary proof of rape as a testament to the superiority of English procedural justice over its French equivalents in both the *ancien régime* and the Revolution.

Throughout the text, Dickens links the illegitimate legal basis for absolute aristocratic privilege to the practice of interclass rape. Early on, the Marquis de Evrémonde complains that "[o]ur not remote ancestors held the right of life and death over the surrounding vulgar" and mentions that "in the next room [of his chateau] . . . one fellow . . . was poniarded on the spot for professing some insolent delicacy respecting his daughter—*his* daughter?"[76] Madame Defarge's brother, on his deathbed after trying to avenge their raped sister, confirms this state of affairs, saying "[t]hey have had their shameful rights, these nobles, in the modesty and virtue of our sisters, many years."[77] The characters' use of "rights" speak—associated with the Enlightenment-era notions of Englishmen's rights against the sovereign—to describe the French aristocracy's right to violate the rights of the lower classes creates an implicit contrast between the legal orders of the two countries. Later on, however, Dickens depicts another form of lawlessness in the Revolutionary tribunal, where Darnay "might have thought that the usual order of things was reversed, and that the felons were trying the honest men."[78] He takes care to nationalize the proceedings, noting that "[t]he lowest, crudest, and worst populace of a city, never without its quantity of low, cruel, and bad, were the directing spirits of the scene."[79] Ultimately, Dickens (like many historians before and since) draws the explicit parallel between the legal illegitimacy of the *ancien régime* and the Reign of Terror:

> [B]efore that unjust Tribunal, there was little or no order of procedure, ensuring to any accused person any reasonable hearing. There could have been no such Revolution, if all laws, forms, and ceremonies had not first been so monstrously abused that the suicidal vengeance of the Revolution was to scatter them all to the winds.[80]

Throughout the novel, and particularly in the character of would-be Englishman Darnay, Dickens maintains the dichotomy between the lawlessness of the French and the possibility of greater procedural and substantive justice across the Channel. Darnay declares of his decision to renounce his aristocratic inheritance that he would prefer "to live by his own industry in England, rather than on the industry of the overladen people of France."[81] The narrator of the novel repeatedly refers to France as "the dawning Republic, One and Indivisible, of Liberty, Equality, Fraternity, or Death."[82] The revolutionaries legitimize their lawlessness along national lines just as the Marquis had along lines of class, declaring that "[e]migrants have no rights."[83] Darnay disclaims the prospect of being "prejudged, and without any means of presenting my case," oblique references to the protections he would have had in his earlier trial for treason in England.[84] While the novel's parallel between pre- and post-Revolution French justice is clear, its implicit comparison to the judicial process in the other of the "two cities" endorses the English.

Yet the rape scene, presented at court via Dr. Manette's letter, functions in a similar manner to the constantly threatened rape in *Ormond*: as a touchstone for both nationalistic and epistemological anxieties. Manette's second-hand account of the dying brother's narrative reveals the inexpressibility of sexual trauma:

> Then, with that man's permission and even with his aid, his brother took her away; in spite of what I know she must have told his brother—and what that is, will not be long unknown to you, Doctor, if it is now—his brother took her away—for his pleasure and diversion, for a little while. I saw her pass me on the road. When I took the tidings home, our father's heart burst; he never spoke one of the words that filled it.[85]

The young man appears to be suggesting that his sister was pregnant, but this fact—like the details of the attack itself—remains buried between parentheticals and several removes away from the listener in the courtroom at Darnay's trial. Similarly, their father's fatal heart attack elided his own account from the record of this abuse. Dr. Manette's framing narrative, composed in the darkness of the Bastille, serves an explicitly evidentiary function itself; like the narrators of *Ormond* and *Clarissa*, he takes care to establish his testimonial competence, noting "[t]here is no confusion or failure in my memory; it can recall, and could detail, every word that was ever spoken between me and those brothers."[86] In short, this trial scene both animates the lurking threat of sexual violence as a component of national identity similar to that in *Ormond,* while also dramatizing the procedural difficulties inherent in vindicating it.

The problem with Darnay's trial is that the wrong legal consequences flow from these concentric accounts of sexual violence. However accurate Manette's account of the rape and his false imprisonment, his then-condemnation of the Evrémondes' future innocent heirs is illegitimate evidence against Darnay. Yet the tribunal treats that condemnation as incontrovertible evidence of Darnay's guilt. This press of failed history on the production of legal truth— while uniquely harmful in the lawless revolutionary tribunal Dickens depicts in the *Tale*—remains an animating feature of the English common law, which he so famously critiques elsewhere. In any case, the novel contributes to the mid-Victorian cultural imagination another example of rape as a product of history and nation, with unique challenges for legal truth production. The unjust action of the past upon the present becomes one of the central themes of the most significant rape novel of the late nineteenth century, *Tess of the d'Urbervilles*, discussed below.

Tess Durbyfield, Evidentiary Reform, and Narrative Justice

The nineteenth century was an age of penal reform and copious legislation in the area of criminal procedure. The increased interest in children as a distinct and protected class, discussed in Chapter 3, was accompanied by legal reform intended to protect certain classes of women; new laws made statutory rape on a girl under ten (and eventually thirteen) a capital crime, and removed the need to prove ejaculation to bring a rape charge generally.[87] The Victorian age also saw some significant changes in the evidentiary jurisprudence of rape cases. The prior chapter discussed the somewhat malleable status of evidence of the victim's character throughout the nineteenth century. But as to the element of force, two cases in particular, *R* v. *Camplin* (1845)[88] and *R* v. *Fletcher* (1859),[89] began more firmly to shift the law away from requiring proof of force and towards the more modern question of whether consent existed. In *Camplin*, the court upheld the defendant's conviction for having sex with an insensible thirteen-year-old after he had given her alcohol "in order to excite her."[90] In *Fletcher* the victim was a developmentally disabled girl who had not resisted the defendant's advances. In upholding his conviction the court said:

> The question is, what is the proper definition of the crime of rape? Is it carnal knowledge of a prosecutrix? If it must be against her will, then the crime was not proved in this case; but if the offence is complete where it was by force and without her consent, then the offence proved that was charged in the indictment, and the prisoner was properly convicted . . . It would be monstrous to say that these poor females are to be subjected to such violence, without the parties inflicting it being liable to be indicted. If so, every drunken woman returning from market, and happening to fall down on the road side, may be ravished at the will of the passers by.[91]

The *Fletcher* court's imagery of the drunken peasant woman sleeping on the roadside introduced into the legal imagination a very particular new scenario —clearly distinct from the narrative of deathly physical struggle that had hitherto predominated—as self-apparently rape. Indeed, several actual cases of rape on a sleeping woman shortly followed, and the courts likewise upheld those convictions.[92] Some treatise writers began to incorporate these newly reconfigured ideas of consent; *Halsbury's Laws of England* says

> If a person by giving a woman liquor makes her intoxicated to such a degree as to be insensible, and then has connection with her, he may be convicted of rape, whether he gave her the liquor to cause insensibility or only to excite her.[93]

Under this new definition, our respectable eighteenth-century character witness Henry Williams, discussed in the previous chapter, could have been convicted for "making a woman drink" in order to "coax her."

This new development, however, had powerful and vehement critics. For example, Charles S. Greaves, one of the most influential forces in mid-nineteenth century criminal legislation,[94] argued that force was a requirement for rape due to the crime's parallel to the crime of robbery:

> it is quite clear that in robbery there must be some violence to the person beyond the force that may be used in taking the articles; for no mere taking from the person, even against the will, can suffice in robbery. It is quite clear that merely taking an article from a man asleep or drunk would not suffice.[95]

What Greaves leaves out, of course, is that in his analogy, the act of stealing from a sleeping man, if not robbery, is at least larceny, which is still a crime.

In the case of sex with a sleeping woman, the only definitional alternative to rape is seduction, which—as discussed above in Chapter 4—is not.

It is also important to note that additional legislation during this era brought about a sea change in the manner in which the facts of a case were presented to a jury. Before 1836, the laws allowed only the prosecution to address the jury directly through opening and closing statements, with no such opportunity for the defense attorney (assuming the defendant was fortunate enough to have one). As a result, the prosecution's capacity to step back and impose narrative order on the pieces of evidence on its side—so crucial to what we now know about jury decision-making—was dramatically disproportionate to the defense's. We can see that defense attorneys felt the absence of this narrative limitation prior to the act. For example in 1800, after Lidwell's prosecutor gave the effective opening statement described in the last chapter, defense counsel pointed out to the court that "a very able address has been made to the jury, whose feelings must be considerably influenced thereby" and asked "that an equal indulgence might be extended to [Lidwell's] counsel."[96] The court declined, noting that "it is the privilege of the crown, to have a case stated on behalf of the prosecutor . . . but the law has drawn the line, and confers no such right upon a prisoner in cases like the present."[97] The absence of direct address by defense counsel, however, required the defendant to take a central testimonial role in his trial. As only the defendant can testify directly to his or her state of mind at the time of the events in question, the absence of statements by defense counsel resulted in what legal scholar John Langbein has referred to as an "accused speaks trial"[98] which, as Schramm puts it, "placed the story of accused persons at the heart of the criminal trial and gave the court access to their own descriptions of their own behavior or their intentions."[99]

In 1836 the Prisoners' Counsel Act gave criminal defendants the right to have their cases presented by professional advocates who, in the past, were only permitted to conduct witness examinations at the discretion of the court. This had the effect of removing criminal defendants from the center of a trial and creating another level of interpretive distance between the narratives produced in court and the underlying factual truth of the matter in question. Schramm has pointed to this development in criminal procedure as the basis for the distrust of lawyers on the parts of Victorian novelists such as George Eliot and Charles Dickens:

> The intervention of the discourse of barristers can only disguise or distort the relationship between appearances and "reality"; authors, on the other hand, can be entrusted with a right reading of the evidence. That lawyers are often selected to perpetrate the author's darkest deeds—and thus carry

the burden of the narrative guilt—is perhaps the product of the author's discomfort at the similarity of their interpretive activities.[100]

This mediated subjectivity—in which the author's interpretive function blends into legal advocacy—would show more benign possibilities than Eliot and Dickens appear to perceive later in the century in the work of Hardy, who depicted failed history and national identity as constitutive of the trauma of both rape and punishment in *Tess of the d'Urbervilles*.

Thomas Hardy's longstanding interest in the law received little scholarly attention until William Davis's *Thomas Hardy and the Law: Legal Presences in Hardy's Life and Fiction* (2003). Hardy served as a local magistrate in Dorchester from 1884 to 1916 and also heard more serious cases while serving at Dorchester's periodic assizes in the company of London justices.[101] He admitted to gathering "novel padding" at law offices, the police, and the divorce courts, and Davis has shown the impact on Hardy's fiction of the material he gathered in the 1880s in a notebook entitled "Facts From Newspapers, Histories, Biographies, & other chronicles—(mainly Local)." This book serves as a record of Hardy's concern with the legal issues affecting women and contains summaries of fifty court cases and newspaper stories dealing with women and such legal events as divorce, rape, and desertion.[102]

Like Richardson and Brockden Brown, Hardy frames *Tess of the d'Urbervilles* as a defense of the character of his rape victim, famously appending, just before publication, the subtitle "A Pure Woman Faithfully Presented" in the face of his contemporary moral critics.[103] The description created great controversy as to its accuracy. Hardy describes a dinner at the Duchess of Albercorn's home in which the table was polarized between those who thought of Tess as a "poor wronged innocent" and those who thought her a "little harlot"[104] (a mixed reaction similar to the public responses to *Clarissa* more than a century earlier). Hardy himself apparently hoped to move past this familiar dichotomy, so formally enshrined in the common law treatment of character evidence in rape cases. He preferred what he describes as a "paradoxical morality" in which Tess is "essentially pure— purer than many a so-called unsullied virgin." Hardy does not appear to view his heroine as faultless but sees her as a literary type who is repeatedly unfairly condemned: "As to my choice of such a character after such a fall," he writes, "it has been borne in upon my mind for many years that justice has never been done to such women in fiction."[105] He seems to acknowledge the role of fiction in generating a particular cultural mythology of the fallen woman, and the resulting potential for injustice. Elsewhere he suggests that the competing myth of the virtuous Lucretia figure is a particularly English cultural ideal, saying, "I have felt that the doll of English fiction must be demolished, if

England is to have a school of fiction at all."[106] Like Brockden Brown, then, Hardy suggests that the cultural construction of rape through evidentiary mechanisms may assume a national character.

While Hardy couches these concerns about false feminine character dichotomies as literary, his understanding of the relationship between cultural narratives and real-life truth production is clear. In the original explanatory note to *Tess* he asserts, similarly to the narrator in *Ormond*, that "the story is sent out in all sincerity of purpose, as representing on the whole a true sequence of things" and refers offended readers to St. Jerome's words: "If an offense come out of the truth, better is it that the offence come than the truth be concealed."[107] The choice of the words "on the whole" and "sequence" underscore the necessarily fragmented construction of "truth" occasioned by the use of a series of subjectivities. Hardy's narrator assumes throughout much of the text a sort of soaring omniscience very unlike the patched-together testimonials in *Ormond*. Indeed in the 1892 edition, acknowledging the literary qualities of his account—the qualities explicitly disclaimed in Brockden Brown's text—he changes this language to "an attempt to give artistic form to a true sequence of things." Despite this commitment to an overall artistic project, however, Hardy frequently begins new movements in the narrative through a more limited, third-person point of view, closer to that deployed by Brockden Brown and Richardson.

The ambiguity of the sexual encounter between Alec and Tess has been famously complicated by the varying degrees of consent depicted in the various editions of the text published by Hardy in his lifetime.[108] In their symbolically-laden first encounter in his mother's garden, Tess accepts Alec's offer of strawberries and roses, including those he feeds to her, suggesting an archetypical, Edenic point of no return for her innocence. Yet in their subsequent physical interactions, Hardy takes care to illustrate the numerous and much more complex ways in which a ravisher may overbear the will of his victim and the difficulties inherent in defining consent. For example, when Tess rejects Alec's attempts to kiss her in his buggy on the way to the Chase, he swears, "I'll never do it again against your will. My life upon it now!" implying that at least on this occasion, the physical encounter had been non-consensual.[109] In the episode of the whistling lesson, "she involuntarily smiled in his face," a concise description which manages to articulate the simultaneous possibility of Alec's subjective belief in her consent and her actual lack of will in fact, as captured by the legally significant adjective "involuntary."[110] At one point Alec hides behind a curtain but "evidently thought better of his freak to terrify her by an ambush of that kind," strongly implying that his intentions would have been unwelcome and criminal.[111]

On the night of the rape itself, the question of consent becomes more complex, though necessarily read in the context of the many preceding pages of plainly stated lack thereof. When Alec "rescues" Tess from the violence threatened by her drunk companions, she is "[i]nexpressibly weary," demonstrating not only what contemporary law would consider lack of capacity but a narratively ineffable state of mind.[112] In other words, the text breaks down in attempting to describe her point of view because her exhaustion itself transcends language. When Alec asks "[m]ay I treat you as a lover?" her response is essentially an ellipsis: "I don't know—I wish—how can I say yes or no when—."[113] At this moment, Tess's state of mind is ambiguous; her question of "how" she can say yes or no implies the categorical impossibility of consent or refusal under the circumstances, though for reasons—a feeling of compulsion? a conflict born from actual desire?—to which the reader is not privy. Our subjective uncertainty may itself model Tess's. When Alec puts his arm around her, "Tess expressed no further negative," which is legally probative of lack of force on his part, given that the law required evidence of the victim's resistance to prove this element of the crime. Nonetheless, Hardy goes on to observe that in this attitude they move "for an unconscionable time." Under the well-established common law doctrine of unconscionability, legal contracts may be rendered void as against public policy if they contain terms judicially determined to be unacceptable. Hardy complicates the legal significance of Tess's earlier silence by implying that the amount of time that had passed would have rendered a contract un-enforceable. In any case, the textual variations complicate the significance of the role of the draught Alec gives her, and the depth of her resulting sleep.

> The obscurity was now so great that he could see absolutely nothing but a pale nebulousness at his feet, which represented the white muslin figure he had left upon the dead leaves. Everything else was blackness alike. D'Urberville stooped; and heard a gentle regular breathing. She was sleeping soundly.[114]

William Davis suggests that Hardy would have been well-aware of the mid-century developments in the case law, discussed in the preceding section, which drew a bright line around the sleeping woman for the purposes of obviating consent; by portraying Tess as asleep, Davis argues, Hardy renders Alec's crime unambiguous.[115] Davis notes that in 1881, Hardy had recorded in one of his notebooks the facts of a Chancery case, *Futcher* v. *Futcher*, in which a husband had fraudulently obtained his wife's property on their wedding day. Hardy's note reads "*Husband, to induce* wife to marry without settlement insists on her drinking some liquid—ceremony of marriage gone through—she does not know what she is doing."[116] In the same notebook Hardy summarizes another case with facts similar to the rape scene in Tess:

Returned soldier—"Exeter Assizes." Wm. Dodd—35—assaulting Sarah German. 21st July . . . Sarah G.—pretty girl, apparently innocent & artless, 15. Servant—Got leave from mistress to go to Moreton Hampstead fair—abt. 2 miles distant, her mother living close to the town of M.H., & she was to sleep at mother's, & return to mistress at 7 in morning. At the fair many hours—with another young woman who afterw[ar]d left her. At the Bell Inn there was dancing—went into dancing room—at about 2 in morning saw prisoner there—asked her in whisper to go with him. She declined also in whisper. Was coming away—prisoner followed. Made her drink from tumbler of spirits. He came out with her & s[ai]d she sh[oul]d not go to mothers [sic] but to her master's. Took her arm by force & led her in that direction . . . Went onward into fields . . . Arrived at mistress's in morning.[117]

Davis observes that Hardy "could certainly have counted on his readers' familiarity with the law in 1891 but apparently preferred to tone down the criminal aspects of the assault after 1892. The effect was to make the assault in the Chase look less like rape."[118] When Hardy *de*-criminalizes Alec's conduct by removing, in the 1892 edition, the draught he forces on Tess, it may indicate Hardy's insistence, clear from his letters, on defending a morally ambiguous heroine.

The other feature of legal epistemology Hardy explores is the extent to which cultural narratives about criminality inflect subjectivity, causing Tess to construct herself as criminal from the very start of the novel. This begins with her inadvertently harming her family: after causing the death of the horse Prince "she regarded herself in the light of a murderess."[119] Later on when, after the rape, she takes a walk near a rabbit warren, Tess imagines herself "as a figure of Guilt intruding into the haunts of Innocence." The allegorical capitalization of "Guilt" shows that Tess has fit herself into a social mythology of corrupted femininity, that she has become a static symbol with no capacity for individuation. However, the narrator immediately breaks down this monolithic construction, noting that "[s]he had been made to break a necessary social law, but no law known to the environment in which she fancied herself such an anomaly."[120] Here the existence of the natural world disrupts the notion of communally constructed evidence of character. Later, when she finds herself briefly enjoying the attentions of the village girls upon her return from the Chase, objectivity descends again and re-consigns her to the realm of the criminal: "the illusion was transient as lightning; cold reason came back to mock her spasmodic weakness, the ghastliness of her momentary pride would convict her."[121] Hardy most clearly dramatizes the gap between socially accepted "truth" and actual truth, which he provides in Tess's subjective experience of the death of her baby, in contrast to the societal construction of the event: "now that her moral sorrows were passing away a fresh one arose on the natural side of her which knew no social law . . . The baby's offence against society in coming into the world was forgotten by the girl-mother."[122] When the baby finally dies Hardy takes the opportunity to make, through bitter satire, what is perhaps the novel's strongest indictment of communal and legal notions of criminality: "So passed away Sorrow the Undesired—that intrusive creature, that bastard gift of shameless Nature who respects not the civil law; a waif to whom the eternal Time had been a matter of days merely."[123]

From the discussion so far we see how the central event of the text —and the various readings of Tess it compels—turns on the subjectively contingent nature of fact. Hardy takes further care to situate this epistemological question in a historically, politically, and legally precise network of authority. *Tess* shares *Ormond's* preoccupation with the grotesqueness of the discourse of historical legitimacy, particularly in legal contexts. The whole tragedy of Tess's fate is, the text suggests, due to her relationship to a corrupted past. Her father, Parson Tringham, reveals, is "the direct lineal representative of the ancient and knightly family of the D'Urbervilles, who derive their descent from Sir Pagan D'Urberville, that renowned knight who came from Normandy with William the Conqueror, as appears by Battle Abbey roll."[124] In one sense, then, Tess shares her point of origin with the very concept of Britishness itself, as embodied in the Norman Conquest of and eventual assimilation with the Saxons to produce the Britons. Yet Tringham's qualification that Tess's father would only be a knight today "if knighthood were hereditary" underscores the necessary discontinuity between present and past, the Durbeyfields' ignorance of which will prove to be Tess's undoing.[125] Later the narrator tells us succinctly that "[p]edigree, ancestral skeletons, monumental record, the D'Urberville lineaments, did not help Tess in her life's battle as yet . . . So much for Norman blood unaided by Victorian lucre."[126] The Norman skeletons and monuments—when appended to a Victorian context—suggest not the triumphant merging of national identity triggered by the Battle of Hastings but gothic decay. This effect recurs later in the novel when Tess and her migrating family are forced to spend a night in the Kingsbere Church where she fatally re-encounters Alec near "the door of her ancestral sepulcher" while "the tall knights of who her father had chanted while in his cups lay inside."[127] Hardy also insistently highlights the difficulties of knowledge production across history—the very project upon which the legitimacy of the common law rests. In contrasting Tess and her mother—whose inability to communicate was one of many links in the chain of causation

resulting in Tess's downfall—he contextualizes Victorian epistemology in
its fractured historical trajectory:

> Between the mother, with her fast-perishing lumber of superstitions, folk-
> lore, dialect, and orally transmitted ballads, and the daughter, with her
> trained National teachings and Standard knowledge under an infinitely
> Revised Code, there were a gap of two hundred years as ordinarily under-
> stood. When they were together the Jacobean and the Victorian ages were
> juxtaposed.[128]

While common law discourse turns on historical continuity and supposed
progress, Hardy presents the persistence of the past in the present as trauma
in the form of insupportable gaps and grotesque hybridities. The codified,
almost statutory nature of Tess's education seems to chafe at the fragmentary,
common law-like knowledge represented by Joan's.

Indeed, Tess's most admirable qualities—from her own perspective, that
of Angel, and that of the narrator—are the individuated ones, explicitly freed
from historical context. Her beauty, inherited from her mother, is "unk-
nightly, unhistorical."[129] Indeed Joan Durbeyfield, at one point, prides herself
on not having fallen from nobility like her husband, who retorts "[d]on't you
be so sure o'that. From your nater 'tis my belief you've disgraced yourselves
more than any o' us, and was kings and queens outright at one time."[130]
Tess attempts to extricate herself from the tyranny of historical precedent—
particularly in its textual form—when she rejects Angel's attempts to get her
to read:

> Because what's the use of learning that I am one of a long row only—
> finding out that there is set down in some old book somebody just like me,
> and to know that I shall only act her part; making me sad, that's all. The
> best is not to remember that your nature and your past doings have been
> just like thousands' and thousands', and your coming life and doings'll be
> like thousands' and thousands'.[131]

For Tess, the written word—like Alec's objective interpretation of her protests, like the common law itself—is coercive in its ability to blur distinctions
between cases and elide the subjective account of truth from the objective.

Throughout the text, Hardy repeatedly takes care to demonstrate how
the pressure history brings to bear upon the present results in traumatic legal
consequence, echoing the legal gothic structure of both *Ormond* and *Jane
Eyre*. The vale of Tess's birth is known as the "Forest of the White Hart"
due to a legend in which Henry III heavily fined a nobleman for having
killed a white hart he had spared.[132] The d'Urberville family legend of the
ghostly coach haunts the descendants of an earlier murderer, reappearing

whenever a latter-day d'Urberville is about to commit another crime.[133] The paintings of Tess's female ancestors in the old d'Urberville estate in which she and Angel spend their ill-fated wedding night—which eventually deter Angel from an impulse to forgive Tess for her revelation—are "suggestive of merciless treachery" and "arrogance to the point of ferocity" and "haunt the beholder afterwards in his dreams."[134] The crimes of betrayal and violence live on through these artifacts through a process of historical haunting. Even the ostensibly humorous tale of the caddish former dairyman at Talbothays, who got tossed in the butter churn by the mother of the girl he had seduced, does violence to Tess's identity by creating a precedent for her situation in which she is read as a figure of absurdity.[135] This haunting of the present by the past becomes explicitly legal in the sequel to this story, wherein the dairyman eventually marries a widow of some means, only to find himself thwarted by the ghost of her late husband whose will—Causabon-like—revoked her dower on the event of her remarriage.

Significantly, Alec's great crime against Tess takes place in "[t]he oldest wood in England"[136] and after the rape Hardy describes the foresters rising from bed nearby in the language of knightly tradition embodied by and enduring in physical space: "some sons of the forest were stirring and striking lights in not very distant cottages; good and sincere hearts among them, patterns of honesty and devotion and chivalry."[137] In one of the most chilling passages in the text, Hardy speculates about the legal relationship between Tess's rape and the rapes committed on peasant girls by her ancestors:

> Why it was that upon this beautiful feminine tissue . . . there should have been traced such a coarse pattern as it was doomed to receive . . . One may, indeed, admit the possibility of a retribution lurking in the catastrophe. Doubtless some of Tess D'Urberville's mailed ancestors rollicking home from a fray had dealt the same wrong even more ruthlessly upon peasant girls of their time. But though to visit the sins of the fathers upon the children may be a morality good enough for the divinities, it is scorned by the average human nature; and it therefore does not mend the matter.[138]

The concept of retribution derives from criminal jurisprudence and mandates parity between the severity of a crime and its punishment. Legal commentators throughout history have used the biblical notion of the "eye for an eye" to illustrate the legal concept of *lex talionis*. Here it is accompanied by another allusion from Exodus when God warns Moses that he will visit the "iniquity of the fathers upon the children." Hardy rejects this theory of punishment through transitive property as inimical to human nature, which implies an earthly system of authority drawn from reason and embodied in the positive laws d'Urberville has here violated. Nonetheless, that he raises the possibility foreshadows the ever-context-dependent interpretation of this sexual encounter, in which Tess's complicity will continue to be re-evaluated.

In the end, Tess's official condemnation and execution for the murder of Alec begin at a site physically implicating deep British history, Stonehenge, where the police finally apprehend her. Her fear of being "only one of a long row" comes to fruition: her younger sister waits to take her place as Angel's wife, and the English readership receives her as yet another example of the literary fallen woman. While Hardy's *Tess* does so much to explore the many sides of subjective truth-production in a legal context, once the formal law descends to distribute justice at the end of the text we have returned to a state of the purely objective: the omniscient narrator observes the observers of Tess's execution and Tess's point of view disappears entirely into the image of the black flag being raised.

This moment resonates with Scarry's conclusions about the impossibility of translating pain; even Hardy's attempts to explore the subjective truth of Tess's sexual violation shuts down at the prison door; the ultimate physical horror of her neck snapping and mental experience of condemnation for a crime against her rapist remains shrouded by the limits of perspective. The question of her "true" desert is left to the reader to puzzle out, even as Angel receives his implied happy ending of marriage. Yet this moment may nonetheless have communicative potential too. Contra Scarry, Sara Ahmed argues that pain, like other emotions, possesses an inherent sociality derived in part from its relation to external objects.[139] For Ahmed, objects— including people—are read as the cause of emotions such as pain in the very process of an individual's taking orientation towards them.[140] Yet because objects themselves circulate through society, orientations toward them are formed socially, not only internally.[141] Because Tess is a figure in the cultural imagination, then, her pain—and that of the real women Hardy intends for her to symbolize—is at least to some extent socially shared, even if objectified. Ahmed, while recognizing that confrontation of another's pain entails a certain degree of what she terms "aboutness" (the sufferer's remaining the object of our feeling rather than a co-sufferer), concludes that the sociality of pain carries an ethical demand that "I must act that which I cannot know, rather than act insofar as I know."[142] A listener to a pain narrative cannot simply hide on the other side of the chasm of ignorance that Scarry theorizes: instead, the incomprehensibility of one's own potential for pain must serve as a point of access for the incomprehensibility of someone else's. In the case of violent acts against an individual, as Ahmed puts it, the body of the community has been damaged.[143] The danger, for her, becomes "the fetishization of the wound" as a commodity, securing the narrative of an injury to the more privileged members of a community.[144] This potential for such fetishizing may be exactly what makes the final scene of Tess so uniquely uncomfortable; even the privileged Angel's mourning of Tess' execution is a sort of commoditization; he derives emotional utility from the ceremony of her expulsion from the world, apparently without any awareness of "ethical demand" for "acting" beyond moving on and marrying her sister, who is essentially a fungible good.

By presenting subjective truths that challenge English legal narratives about rape victim character, Hardy may make such demands upon his readers. We are left with the question of whether the common law may self-correct the structural, cultural trauma it creates whenever its reliance on failed history creates injustice. *Tess* dramatizes how the weight of failed English history may result in the same sexual outrages as those associated with French lawlessness in Brockden Brown and Dickens. Yet by participating within the slow-moving apparatus of the common law imagination Hardy's text itself serves a potentially disruptive role.

Notes

1. Blackstone, *Commentaries*, vol. 4, p. 141.
2. Burke, *Revolution in France*, p. 71.
3. Stoebuck describes the influence of Hebraic law and local custom as competitors to the common law at the birth of the American republic. Stoebuck, "Reception of Common Law," pp. 394–5.
4. Ibid. p. 410.
5. Ibid. p. 426.
6. For the most complete account of Brockden Brown's role in the creation of the American Gothic genre, see Kafer, *Charles Brockden Brown's Revolution*.
7. Sedgwick, *Coherence of Gothic Conventions*, p. 12.
8. Kafer, *Charles Brockden Brown's Revolution*, p. 1.
9. Ibid. pp. 49–50.
10. Ibid. p. 198.
11. Brockden Brown, *Wieland*, p. 25.
12. This dichotomy was perhaps most famously embodied by the Founding rivals John Adams and Thomas Jefferson.
13. Brockden Brown, *Wieland*, p. 26.
14. Peter Okun has studied the new theories of penology at Philadelphia's Walnut Street Prison, which was the first to utilize periods of incarceration and rehabilitative goals, in place of broad capital punishment and retributive ideology, with the same Foucauldian effects that would occur in England half a century later. Okun found that crime was defined in terms of its relationship to the new nation: "The scientific rhetoric of Philadelphia prison reform was bound . . . to a post-Revolutionary, nationalizing aesthetic. The same logic that differentiated

the normal from the abnormal, for instance, divided the useful from the useless and the citizen from the criminal." Okun, *Crime and the Nation*, p. 149.

15. Brockden Brown, *Wieland*, p. 230.

16. Lewis, "Brown and the Gendered Canon," p. 170. Brockden Brown generated a fair amount of controversy among feminist scholars in the last couple of decades of the twentieth century. Lewis urges that Brockden Brown's fiction, with its survivor heroines, should be included "in the tradition of women's fiction" and would itself "move us toward gender balance in the study of feminist ideology in the early American novel." Ibid. p. 183. Other scholars such as Jane Tompkins have argued that Brown's belated reputation as the "father of the American novel" came at the expense of other, more popular, female novelists.

17. Stern, "State of 'Women' in *Ormond*," p. 185.

18. Ibid. p. 185.

19. Ibid. p. 182.

20. Ibid. p. 184.

21. Brockden Brown, *Ormond*, p. 37.

22. Ibid. p. 37.

23. Ibid. p. 37.

24. This narrative moment exemplifies Schramm's observation that "In fictional texts where formal accusations of guilt are made and subsequently proven or rejected in a legal forum, we see a particular sensitivity to many of the most important epistemological issues of the age." Schramm, *Testimony and Advocacy*, p. 4. She names as the "essential ambiguity" of the term "testimony" the fact that it "not only encompasses narratives of experience which need lay no immediate claim to issues of truth or falsehood, but that it seeks to be regarded as a species of evidence," which is precisely the contradiction with which Sophia seems to struggle. Ibid. p. 5.

25. Brockden Brown, *Ormond*, p. 230.

26. Ibid. p. 230.

27. Ibid. p. 37.

28. Michael J. Drexler and Ed White argue that in *Ormond* "republicanism is itself a fantasy structure accessible through the figure of the 'secret witness'" which "denotes a self-witnessing divorced from consciousness—the structure of consciousness whereby we secretly observe ourselves acting as republicans." Drexler & White, "Secret Witness," p. 334. While I take "witness" at its narrower, legal meaning, this section will explore, as they do, the relationship between competing fantasies of republicanism that seem to drive much of the action in the novel, but endeavor to link those abstract political structures to the procedural mechanisms through which they manifest coercively in the law.

29. Brockden Brown, *Ormond*, pp. 275–6.

30. See McCormick § 195, at 584–5, for the distinction between evidence of habit and that of character.

31. Brockden Brown, *Ormond*, p. 276.

32. Ibid. pp. 37–8.

33. Ibid. p. 220. Sophia's observations about America echo those of Danford, in Wollstonecraft's *Maria*, who observes that in America

> the only pleasure wealth afforded, was to make an ostentatious display of it; for the cultivation of the fine arts or literature, had not introduced into the first circles that polish of manners which renders the rich so essentially superior to the poor in Europe.

34.

> If among all these diverse features I seek the one that appears to me the most general and the most striking, I come to see that what may be remarked in fortunes is represented in a thousand other forms. Almost all extremes become milder and softer; almost all prominent points are worn down to make a place for something middling that is at once less high and less low, less brilliant and less obscure than what used to be seen in the world.

de Tocqueville, *Democracy in America*, p. 674.

35. Brockden Brown, *Ormond*, p. 51.

36. An aversion, for Dickens, embodied in the tragic, disembodied Nemo who haunts *Bleak House* (1852–1853).

37. Brockden Brown, *Ormond*, p. 109.

38. Ibid. p. 110.

39. Ibid. pp. 125–6.

40. Ibid. p. 43.

41. Ibid. p. 102.

42. Ibid. p. 103. "[E]very man has a *property* in his own *person*; this no body has any right to but himself. The *labour* of his body, and the *work* of his hands, we may say, are properly his." Locke, *Second Treatise*, p. 19.

43. "But should it be proved that woman is naturally weaker than man, whence does it follow that it is natural for her to labour to become still weaker than nature intended for her to be?" Wollstonecraft, *Maria*, p. 40.

44. Brockden Brown, *Ormond*, p. 104.

45. This seems to be another example supporting Gillian Brown's argument, discussed in the last chapter, that eighteenth-century literary depictions of forced marriages often invoked the American revolutionary republican rhetoric of illegitimate consent.

46. See Tompkins, *Sensational Designs*, and Samuels, *Romances of the Republic*.

47. Layson, "Rape and Revolution," p. 161.

48. Brockden Brown, *Ormond*, p. 64.

49. The idea of the plague as a symbol of European dissipation in American gothic fiction would be memorably reprised in Edgar Allan Poe's "The Masque of the Red Death" (1842).
50. Richardson, *Clarissa*, p. 583.
51. Brockden Brown, *Ormond*, p. 205.
52. Ibid. p. 205.
53. Ibid. p. 205.
54. Ibid. pp. 127–8.
55. Ibid. pp. 134–5.
56. Ibid. p. 135.
57. Ibid. p. 139.
58. Ibid. p. 274.
59. Ibid. p. 182.
60. Ibid. p. 182.
61. Ibid. p. 251.
62. Ibid. p. 246.
63. Even Lidwell's prosecutor implicitly criticized Sarah Sutton for a similar lack of vigilance when he

> left it to the Jury to consider, whether [Lidwell's initial rude behavior] was not an indication of an intention to take greater liberties with her; and whether it did not furnish a caution to her, not again to expose herself to a repetition of such, and perhaps greater freedoms.

Lidwell's Trial, p. 85.
64. Brockden Brown, *Ormond*, p. 258.
65. Ibid. p. 258.
66. Ibid. p. 261.
67. Ibid. pp. 261–2.
68. Ibid. p. 272.
69. Ibid. p. 272.
70. Ibid. pp. 273–4.
71. Brockden Brown, *Ormond*, p. 274.
72. Hutter, "Nation and Generation," p. 448.
73. Ibid. p. 449.
74. See, for example, James Buzard's observation that "Britain's culture vouchsafed in *Bleak House* and exemplified in the tentacular Court of Chancery presents 'a state of disastrous and inescapable interconnection,' 'a culture-like vision of social totality that is simply marked with a minus sign.'" Buzard, "Country of the Plague," p. 413 (citing Buzard, *Disorienting Fiction*, p. 21).
75. Amanda Anderson presents this argument in Anderson, *The Powers of Distance*.
76. Dickens, *A Tale of Two Cities*, p. 127.

77. Ibid. p. 334.
78. Ibid. p. 292.
79. Ibid. p. 292.
80. Ibid. p. 325.
81. Ibid. p. 293.
82. Ibid. p. 255.
83. Ibid. p. 261.
84. Ibid. p. 261.
85. Ibid. p. 335.
86. Ibid. p. 338.
87. An Act for Consolidating and Amending the Statutes in England Relative to Offences Against the Person 1828, 9 Geo. 4 c. 31; An Act to Make Further Provision for the Protection Girls, the Suppression of Brothels, and Other Purposes, Criminal Law Amendment Act 1885, 48 & 49 Vict. c. 69.
88. 1 Cox C.C. 220.
89. 8 Cox C.C. 131.
90. 1 Cox C.C. 220.
91. 8 Cox C.C. 134.
92. *R* v. *Mayers* (1872), 12 Cox C.C. 311; *R* v. *Young* (1873), 14 Cox C.C. 114.
93. *Halsbury's Laws of England*, vol. 9, p. 612.
94. Greaves, apart from being a magistrate, drafted the Criminal Procedure Act of 1851 and the Criminal Law Consolidation Acts of 1861, and became Secretary to the Criminal Law Commission in 1878.
95. Quoted in MacFarlane, "Historical Development of the Offense of Rape," p. 24.
96. *Lidwell's Trial*, p. 8.
97. Ibid. p. 8.
98. Langbein, "Prosecutorial Origins of Defence of Counsel," p. 48.
99. Schramm, *Testimony and Advocacy*, p. 6.
100. Ibid. p. 144.
101. Davis, *Thomas Hardy and the Law*, p. 191.
102. Ibid. pp. 20–3.
103. Hardy, *Tess of the d'Urbervilles*, p. 1.
104. Higgonet, "Introduction," p. xix.
105. Hardy, *Collected Letters*, vol. 1, p. 251.
106. Ibid. p. 250.
107. Hardy, *Tess of the d'Urbervilles*, p. 3.
108. Prior to Davis's work much of the scholarship surrounding the question of consent in this scene focused on the impossibility of knowing the "truth" about this question. H. M. Daleski describes the scene as "ambiguously presented" to invite "mutually contradictory readings," Daleski, "*Tess:* Mastery and

Abandon," p. 331. Ellen Rooney says that "the scene of sexual violence, Tess and the female subject all appear as radically unreadable figures." Rooney, "A Little More Than Persuading," p. 97. Kristin Brady describes it as "impossible to ascertain" what happened on The Chase and claims "the debate has still not been resolved with perfect clarity." Brady, "Tess and Alec," p. 131.

109. Hardy, *Tess of the d'Urbervilles*, p. 57.
110. Ibid. p. 62.
111. Ibid. p. 63.
112. Ibid. p. 70.
113. Ibid. p. 70.
114. Ibid. p. 73.
115. Davis, *Thomas Hardy and the Law*, p. 80.
116. Quoted in ibid. p. 81.
117. Quoted in ibid. pp. 81–2.
118. Ibid. p. 82.
119. Hardy, *Tess of the d'Urbervilles*, pp. 34–5.
120. Ibid. p. 86.
121. Ibid. p. 84.
122. Ibid. p. 92.
123. Ibid. p. 96.
124. Ibid. p. 8.
125. Ibid. p. 8.
126. Ibid. p. 17.
127. Ibid. p. 363.
128. Ibid. p. 23.
129. Ibid. p. 20.
130. Ibid. p. 29.
131. Ibid. p. 126.
132. Ibid. p. 13.
133. Ibid. pp. 166, 213–14.
134. Ibid. p. 217.
135. Ibid. p. 179.
136. Ibid. p. 71.
137. Ibid. p. 74.
138. Ibid. p. 74.
139. Ahmed, *Cultural Politics of Emotion*, pp. 5–7.
140. Ibid. p. 8.
141. Ibid. p. 8.
142. Ibid. p. 30.
143. Ibid. p. 33.
144. Ibid. p. 33.

Coda: Leaving *Midlothian*

Returning again to where we started in *The Heart of Midlothian* (1818), the door of Edinburgh's Tolbooth Prison is a site of concentric acts of criminal violence: the lynching of Edinburgh City Guard Captain James Porteous, whose death sentence for the lawless shooting of six citizens during a riot had been deferred at the intervention of Sir Robert Walpole. (The Jacobite-inflected riot itself resulted from the execution of smuggler Andrew Wilson, who had gained popular sympathy due in part to Scottish dissatisfaction at customs and excise taxes imposed from London.) The Tolbooth is thus a point of access to a historical narrative of the struggle for Scottish legal sovereignty encoded in the operation of the criminal law.

But the Tolbooth also marks the start of Sir Walter Scott's heroine Jeanie Deans's journey to London to seek English sovereign intervention in the operation of specifically Scottish criminal law. Jeanie's sister Effie had been convicted of the murder of her baby, based solely on evidence of the child's disappearance and her earlier failure to report its birth. Jeanie wins the attention of the Scottish Duke of Argyle who, despite tensions with King George II over his countrymen's lawlessness in the Porteous matter, manages to get her an audience with Queen-consort Caroline of Ansbach. The Duke suggests Caroline might intercede to win a royal pardon from her spouse on the basis of the harshness of the evidentiary presumptions permitted under the Scottish infanticide statute (which, even after the Act of Union, was specifically a question of Scottish law). He argues that "[i]t seems contrary to the genius of British law . . . to take that for granted which is not proved, or to punish with death for a crime, which, for aught the prosecutor has been able to show, may not have been committed at all."[1] According to this argument, the project of defining criminality has a distinctly national character, and this Scottish law is an aberration from the general pattern of good "British" justice.

This is a strange argument for Scott to put into the mouth of a character in defense of his heroine. Scott was, himself, involved in the Scottish criminal law in his capacity as Sheriff of Selkirkshire, supervising criminal investigations and, when the Court of Session was in recess, acting as a magistrate in the Sheriff Court.[2] He considered the Scottish law to be crucial to Scottish identity as distinct from English and deplored the speed with which cases made their way through Scottish courts only to be appealed in Chancery. "The consequence," he wrote emotionally in his journal

> will in time be that the Scottish Supreme court will be in effect situated in London. Then down fall — as national objects of respect and veneration — the Scottish bench — the Scottish Bar — the Scottish Law herself — And — And — there is an end of an auld Sang. Were I as I have been I would fight knee deep in blood ere it came to that — But it is a catastrophe which the great course of events brings daily nearer.[3]

He resolves *Midlothian,* then, through a compromise that subsumes this "catastrophic" trauma of pending Scottish legal obliteration into a narrative happy ending.

Queen Caroline agrees with Argyle that the Scottish statute is "a severe law" but notes that "it is adopted upon good grounds, I am bound to suppose, as the law of the country, and the girl has been convicted under it."[4] Nonetheless, she does secure Effie a pardon, but only one that commutes her death sentence to the familiar punishment of transportation. We learn that "[t]he King's Advocate had insisted . . . upon this qualification of the pardon, having pointed out to his Majesty's ministers, that, within only seven years, twenty-one instances of child-murder had occurred in Scotland."[5] The half-pardon gives Jeanie narrative vindication for her martyr-like struggles on behalf of her actually-innocent sister, while still partially vindicating the Scottish law's response to the recent trauma of infanticide by removing the legally "guilty" party from the sovereign space of Scotland.

The multiple crimes associated with the Tolbooth—both historical and fictitious—demonstrate the power of the criminal law both to generate and ease cultural trauma. Even as the specter of English law threatens a form of trauma to Scottish national identity, its forms and processes allow discursive counterpoints to reside simultaneously in a narrative whole. The pardon both saves Effie and excludes her, the English crown retains sovereignty over the engines of justice—in this case guided by the advocacy of a Scottish lord—and the persistence of the infanticide law reifies the relevant historical reality of child murders. The text itself—like the physical door Scott acquired in real life—serves as a legal artifact encoding the deeper historical reality of Anglo-Scotch violence. Like so many other episodes of violence explored in this study, it persists in the memory of the common law.

Notes

1. Scott, *Heart of Midlothian,* p. 422.
2. Anderson, "Introduction", *The Journal of Sir Walter Scott,* pp.xxv–xxvii.
3. Scott, Entry for Thursday, 8 June 1826, *The Journal of Sir Walter Scott,* pp.179–80.
4. Scott, *Heart of Midlothian,* p. 439.
5. Ibid. p. 456.

Bibliography

Primary Sources

Adams, Abigail, "Letter to Lucy Cranch" (27 August 1785), in Lois E. Bueler (ed.), Clarissa: *The Eighteenth-Century Response* (New York: AMS Press, 2010), vol. 1, pp. 279–80.

Anonymous (1830), York Sp. Assizes, 1 Lewin 293.

Aquinas, Thomas, *Summa Theologica*, Fathers of the English Dominican Province (eds), 5 vols [1265–1274] (Westminster, MD: Christian Classics, 1981).

Arnold, Matthew, "Letter to Arthur Hugh Clough" [21 March 1853], in *The Letters of Matthew Arnold*, Cecil Y. Lang (ed.), 6 vols (Charlottesville: University of Virginia Press, 1996).

Austen, Jane, *Mansfield Park* [1814] (London: Penguin Books, 2003).

Blackstone, William, *The Oxford Edition of Blackstone: Commentaries on the Laws of England: Book II: Of the Right of Things*, Simon Stern (ed.), (Oxford: Oxford University Press, 2016).

Blackstone, William, *The Oxford Edition of Blackstone: Commentaries on the Laws of England: Book IV: Of Public Wrongs*, Ruth Paley (ed.), (Oxford: Oxford University Press, 2016).

The Bloody Register: Being a Collection of the Most Remarkable Trials for Murder, Treason, Rape, Sodomy, &c., 4 vols (London: E. & M. Viney, 1764).

Bracton, Henry de, *De Legibus et Consuetudinibus Angliae*, G. E. Woodbine (ed.). Samuel Thorne. (trans.), 4 vols (Cambridge, MA: Harvard University Press, 1968–77).

Britton: Containing the Ancient Pleas of the Crown, Robert Kelhan (trans.) [1290?] (London: Woodfall & Strahan, 1762).

Brockden Brown, Charles, *Ormond* [1799] (Peterborough, ON: Broadview Press, Ltd., 1999).

_____, *Wieland* [1798] (Kent, OH: Kent State University Press, 1978).

Brontë, Charlotte, *Jane Eyre* [1847] (London: Penguin Books, 1996).

_____, "Letter to Constantin Heger" (8 January 1845), in Margaret Smith (ed.), *The Letters of Charlotte Brontë: With a Selection of Letters by Family and Friends* (Oxford: Clarendon Press, 2004), vol. 1, pp. 329–30.

Browning, Robert, *The Ring and the Book*, Richard Altick (ed.) [1868–9] (London: Penguin Books, 1990).

Buchanan, Robert, "Immorality in Authorship", *Fortnightly Review*, 15 September 1866, p. 6.

Burke, Edmund, *Reflections on the Revolution in France*, L. G. Mitchell (ed.) [1790] (Oxford: Oxford University Press, 1993).

Captain Leeson's Case (London: J. Roberts, 1715).

Carpenter, Mary, "A Letter addressed to the Editor of the *Bristol Gazette*", in Jelinger Symons (ed.), *On the Reformation of Young Offenders: A Collection of Papers, Pamphlets, & Speeches on Reformatories, and the Various Views Held on the Subject of Juvenile Crime and its Treatment*, (London: Routledge, 1855), pp. 138–40.

The Case of the Lord John Drummond (London: J. Roberts, 1715).

Coke, Edward, *Institutes of the Laws of England*, 3 vols (London: E. & R. Brooke, 1794).

Coleridge, Samuel Taylor, *The Collected Letters of Samuel Taylor Coleridge*, Earl Leslie (ed.), 6 vols (Oxford: Oxford University Press, 1971).

_____, "The Rime of the Ancient Mariner" in Stephen Greenblatt (ed.), *Norton Anthology of English Literature*, vol. 2. (New York: Norton, 2006), pp. 430–46.

The Criminal Law Amendment Act 1885, 48 & 49 Vict. c. 69.

Darwin, Charles, *On the Origin of Species by Means of Natural Selection*, 2nd edn (London: John Murray, 1860).

"Debate in the Lords on the Standing Order respecting Divorce Bills", in *The Parliamentary History of England*, vol. 34 (1798–1800) (London 1819), cols 1551–61.

Dickens, Charles, *A Tale of Two Cities* [1859] (New York: Signet, 1997).

_____, *Bleak House* [1852–53] (London: Penguin Books, 2003).

_____, *David Copperfield* [1849–50] (London: Penguin Books, 2003).

_____, *Great Expectations* [1861] (London: Penguin Books, 2003).

_____, *Oliver Twist* [1837–39] (London: Penguin Books, 2003).

The Earl of Halsbury (ed.), *The Laws of England: Being a Complete Statement of the Whole Law of England*, 31 vols (London: Butterworth, 1907–1917)

East, Edward Hyde, *Pleas of the Crown*, 2 vols (London: A. Strahan, 1803).

Edgeworth, Maria, *Practical Education*, Susan Manly (ed.), 2 vols (London: Pickering & Chatto, 2003).

Emlyn, Sollum, *State Trials* (London: Timothy Goodwin, 1730).

Farr, Samuel, *The Elements of Medical Jurisprudence* (London: T. Becket, 1787).

Fielding, Henry, "Letter to *The Jacobite's Journal*" (2 January 1748), in Lois E. Bueler (ed.), *Clarissa: The Eighteenth-Century Response* (New York: AMS Press, 2010), vol. 1, pp. 7–8.

_____, *The Modern Husband* [1730] (London: J. Watts, 1732).

Filmer, Sir Robert, *Patriarcha, or the Natural Power of Kings* (London: Walter Davis, 1680).

Fordyce, James, "Sermons to Young Women" [1766], in Lois E. Bueler (ed.), *Clarissa: The Eighteenth-Century Response* (New York: AMS Press, 2010), vol. 1, pp. 340–1.

Gally, Henry, "A Critical Essay on Characteristic-Writing", in Henry Galley (trans.), *The Moral Characters of Theophrastus* (London: John Hooke, 1725).

Graham, Catharine Sawbridge MacAulay, *Letters on Education. With Observations on Religious and Metaphysical Subjects* [1790] in Lois E. Bueler (ed.), *Clarissa: The Eighteenth-Century Response* (New York: AMS Press, 2010), vol. 1, pp. 352–5.

Grant, Anne McVicar, "Letter to Miss Ewing" [3 October 1778], in Lois E. Bueler (ed.), Clarissa: *The Eighteenth-Century Response* (New York: AMS Press, 2010), vol. 1, pp. 277–8.

Hale, Matthew, "Consideration Touching the Amendment or Alteration of Lawes", in Francis Hargrave (ed.), *A Collection of Legal Tracts Relating to the Law of England* (1787).

_____, *The History of the Pleas of the Crown*, W. A. Stokes & E. Ingersoll (eds), 2 vols [1736] (Philadelphia: Robert Small, 1847).

Hall, Robert, "Extract from a Lecture on Mettray", in Jelinger Symons (ed.), *On the Reformation of Young Offenders: A Collection of Papers, Pamphlets, & Speeches on Reformatories, and the Various Views Held on the Subject of Juvenile Crime and its Treatment*, (London: Routledge, 1855), pp. 37–82.

Hall, W. Clarke, *The Law Relating to Children: A Short Treatise on the Personal Status of Children* (London: Stevens & Sons, Ltd., 1905).

Hansard's Parliamentary Debates, 3rd ser., vol. 146 (1857).

Hardy, Thomas, *Tess of the D'Urbervilles*, Tim Dolin (ed.) [1891] (London: Penguin Classics, 2003).

_____, *The Collected Letters of Thomas Hardy*, Richard Little Purdy & Michael Millgate (eds), 5 vols (Oxford: Oxford University Press, 1978).

Hawkins, William, *Pleas of the Crown*, 2 vols (London: 1716).

Hill, Matthew Davenport, "Practical Suggestions to the Founders of Reformatory Schools", in Jelinger Symons (ed.), *On the Reformation of Young Offenders: A Collection of Papers, Pamphlets, & Speeches on Reformatories, and the Various Views Held on the Subject of Juvenile Crime and its Treatment* (London: Routledge, 1855), pp. 1–7.

Hitchcock, Enos, *Memoirs of the Bloomsgrove Family. In a Series of Letters to a respectable citizen of Philadelphia, containing the Sentiments on a mode of domestic education, suited to the present state of society, government, and manners, in the United States of America: and on the dignity and importance of the female character. Interspersed with a variety of interesting anecdotes* [1790] in Lois E. Bueler (ed.), Clarissa: *The Eighteenth-Century Response* (New York: AMS Press, 2010), vol. 1, pp. 351–2.

Hume, David, *Commentaries on the Laws of Scotland Respecting Crimes*, vol. 1 (Edinburgh: Bell & Bradfete, 1819).

The Important and Eventful Trial of Queen Caroline, Consort of George IV, for "Adulterous Intercourse," with Bartolomo Bergami (London 1820).

Jacob, Giles, *Every Man His Own Lawyer, or A Summary of the Laws of England, in a New and Instructive Method* (London: Hugh Gaine, 1768).

_____, *Law Dictionary*, T. E. Tomlins (ed.), 6 vols [1732] (New York: I. Riley, 1811).

Johnson, Samuel, 'Introduction', in *The Rambler* No. 97, 19 February 1751, <http://www.johnsonessays.com/the-rambler/advice-unmarried-ladies/> (last accessed 25 April 2019).

Kingsley, Charles, *Alexandria and her Schools: Four Lectures Delivered at the Philosophical Institution, Edinburgh* (Cambridge: Macmillan, 1854).

_____, "Capital Punishment" [Eversley, 1872], in *All Saints' Day and Other Sermons*, W. Harrison (ed.), 3rd edn (London: C. Kegan Paul & Co., 1878), pp. 53–64.

_____, "The Comforter" [Eversley, 1868], in *All Saints' Day and Other Sermons*, W. Harrison (ed.), 3rd edn (London: C. Kegan Paul & Co., 1878), pp. 124–33.

_____, "David's Deserts", in *Five Lectures on David* (London: Macmillan, 1874), pp. 69–89.

_____, "Discipline" [Wimbledon, 14 July 1867], in *Discipline, and Other Sermons* (London: Macmillan & Co., 1899), pp. 1–10.

_____, "England's Strength", in *Sermons for the Times* (London: Macmillan, 1898), pp. 188–97.

_____, *Glaucus, or The Wonders of the Shore* [1855] (London: Macmillan, 1899).

_____, *His Letters and Memories of his Life*, F. Kingsley (ed.) (New York: Scribner, 1877).

_____, "Human Soot" [Liverpool, 1870], in W. Harrison (ed.), *All Saints' Day and Other Sermons*, 3rd edn (London: C. Kegan Paul & Co., 1878), pp. 302–11.

_____, "The Natural Theology of the Future" [Sion College, 10 January 1871], in *The Works of Charles Kingsley: Scientific Lectures and Essays*, vol. XIX (London: Macmillan, 1880), pp. 313–36.

_____, "On Bio-geology" [Winchester, 1871], in *The Works of Charles Kingsley: Scientific Lectures and Essays*, vol. XIX (London: Macmillan & Co, 1880), pp. 155–80.

_____, "Preparation for Advent" [Westminster Abbey, 15 November 1874], in W. Harrison (ed.), *All Saints' Day and Other Sermons*, 3rd edn (London: C. Kegan Paul & Co., 1878), pp. 9–29.

_____, *The Water-Babies* [1862–63] (Mineola, NY: Dover Publications, 2006).

Knapp, Andrew & William Baldwin, *The Newgate Calendar*, 5 vols (London: J. Robins & Co., 1825)

Lidwell's Trial: An Authentic Report of the Trial of Thomas Lidwell, Esq. on an Indictment for a Rape Committed on the Body of Sarah Sutton (Dublin: Robert Marchbank, 1800).

Littell, Eliakim, *Littell's Living Age* (New York: The Living Age Co., Inc., 1847).

Locke, John, *Second Treatise on Government*, C. B. Macpherson (ed.) [1690] (Indianapolis: Hackett Publishing, 1980).

_____, *Some Thoughts Concerning Education and Of the Conduct of the Understanding*, Ruth W. Grant & Nathan Tarcov (eds) (Indianapolis: Hackett Publishing Co., 1996).

_____, *Two Treatises of Government*, Peter Laslett (ed.) [1689] (Cambridge: Cambridge University Press, 1988)

MacDonald, George, "Abba, Father!", in *Unspoken Sermons: Second Series* (London: Longmans, Green, and Co., 1885), pp. 139–65.

_____, *An Expression of Character: the Letters of George MacDonald*, Glenn Edward Sadler (ed.) (MI: Eerdman's Publishing, 1994)

_____, "The Child in the Midst", in *Unspoken Sermons: First Series* (London: Longmans, Green, and Co. 1887), pp. 1–26.

_____, *The Complete Fairy Tales*, U. C. Knoepflmacher (ed.) (New York: Penguin, 1999).

_____, "The Creation in Christ", in *Unspoken Sermons: Third Series* (London: Longmans, Green, and Co., 1889), pp. 1–24.

_____, *An Expression of Character: The Letters of George MacDonald*, Glenn Edward Sadler (ed.) (Grand Rapids, MI: William B. Eerdman's Publishing Co., 1994).

_____, "Hands of the Father", in *Unspoken Sermons: First Series* (London: Longmans, Green, and Co., 1887), pp. 180–8.

_____, "The Higher Faith", in *Unspoken Sermons: First Series* (London: Longmans, Green, and Co., 1887), pp. 50–65

_____, *Lilith* (Grand Rapids, MI: William B. Eerdman's Publishing Co., 1981).

_____, "Wordsworth's Poetry", in *A Dish of Orts* (London: George Newnes, Ltd., 1905), pp. 245–63.

Malory, Thomas, *The Works of Sir Thomas Malory*, Eugène Vinaver (ed.), 3 vols (Oxford: Oxford University Press, 1990).

The Matrimonial Causes Act, 20 & 21. Vict. c. 85 (1857).

McCormick, Charles T, Kenneth S Broun & George E Dix, *McCormick on Evidence*, 7th edn (MN: Thomson/West, 2013)

Montagu, Mary Wortley, "Letter to Lady Bute" [1 March 1752], in Lois E. Bueler (ed.), Clarissa: *The Eighteenth-Century Response* (New York: AMS Press, 2010), vol. 1, pp. 56–7.

A New and Complete Collection of the Most Remarkable Trials for Adultery &c., 2 vols (London: J. Fleeming. 1780).

Norton, Caroline, *A Letter to the Queen on Lord Chancellor Cranworth's Marriage and Divorce Bill* (London: Longman, Brown, Green, and Longmans, 1855).

_____, "Letter to Lady Dacre" (12 January 1848), archived at the Brontë Parsonage Museum.

_____, *Plain Letter to the Lord Chancellor on the Infant Custody Bill* (London: James Ridgway, 1839) (using pseudonym of "Pearce Stevenson").

The Offenses Against the Person Act 1828, 9 Geo. 4 c. 31.

People v. *Abbot* (NY 1838), 19 Wend. 192.

Phipson, Sidney L., *The Law of Evidence*, 5th edn (London: Stevens & Haynes, 1911).

Pollock, Sir Frederick & Frederic William Maitland, *The History of English Law Before the Time of Edward I*, 2 vols (Cambridge: Cambridge University Press, 1898).

de la Porte, Joseph, "*The Rest of the Letters of Clarissa, translated from the English*", [1752] in Lois E. Bueler (ed.), Clarissa: *The Eighteenth-Century Response* (New York: AMS Press, 2010), vol. 1, pp. 72–79.

R v. *Adkins*, Old Bailey Proceedings, sessions ending 18 September 1751.

_____ v. *Barker* (1829), 3 C. & P. 588, 590.

_____ v. *Camplin* (1845), 1 Cox C.C. 220.

_____ v. *Clarke* (1817), 2 Stark. Rep. 241, 243.

_____ v. *Clay* (1851), 5 Cox C.C. 146.

_____ v. *Cockcroft* (1870), 11 Cox C.C. 410.

_____ v. *Fletcher* (1859), 8 Cox C.C. 131, 134.

_____ v. *Hodgson* (1812), Russ. & Ry. 211.

_____ v. *Holmes & Furness* (1871), 25 LT. 669.

_____ v. *Martin* (1834), 6 C. & P. 562.

_____ v. *Mayers* (1872), 12 Cox C.C. 311.

_____ v. *Robins* (1843), 1 Cox C.C. 55.

_____ v. *Rowton* (1865), 169 ER. 1497.

_____ v. *Rudland* (1865), 4 F. 495.

_____ v. *Ryan* (1846), 2 Cox C.C. 115.

_____ v. *Sherwin*, Old Bailey Proceedings, sessions beginning 31 January 1779.

_____ v. *Yorke* (1748), 1 Fost. 70.

_____ v. *Young* (1873), 14 Cox C.C. 114.

Richardson, Samuel, *Clarissa* [1748] (London: Penguin Books, 1985).

Rowe, Richard Radford, *Reports of Interesting Cases: Argued and Determined in the King's Law Courts of England and Ireland, the House of Parliament, and Military Courts* (1824).

Russell, William Oldnall, *A Treatise on Crimes and Indictable Misdemeanors*, 2 vols (London: Butterworth and Son, 1826).

Saunders, Thomas, William & William Edgar Saunders, *The Law as Applicable to the Criminal Offences of Children and Young Persons* (London: Horace Cox, 1887).

Scott, Walter, Entry for Thursday, 8 June 1826, in W. E. K. Anderson (ed.), *The Journal of Sir Walter Scott*, (Edinburgh: Canongate Books, 1998), pp.179–80.

Scott, Walter, *The Heart of Midlothian* [1818] (New York: Charles Scribner's Sons, 1918).

Shenstone, William, "Letter to Lady Luxborough" [23 March 1750], in Lois E. Bueler (ed.), Clarissa: *The Eighteenth-Century Response* (New York: AMS Press, 2010), vol. 1, pp. 245.

The Statute of Uses 1536, 27 Hen. 8 c. 10.

Statutes of the Realm, 9 vols (London: G. Eyre and A. Strahan, 1810–1828).

Stephen, Fitzjames, *History of the Criminal Law of England*, 2 vols (London: Macmillan and Co., 1883).

_____, "Madame Bovary", *Saturday Review* (11 July 1847), pp. 40–1.

Swabey, M. C. Merttins, *The Act to Amend the Law Relating to Divorce and Matrimonial Causes in England, Etc.* (London: Shaw & Sons, 1857).

Swinburne, Algernon, "A. C. Swinburne on the *Idylls*" [1872], in John D. Jump (ed.), *Tennyson: The Critical Heritage* (London: Routledge, 2013), pp. 318–21.

Symons, Jerlinger, "On Juvenile Crime as it affects Commerce, and the best Means of repressing it", in Jelinger Symons (ed.), *On the Reformation of Young Offenders: A Collection of Papers, Pamphlets, & Speeches on Reformatories, and the Various Views Held on the Subject of Juvenile Crime and its Treatment* (London: Routledge, 1855), pp. 82–102.

Tennyson, Alfred, "Idylls of the King" [1859], in Charles Howard Johnson (ed.), *The Complete Works of Lord Tennyson* (New York: Frederick A. Stokes, 1891).

Thackeray, William Makepeace, Letter to Hallam Tennyson [1874], in Hester Thackeray Ritchie (ed.), *Thackeray and his Daughter: The Letters and Journals of Anne Thackeray Ritchie, with Many Letters of William Makepeace Thackeray* (New York: Harper, 1924), pp. 170–1.

de Tocqueville, Alexis. *Democracy in America*, Harvey Mansfield & Delba Winthrop (eds) [1835] (Chicago: University of Chicago Press, 2000).

Trial of Hugh Leeson and Sarah Blandford (27 April 1715), Old Bailey Proceedings Online, <http://www.oldbaileyonline.org> (last accessed 2 March 2019) (search for reference number t17150427-43).

Trials for Adultery, or A History of Divorces, 7 vols (London: S. Blandon, 1799).

de Troyes, Chrètien, "Lancelot (The Knight of the Cart)", in *Arthurian Romances*, D. D. R. Owen (trans.) (London: Dent, 1987).

von Haller, Albrecht, *A Critical Account of* Clarissa *in 7 Volumes* [1749], in Lois E. Bueler (ed.), Clarissa: *The Eighteenth-Century Response* (New York: AMS Press, 2-10), vol. 1, pp. 20–24.

Whipping Act 1862, 25 & 26 Vict. c. 18.

Wigmore, John Henry, *Evidence in Trials at Common Law*, 3rd edn (Boston: Little, Brown & Co., 1940)

Wollstonecraft, Mary, *Maria* [1797] (New York: Dover Publications, 2005).

_____, *A Vindication of the Rights of Woman* [1792], Stanley Appelbaum (ed.) (Mineola, NY: Dover Publications Ltd., 1996).

Wordsworth, William, *The Major Works*, Stephen Gill (ed.) (Oxford: Oxford University Press, 2000).

_____, "The Prelude: Book Five", in *Selected Poems and Prefaces*, Jack Stillinger (ed.) (Boston: Houghton Mifflin, 1965), pp. 241–55.

Secondary Sources

Ahmed, Sarah, *The Cultural Politics of Emotion* (New York: Routledge, 2004).

Alexander, Jeffrey, "Toward a Theory of Cultural Trauma", in Jeffrey Alexander, Ron Eyerman, Bernhard Giesen, Neil J. Smelser & Piotr Sztompka (eds), *Cultural Trauma and Collective Identity* (Berkeley: University of California Press, 2004)

Altick, Richard. D., "Introduction", in Robert Browning, *The Ring and the Book* (London: Penguin, 1990), pp. 11–15.

Amussen, Susan Dwyer, *An Ordered Society: Gender and Class in Early Modern England* (New York: Columbia University Press, 1988).

Anderson, Amanda, *The Powers of Distance: Cosmopolitanism and the Cultivation of Detachment* (Princeton: Princeton University Press, 2001).

Anderson, W. E. K., "Introduction", in Walter Scott, *The Journal of Sir Walter Scott*, (Edinburgh: Canongate Books, 1998).

Andrew, Donna, "The Code of Honour and its Critics: the Opposition to Duelling in England, 1700–1850." *Social History*, 5:3, 409–34 (1980).

Annuschat, Katherine. "An Affair to Remember: the State of the Crime of Adultery in the Military", *San Diego Law Review* 47:4, 1161–1204 (2010).

Armstrong, Isobel, "Browning and Victorian Poetry of Sexual Love", in Isobel Armstrong (ed.), *Robert Browning* (Athens: Ohio University Press, 1975), pp. 267–98.

Armstrong, Judith, *The Novel of Adultery* (New York: Macmillan, 1976).

Armstrong, Nancy, "Gender Must Be Defended", *The South Atlantic Quarterly*, 111:3, 529–47 (2012).

Atiyah, P. S., *Accidents, Compensation and the Law*, 3rd edn (London: Weidenfeld and Nicolson, 1980).

Atkinson, Diane, *The Criminal Conversation of Mrs. Norton* (New York: Random House, 2012).

Bakhtin, Mikhail, *Speech Genres and Other Late Essays*, Vern W. McGee (trans.) (Austin: University of Texas Press, 1986).

Ballaster, Ros, *Seductive Forms: Women's Amatory Fiction from 1684 to 1740* (Oxford: Oxford University Press, 1998).

Banerjee, Jacqueline P., "Ambivalence and Contradictions: the Child in Victorian Fiction", *English Studies*, 65:6, 481–94 (1984).

Barr, Alan P., "Mourning Becomes David: Loss and the Victorian Restoration of Young Copperfield", *Dickens Quarterly*, 24:2, 63–79 (2007).

Barrett, Andrew & Harrison, Christopher, *Crime and Punishment in England: A Sourcebook* (London: Routledge, 1999).

Beatty, C. J. P., "Charles Dickens's *Great Expectations* (1860–1) and the Probable Source of the Expression 'Brought Up by Hand'", *Notes and Queries*, 38:3, 315 (1991).

Beebe, Thomas, "Doing Clarissa's Will: Samuel Richardson's Legal Genres", *International Journal for the Semiotics of Law*, 2:5, 159–72 (1989).

Beer, Gillian, *Darwin's Plots: Evolutionary Narrative in Darwin, George Eliot and Nineteenth-Century Fiction* (London: Routledge & Kegan Paul, 1983).

Bell, Ian, *Literature and Crime in Augustan England* (London: Routledge, 1991).

Bender, John, *Imagining the Penitentiary: Fiction and the Architecture of Mind in Eighteenth-Century England* (Chicago: University of Chicago Press, 1987).

Ben-Yishai, Ayelet, *Common Precedents: The Presentness of the Past in Victorian Law and Fiction* (Oxford: Oxford University Press, 2013).

_____, "Victorian Precedents: Narrative Form, Law Reports, and *Stare Decisis*", *Law, Culture & the Humanities*, 4:3, 382–402 (2008).

Bowers, Toni, *By Force or Fraud: British Seduction Stories and the Problem of Resistance, 1660–1760* (Oxford: Oxford University Press, 2011).

Brady, Kristin, "Tess and Alec: Rape or Seduction", in Norman Page (ed.), *Thomas Hardy Annual No. 4* (London: Macmillan,1986), pp. 127–47.

Brescó de Luna, Ignacio, "How the Future Weights on the Past. Prolepsis and Other Ways of Reconstructing the Past in Relation to Different Imagined Futures", in Constance de Saint-Laurent, Sandra Obradovic & Kevin Carriere (eds), *Imagining Collective Futures: Perspectives from Social, Cultural and Political Psychology* (London: Palgrave Macmillan, 2018), pp. 109–28.

Brewer, Holly, *By Birth or Consent: Children, Law & the Anglo-American Revolution in Authority* (Raleigh: North Carolina University Press, 2005).

Brooks, Peter, *Troubling Confessions: Speaking Guilt in Law and Literature* (Chicago: University of Chicago Press, 2000).

_____ & Paul Gewirtz, *Law's Stories: Narrative and Rhetoric in Law* (New Haven: Yale University Press, 1996).

Broome, F. Hal, "The Scientific Basis of George MacDonald's Dream Frame", in William Raeper (ed.), *The Gold Thread* (Edinburgh: Edinburgh University Press, 1990), pp. 87–108.

Brown, Eric, "The Influence of Queen Victoria on England's Literary Fairy Tale", *Marvels & Tales*, 13:1, 31–51 (1999).

Brown, Gillian, "Consent, Coquetry, and Consequences", *American Literary History*, 9:4, 625–52 (1997).

Bueler, Lois E., "Introduction", in Lois E. Bueler (ed.), *Clarissa: The Eighteenth-Century Response* (New York: AMS Press, 2010), vol. 1, pp. xi–xv.

Burke, Alafair S., "Equality, Objectivity, and Neutrality", *Michigan Law Review*, 103:6, 1043–80 (2005).

Buzard, James, *Disorienting Fiction: The Autoethnographic Work of Nineteenth-Century British Novels* (Princeton: Princeton University Press, 2005).

_____, "'The Country of the Plague': Anticulture and Autoethnography in Dickens's 1850s", *Victorian Literature and Culture*, 38:2, 413–19 (2010).

Calabresi, Guido, *The Costs of Accidents: A Legal and Economic Analysis* (New Haven, CT: Yale University Press, 1970).

Carter, John Marshall, "Rape in Medieval England: An Historical and Sociological Study", *Speculum*, 61:3, 633–5 (1986).

A Catalogue of Prints and Drawings in the British Museum (London: Chiswick Press, 1873).

Chase, Kevin & Michael Levenson, *The Spectacle of Intimacy: A Public Life for the Victorian Family* (Princeton: Princeton University Press, 2000).

Chute, Chaloner William, *Equity Under the Judicature Act, or the Relation of Equity to the Common Law* (London: Butterworths, 1874).

Cornett, Judy, "The Treachery of Perception: Evidence and Experience in *Clarissa*", *University of Cincinnati Law Review*, 63:1, 165–93 (1994).

Cox, Pamela & Heather Shore, "Re-inventing the Juvenile Delinquent in Britain and Europe 1650–1950", in Pamela Cox & Heather Shore (eds), *Becoming Delinquent: British and European Youth, 1650–1950* (Hampshire: Ashgate, 2002).

Crane, Susan, "Writing the Individual Back into Collective Memory", *American Historical Review*, 102:5, 1372–85 (1997).

Daleski, H. M., "Tess of the d'Urbervilles: Mastery and Abandon", *Essays in Criticism*, 30:4, 326–45 (1980).

Davis, William, "'But he can be prosecuted for this': Legal and Sociological Backgrounds to the Mock Marriage in Hardy's Serial *Tess*", *Colby Library Quarterly*, 25:1, 28–41 (1989).

_____, *Thomas Hardy and the Law: Legal Presences in Hardy's Life and Fiction* (Newark: University of Delaware Press, 2003).

Devereaux, Simon, "Imposing the Royal Pardon: Execution, Transportation, and Convict Resistance in London, 1789", *Law and History Review*, 25:1, 101–38 (2007).

Drexler, Michael & Ed White, "Secret Witness, or, the Fantasy Structure of Republicanism", *Early American Literature*, 44:2, 333–61 (2009).

Durston, Gregory, "Rape in the Eighteenth-Century Metropolis: Part 2", *British Journal for Eighteenth-Century Studies*, 29:1, 15–31 (2006).

_____, *Whores and Highwaymen: Crime and Justice in the Eighteenth-Century Metropolis* (Winchester: Waterside Press, 2012).

Dunn, Caroline, *Stolen Women in Medieval England* (Cambridge: Cambridge University Press, 2014).

Edwards, Susan S. M., *Female Sexuality and the Law* (Oxford: Martin Robertson, 1981).

Elden, Stuart, *Foucault's Last Decade* (Cambridge: Polity Press, 2016).

Ellis, Karen Elizabeth, "Gaol Delivery in Yorkshire, 1399–1407" (MA thesis, Carleton University, Canada, 1983).

Faller, Lincoln, *Turned to Account: the Forms and Functions of Criminal Biography in Late Seventeenth- and Early Eighteenth-Century England* (Cambridge: Cambridge University Press, 1987).

Ferguson, Frances, "Rape and the Rise of the Novel", *Representations*, No. 20, 88–112 (1987).

Fish, Stanley, *Doing What Comes Naturally: Change, Rhetoric and the Practice of Theory in Literary and Legal Studies* (Durham: Duke University Press, 1989).

_____, *Is There a Text in this Class? The Authority of Interpretive Communities* (Cambridge, MA: Harvard University Press, 2003).

Fleming, John G., *An Introduction to the Law of Torts* (Oxford: Clarendon Press, 1967).

Foucault, Michel, *The Foucault Reader*, Paul Rabinow (ed.) (New York: Pantheon Books, 1984).

_____, "*From* Discipline and Punish: The Birth of the Prison", in Vincent Leitch (ed.), *Norton Anthology of Theory and Criticism* (New York: Norton, 2001), pp. 1636–47.

_____, *The Government of Self and Others: Lectures at the Collège de France 1982–1983*, Arnold I. Davidson (ed.), Graham Burchell (trans.) (New York: Palgrave Macmillan, 2010).

_____, "Governmentality" [1978], *Ideology and Consciousness*, No. 6, 5–26 (1979).

_____, *History of Sexuality*, Robert Hurley (trans.), 4 vols (New York: Vintage, 1990).

_____, "Human Nature: Justice versus Power", in Fons Elders (ed.), *Reflexive Water: The Basic Concerns of Mankind* (London: Souvenir Press, 1974).

_____, *Language, Counter-Memory, Practice*, Donald F. Bouchard (ed.) & Sherry Simon (trans.) (Ithaca: Cornell University Press, 1980).

_____, "Truth and Power", in Vincent Leitch (ed.), *Norton Anthology of Theory and Criticism* (New York: Norton, 2001), pp. 1667–70.

Fraser, Antonia, *The Wives of Henry VIII* (New York: Vintage, 1993).

Gattrell, V. A. C., *The Hanging Tree: Execution and the English People 1770–1868* (Oxford: Oxford University Press, 1996).

Gilbert, Sandra M. & Susan Gubar, *The Madwoman in the Attic: The Woman Writer and the Nineteenth Century Literary Imagination* (New Haven: Yale University Press, 1979).

Goldberg, John C. P. & Benjamin C. Zipursky, "Torts as Wrongs", *Texas Law Review*, 88:5, 917–86 (2010).

Goodrich, Peter, "Antirrhesis: Polemical Structures of Common Law Thought", in Austin Sarat and Thomas R. Kearns (eds), *The Rhetoric of Law* (Ann Arbor: University of Michigan Press, 1994).

Gordon, Scott Paul, "Disinterested Selves: *Clarissa* and the Tactics of Sentiment", *ELH*, 64:2, 496–513 (1997).

Gowing, Laura, *Domestic Dangers: Women, Words, and Sex in Early Modern London* (Oxford: Clarendon Press, 1996).

Gray, J. M., "Tennyson and Geoffrey of Monmouth", *Notes and Queries*, 14:2 (new series), 52–53 (1967).

Green, Anna, "Individual Remembering and 'Collective Memory': Theoretical Presuppositions and Contemporary Debates", *Oral History*, 32:2, 35–44 (2004).

Greenfield, Anne, "The Question of Marital Rape in Nicholas Rowe's *Tamerlane*", *Restoration and 18th-Century Theater Research*, 26:1–2, 57–72 (2011).

Groot, Roger D., "The Crime of Rape *temp.* Richard I and John", *Journal of Legal History*, 9:3, 324–34 (1988).

Grosrichard, Alain, *The Sultan's Court: European Fantasies of the East* (London: Verso, 1998).

Gruber, Aya, "A Provocative Defense", *California Law Review*, 103:2, 273, 334 (2014).

Hager, Kelly, "Chipping Away at Coverture: The Matrimonial Causes Act of 1857", in Dino Franco Felluga (general ed.), *BRANCH: Britain, Representation and Nineteenth-Century History* <https://www.branchcollective.org/?ps_articles

=kelly-hager-chipping-away-at-coverture-the-matrimonial-causes-act-of-1857> (last accessed 9 September 2017).

Halbwachs, Maurice, *The Collective Memory*, Francis J. Ditter & Vida Yazdi Ditter (trans.) (New York: Harper Colophon, 1980).

Hamburger, Philip, *Law and Judicial Duty* (Cambridge, MA: Harvard University Press, 2008).

Hanawalt, Barbara, *Crime and Conflict in English Communities, 1300–1348* (Cambridge, MA: Harvard University Press, 1979).

Hargraves, Neil, "Revelation of Character in Eighteenth-Century Historiography and William Robertson's *History of the Reign of Charles V*", *Eighteenth-Century Life* 27:2, 23–48 (2003).

Harrington, Henry, "Charles Kingsley's Fallen Athlete", *Victorian Studies*, 21:1, 73–86 (1977).

Hartsock, Nancy, "Foucault on Power: A Theory for Women?" in Linda Nicholson (ed.), *Feminism/Postmodernism (Thinking Gender)* (Abingdon: Routledge, 1989), pp. 157–75.

_____, "Postmodernism and Political Change: Issues for Feminist Theory", *Cultural Critique*, No. 14, 15–33 (1989–1990) (special issue: "The Construction of Gender and Modes of Social Division II").

Hawley, John C., "Charles Kingsley and the Book of Nature", *Anglican and Episcopal History*, 60:4, 461–79 (1991).

Heiniger, Abigail, "Faery and the Beast", *Brontë Studies*, 31:1, 23–29 (2006).

Heinzelman, Susan, *Riding the Black Ram: Law, Literature and* Gender (Stanford: Stanford University Press, 2010).

Heisler, Aaron Yale, "The English Destiny of Tennyson's Camelot", *Philological Quarterly*, 88:1–2, 151–70 (2009).

Hendrick, Harry, "Constructions and Reconstructions of British Childhood: An Interpretive Survey 1800 to the Present", in Allison James & Alan Prout (eds), *Constructing and Reconstructing Childhood* (London: Falmer Press, 1997).

Higgonet, Margaret, "Introduction", in Thomas Hardy, *Tess of the d'Urbervilles*, Tim Dolin (ed.) [1891] (London: Penguin Classics, 2003).

Hirschberger, Gilad, "Collective Trauma and the Social Construction of Meaning", *Frontiers in Psychology*, 9, article 1441 (2018).

Horder, Jeremy, *Provocation and Responsibility* (Oxford: Clarendon Press, 1992).

Hughes, Derek, "Rape on the Restoration Stage", *The Eighteenth Century* 46:3, 225–36 (2005).

Hume, Robert, *Henry Fielding and the London Theater, 1728–1737* (Oxford: Clarendon Press, 1988).

Hutter, Albert D., "Nation and Generation in *A Tale of Two Cities*", *PMLA*, 93:3, 448–62 (1978).

Immel, Andrea, U. C. Knoepflmacher & Julia Briggs, "Fantasy's Alternative Geography for Children", in *The Cambridge Companion to Children's Literature* (Cambridge: Cambridge University Press, 2009), pp. 229–41.

Ingram, Martin, *Church Courts, Sex and Marriage in England, 1570–1640* (Cambridge: Cambridge University Press, 1987).

Jackson, Jeffrey E, "The Once and Future Sword: Excalibur and the Poetics of Imperial Heroism in *Idylls of the King*", *Victorian Poetry*, 46:2, 207–29 (2008).

Janes, Dominic, *Victorian Reformation: The Fight Over Idolatry in the Church of England, 1840–1860* (Oxford: Oxford University Press, 2009).

Jardine, David, *Criminal Trials*, 2 vols (London: M. A. Nattali, 1832).

Johnson, Nancy, "The 'French Threat' in Anti-Jacobin Novels of the 1790s", in Thomas DiPiero & Pat Gills (eds), *Illicit Sex: Identity Politics in Early Modern Culture* (Athens: University of Georgia Press, 1996), pp. 181–202.

Johnston, Arthur, "*The Water-Babies*: Kingsley's Debt to Darwin", *English*, 12:72, 215–19 (1959).

Jussawalla, Feroza F, "*The Red King's Dream or Lewis Carroll in Wonderland*, and: *The Alice Companion: A Guide to Lewis Carroll's Alice Books*, and *Lewis Carroll and New Horizons*" (review), *The Lion and the Unicorn*, 24:1, 157–61 (2000).

Kafer, Peter, *Charles Brockden Brown's Revolution and the Birth of American Gothic* (Philadelphia: University of Pennsylvania Press, 2004).

Kant, Immanuel, *Metaphysical Elements of Justice*, John Ladd (trans.) (New York: Hackett, 1999).

Kauffman, Linda S., *Discourses of Desire: Gender, Genre, and Epistolary Fiction* (Ithaca: Cornell University Press, 1988).

Kenny, Michael, "A Place for Memory: The Interface between Individual and Collective History", *Comparative Studies in Society and History*, 41:3, 420–37 (1999).

Kesselring, K. J., "No Greater Provocation: Adultery and the Mitigation of Murder in English Law", 34 *Law and History Review*, 34:1, 199–225 (2016).

Keymer, Tom, *Richardson's* Clarissa *and the Eighteenth-Century Reader* (Cambridge, Cambridge University Press, 1992).

Kincaid, James, *Child-Loving: The Erotic Child and Victorian Culture* (Routledge, 1994).

Klein, Eric K., "Dennis the Menace or Billy the Kid: An Analysis of the Role of Transfer to Criminal Court in Juvenile Justice", *American Criminal Law Review*, 35:2, 371–410 (1998).

Knell, B. E. F, "Capital Punishment: Its Administration in Relation to Juvenile Offenders in the Nineteenth Century and Its Possible Administration in the Eighteenth", *The British Journal of Criminology* 5:2: 198–207 (1965).

Knoepflmacher, U. C., *Ventures into Childland* (Chicago: University of Chicago Press, 1998).

Komisaruk, Adam, "The Privatization of Pleasure: 'Crim-Con' in Wollstonecraft's *Maria*", *Law and Literature* 16:1, 33–63 (2004).

Langbein, John, "The Prosecutorial Origins of Defence of Counsel in the Eighteenth Century: The Appearance of Solicitors", *Cambridge Law Journal*, 58:2, 314–65 (1999).

Laurence, John, *A History of Capital Punishment* (London: Sampson, Low, Marston & Co, 1932).

Layson, Hana, "Rape and Revolution: Feminism, Antijacobinism, and the Politics of Injured Innocence in Brockden Brown's *Ormond*", *Early American Studies*, 2:1, 160–91 (2004).

Leckie, Barbara, *Culture and Adultery: The Novel, the Newspaper, and the Law, 1857–1914* (Philadelphia: University of Pennsylvania Press, 1999).

Lennon, Florence Becker, *Victoria Through the Looking-Glass: The Life of Lewis Carroll* (New York: Simon and Schuster, 1945).

Levy, David and Sandra Peart, "Charles Kingsley and the Theological Interpretation of Natural Selection", *Journal of Bioeconomics*, 8:3, 197–218 (2006).

Lewis, James, "Images of Captive Rape in the Nineteenth Century", *Journal of American Culture*, 15:2, 69–77 (1992).

Lewis, Paul, "Charles Brockden Brown and the Gendered Canon of Early American Fiction", *Early American Literature*, 31:2, 167–88 (1996).

Linebaugh, Peter, *The London Hanged: Crime and Civil Society in the Eighteenth Century*, 2nd edn (New York: Verso, 2006).

Loewen-Schmidt, Chad. "Pity and the Providence of the Body in Richardson's *Clarissa*", *Eighteenth-Century Fiction*, 22:1, 1–28 (2008).

"Lord Abergavenny Against Richard Lyddel, Esq.", in *Trials for Adultery: or, the History of Divorces from the Year 1760 to the Present Time* (London: 1780).

Lynch, Deirdre Shauna, *The Economy of Character* (Chicago: University of Chicago Press, 1998).

MacAndrew, Elizabeth, *The Gothic Tradition in* Fiction (New York: Columbia University Press, 1979).

MacFarlane, Bruce A, "Historical Development of the Offence of Rape" (1993), <https://archive.org/details/413655-hist-devel-of-offence-of-rape> (last accessed 27 April 2019).

Machann, Clinton, *Masculinity in Four Victorian Epics: A Darwinist Reading* (Burlington, VT: Ashgate, 2010).

MacPherson, Sandra, "Lovelace, Ltd.", *ELH*, 65:1, 99–121 (1998).

_____, *Harms Way, Tragic Responsibility and the Novel Form* (Baltimore: Johns Hopkins University Press, 2010).

Maddern, Philippa, *Violence and Social Order: East Anglia, 1422–1442* (Oxford: Oxford University Press, 1992).

Makman, Lisa Hermine, "Child's Work is Child's Play: The Value of George MacDonald's Diamond", *Children's Literature Association Quarterly*, 24:3, 119–29 (1999).

Margery, Susan, "The Invention of Juvenile Delinquency in Early Nineteenth-Century England", in Gordon Hughes, Eugene McLaughlin & John Muncie (eds), *Youth Justice: Critical Readings* (London: Sage Publications, 2006).

Marsden, Jean I., "Rape, Voyeurism, and the Restoration Stage", in Katherine M. Quinsey (ed.), *Broken Boundaries: Women & Feminism in Restoration Drama* (Lexington: University of Kentucky Press, 1996), pp. 185–200.

McGillis, Roderick, "Childhood and Growth: George MacDonald and William Wordsworth", in James Holt MacGavarn, Jr. (ed.), *Romanticism and Children's Literature in Nineteenth-Century England* (Athens: University of Georgia Press, 1991), pp. 150–67.

McIlwain, Charles Howard, *The Political Works of King James I* (Cambridge: Cambridge University Press, 1918).

Michalik, Kerstin, "The Development of the Discourse of Infanticide in the Late Eighteenth Century and the New Legal Standardization of the Offense in the Nineteenth Century", in Ulrike Gleixner & Marion W. Gray (eds), *Gender in Transition: Discourse and Practice in German-Speaking Europe 1750–1830* (Ann Arbor: University of Michigan Press, 2006), pp. 51–71.

Miller, D. A., *The Novel and the Police* (Berkeley: University of California Press, 1989).

Moretti, Franco, *The Way of the World: The* Bildungsroman *in European Culture* (London: Verso, 1987).

Morris, Marilyn, "Marital Litigation and English Tabloid Journalism: Crim. Con. in the *Bon Ton* (1791–1796)", *British Journal for Eighteenth-Century Studies*, 28:1, 33–54 (2005).

"Muscular Christianity", in *Tait's Edinburgh Magazine from January to December 1858, Vol. XXV* (Edinburgh: Sutherland & Knox, 1858), pp. 100–2.

Neal, Arthur, *National Trauma and Collective Memory: Major Events in the American Century* (New York: M. E. Sharpe, 1998).

Nickelsberg, Marilyn, "Rending the Veil of Sin: Idolatry and Adultery in *Jane Eyre* in Light of Ezekiel 16 and I and II Corinthians", *Brontë Studies*, 37:4, 292–8 (2012).

Nodelman, Perry, *The Hidden Adult* (Baltimore: Johns Hopkins University Press, 2008).

Nora, Pierre, "Between Memory and History: Les Lieux de Mémoire", *Representations*, No. 26, 7–24 (1989).

Norton, Mary Beth, *Founding Mothers and Fathers: Gendered Power and the Forming of American Society* (New York: Vintage, 1996).

Nussbaum, Martha, *Poetic Justice: the Literary Imagination and Public Life* (Boston: Beacon Press, 1997).

Olick, Jeffrey, "Collective Memory: The Two Cultures", *Sociological Theory*, 17:3, 333–48 (1999).

Okun, Peter, *Crime and the Nation: Prison Reform and Popular Fiction, Philadelphia 1786–1800* (New York: Routledge, 2002).

Owen, David G., "A Punitive Damages Overview: Functions, Problems and Reform", *Villanova Law Review*, 39:2, 363–413 (1994).

Pennington, Nancy & Reid Hastie, "A Cognitive Theory of Juror Decision Making: The Story Model", *Cardozo Law Review*, 13:2–3, 519–57 (1991).

Petch, Simon, "Equity and Natural Law in *The Ring and the Book*", *Victorian Poetry*, 35:1, 105–11 (1997).

———, "Law, Equity, and Conscience in Victorian England", *Victorian Literature and Culture*, 25:1, 123–39 (1997).

Platt, Anthony, *The Child-Savers: The Invention of Delinquency* (Chicago: University of Chicago Press, 1977).

Potkay, Adam, "The Problem of Identity and the Grounds for Judgment in *The Ring and the Book*", *Victorian Poetry*, 25:2, 143–57 (1987).

Potter, Jr., Parker B., "Punishment in Wonderland", *International Journal of Punishing and Sentencing*, 4:2, 82–109 (2008).

Powell, Edward, "Jury Trial at Gaol Delivery in the Late Middle Ages: The Midland Circuit, 1400–1429", in James S. Cockburn & Thomas A. Green (eds), *Twelve Men Good and True: The Criminal Jury in England, 1200–1800* (Princeton: Princeton University Press, 1988).

Radzinowicz, Leon, *A History of English Criminal Law and its Administration from 1750*, vol. 3 (New York: Macmillan, 1956).

Ramsey, Carolyn B., "Sex and Social Order: The Selective Enforcement of Colonial American Adultery Laws in the English Context", *Yale Journal of Law and the Humanities*, 10:1, 191–228 (1998).

Rawlings, Philip, *Drunks, Whores, and Idle Apprentices: Criminal Biographies of the Eighteenth Century* (London: Routledge, 1992).

Rawlins, Jack P., "Great Expiations: Dickens and the Betrayal of the Child", *Nineteenth Century*, 23:4, 667–83 (1983).

Rea, Joanne E., "Brontë's *Jane Eyre*", *Explicator*, 50:2, 75–78 (1992).

Richards, Judith M., *Elizabeth I* (London: Routledge, 2011).

Riga, Frank, "The Platonic Imagery of George MacDonald and C. S. Lewis: The Allegory of the Cave Transfigured", in Roderick McGillis (ed.), *For the Childlike: George MacDonald's Fantasies for Children* (Metuchen, New Jersey: Scarecrow Press, 1992), pp. 111–32.

Rippon, Maria, *Judgment and Justification in the Nineteenth Century Novel of Adultery* (Westport, CT: Greenwood Press, 2002).

Rivero, Albert, *The Plays of Henry Fielding: A Critical Study of his Dramatic Career* (Charlottesville: University of Virginia Press, 1989).

Robins, Jane, *Rebel Queen: How the Trial of Caroline Brought England to the Brink of Revolution* (New York: Simon and Schuster, 2006).

Rodas, Julia Miele, "Brontë's *Jane Eyre*", *The Explicator*, 61:3, 149–51 (2003).

Rodensky, Lisa, *The Crime in Mind: Criminal Responsibility and the Victorian Novel* (Oxford: Oxford University Press, 2003).

Rooney, Ellen, "'A Little More than Persuading': Tess and the Subject of Sexual Violence", in Lynn A. Higgins & Brenda R. Silver (eds), *Rape and Representation* (New York: Columbia University Press, 1991), pp. 87–113.

Rose, Jacqueline, *The Case of Peter Pan, or the Impossibility of Children's Literature* (Philadelphia: University of Pennsylvania Press, 1992).

Said, Edward, *Orientalism* (New York: Vintage Books, 1979).

de Saint-Laurent, Constance, "Thinking Through Time. From Collective Memory to Collective Imagination", in Constance de Saint-Laurent, Sandra Obradovic & Kevin Carriere (eds), *Imagining Collective Futures: Perspectives from Social, Cultural and Political Psychology* (London: Palgrave Macmillan, 2018), pp. 59–81.

de Saint-Laurent, Constance & Sandra Obradovic, "Uses of the Past: History as a Resource for the Present", *Integrative Psychological and Behavioral Science*, 53:1, 1–13 (2019).

Samuels, Shirley, *Romances of the Republic: Women, the Family, and Violence in the Literature of the Early American Nation* (Oxford: Oxford University Press,1996).

Scarry, Elaine, *The Body in Pain* (Oxford: Oxford University Press, 1985).

Schramm, Jan-Melissa, *Testimony and Advocacy in Victorian Law, Literature, and Theology* (Cambridge: Cambridge University Press, 2000).

Schudson, Michael, "Dynamics of Distortion in Collective Memory", in Daniel Schacter (ed.), *Memory Distortion: How Minds, Brains and Societies Reconstruct the Past* (Cambridge, MA: Harvard University Press, 1995), pp. 346–7.

Sedgwick, Eve, *The Coherence of Gothic Conventions* (New York: Routledge, 1986).

Sheley, Erin, "Reverberations of the Victim's 'Voice': Victim Impact Statements and the Cultural Project of Punishment", *Indiana Law Journal*, 87:3, 1247–86 (2012).

_____, "From Eden to Eternity: The Timescales of Genesis in George MacDonald's 'The Golden Key' and *Lilith*", *Children's Literature Association Quarterly*, 29:4, 329–44 (2004).

Shoemaker, Karl, "The Problem of Pain in Punishment: Historical Perspectives", in Austin Sarat (ed.), *Pain, Death and the Law* (Ann Arbor: University of Michigan Press, 2001), pp. 15–42.

Shore, Heather, *Artful Dodgers: Youth and Crime in Early Nineteenth-Century London* (Boydell Press, 2002).

Smith, Steven D., "The Critics and the 'Crisis': A Reassessment of Current Conceptions of Tort Law", *Cornell Law Review*, 72:4, 765–98 (1987).

Staves, Susan, "Fielding and the Comedy of Attempted Rape", in Beth Fowkes Tobin (ed.), *History, Gender & Eighteenth-Century Literature* (Athens: University of Georgia Press, 1994), pp. 86–112.

_____, "Money for Honor: Damages for Criminal Conversation", in Harry C. Payne (ed.), *Studies in Eighteenth-Century Literature*, vol. 11 (Madison: University of Wisconsin Press, 1982), pp. 279–97.

Stern, Julia, "The State of 'Women' in *Ormond*; or, Patricide in the New Nation", in Philip Barnard, Mark L. Kamrath & Stephen Shapiro (eds), *Revising Charles Brockden Brown: Culture, Politics, and Sexuality in the Early Republic* (Knoxville: University of Tennessee Press, 2004), pp. 182–215.

Stoebuck, William B., "Reception of Common Law in the American Colonies", *William and Mary Law Review*, 10:2, 393–426 (1968).

Stoffel, Stephanie Lovett, *Lewis Carroll and Alice: New Horizons* (London: Thames and Hudson, 1997).

Stone, Harry, *Dickens and the Invisible World: Fairy Tales, Fantasy, and Novel-Making* (Bloomington: Indiana University Press, 1979).

Stone, Lawrence, *Family, Sex, and Marriage in England 1500–1800* (New York: Harper & Row, 1977).

_____, *Road to Divorce: England 1530–1987* (Oxford: Oxford University Press, 1990).

Struve, Laura, "'This Is No Way to Tell a Story': Robert Browning's Attack on the Law in *The Ring and the Book*", *Law and Literature*, 20:3, 423–43 (2008).

Sturken, Marita, *Tangled Memories: the Vietnam War, the AIDS Epidemic, and the Politics of Remembering* (Berkeley: University of California Press, 1997).

Summerfield, Penny, *Reconstructing Women's Wartime Lives* (Manchester: Manchester University Press, 1998).

Talairach-Vielmas, Laurence, "'Portrait of a Governess, Disconnected, Poor, and Plain': Staging the Spectral Self in Charlotte Brontë's *Jane Eyre*", *Brontë Studies*, 34:2, 127–37 (2009).

Tanner, Tony, *Adultery in the Novel: Contract and Transgression* (Baltimore: Johns Hopkins University Press, 1979).

Temple, Kathryn, "Imagining Justice: Gender and Juridical Space in the Gothic", in Thomas DiPiero & Pat Gills (eds), *Illicit Sex: Identity Politics in Early Modern Culture* (Athens: University of Georgia Press, 1996), pp. 68–85.

Terdiman, Richard, *Present Past: Modernity and the Memory Crisis* (Ithaca: Cornell University Press, 1993).

Thomson, R. L., "Owain: Chwedl Iarlles y Ffynnon", in Rachel Bromwich, A. O. H. Jarman & Brynley F. Roberts (eds), *The Arthur of the Welsh: The Arthurian Legend in Medieval Welsh Literature* (Cardiff: University of Wales Press, 1991), pp. 159–69.

Tompkins, Jane, *Sensational Designs: The Cultural Works of American Fiction, 1790–1860* (New York: Oxford University Press 1985).

Turcotte, Gerry, "Geoffrey of Monmouth and Tennyson: A Paradoxical Parallel", *ANQ: A Quarterly Journal of Short Articles, Notes, and Reviews*, 1:4, 140–1 (1988).

Turner, David, *Fashioning Adultery: Gender, Sex and Civility in England, 1660–1740* (Cambridge, Cambridge University Press, 2002).

Wallace, Diana, *Female Gothic Histories: Gender, History, and the Gothic* (Cardiff: University of Wales Press, 2013).

Ward, Ian, *Law and the Brontës* (London: Palgrave, 2012).

_____, *Sex, Crime and Literature in Victorian England* (Oxford: Hart Publishing, 2014).

Warner, William Beatty, "Proposal and Habitation: The Temporality and Authority of Interpretation in and about a Scene of Richardson's *Clarissa*", *boundary 2*, 7:2, 169–200 (1979).

Watson, Jeanie, *Risking Enchantment: Coleridge's Symbolic World of Faery* (Lincoln: University of Nebraska Press, 1990).

Watt, Ian, *The Rise of the Novel* (Berkeley: University of California Press, 1957).

Weinrib, Ernest J., *The Idea of Private Law* (Cambridge, MA: Harvard University Press, 1995).

Welsh, Alexander, *Strong Representations: Narrative and Circumstantial Evidence in England* (Baltimore: Johns Hopkins University Press, 1995).

Whitaker, Muriel, "The Proper Bringing Up of Young Pip", *Children's Literature*, 2, 152–58 (1973).

White, James Boyd, *Acts of Hope: Creating Authority in Literature, Law, and Politics* (Chicago: University of Chicago Press, 1994).

Willard, Nancy, "The Goddess in the Belfry: Grandmothers and Wise Women in George MacDonald's Books for Children", in Roderick McGillis (ed.), *For the Childlike: George MacDonald's Fantasies for Children* (Metuchen, NJ: Scarecrow Press, 1992), pp. 67–74.

Wilputte, Earla, "Wife Pandering in Three Eighteenth-Century Plays", *Studies in English Literature*, 38:3, 447–64 (1998).

Wilson, Jean, "Heinrich von Kleist's *Amphitryon*: Romanticism, Rape and Comic Irresolution", *Papers on Language and Literature*, 37:2, 115–31 (2001).

Wood, Naomi, "A (Sea) Green Victorian: Charles Kingsley and *The Water-Babies*", *The Lion and the Unicorn* 19:2, 233–52 (1995).

Wootton, David (ed.), *Divine Right and Democracy: an Anthology of Political Writing in Stuart England* (Indianapolis: Hackett Publishing, 1986).

Wright, Jane, "An Unnoticed Allusion to *Henry V* in Tennyson's *Idylls of the King*", *ANQ: A Quarterly Review of Short Articles, Notes, and Reviews*, 25:2, 109–11 (2012).

Zietlow, Paul, "Psychological Exploration in *Idylls of the King*: The Case of Geraint and Enid", *Studies in English Literature 1500–1900*, 24:4, 731–47 (1984).

Index

Wilputte, Earla, 45
witnesses, protection of, 179
Wollstonecraft, Mary, 38–9, 45, 46, 47, 63,
    192, 198
women
  commoditization of, 24, 38–9, 44–6
  feminist resistance, 46–8

friendship in *Ormond*, 193
and justice, Hardy's interest in, 211
objectified subjects, 25
and revolutionary ideals, 198, 199–200
see also female adultery; Gothic genre
World War II, movies, 3
Wykes, Jacob, 155–7